Praise for *Framework Design Guidelines*

"*Framework Design Guidelines* is one of those rare books that can be read at different reading levels and can be useful to different kinds of developers. Regardless of whether you want to design an effective object model, improve your understanding of the .NET Framework, borrow from the experience of software gurus, stay clear of the most common programming mistakes, or just get an idea of the huge effort that led to the .NET initiative, this book is a must-read."

—Francesco Balena, The VB Migration Partner Team (www.vbmigration.com), Code Architect, Author, and Microsoft Regional Director, Italy

"Frameworks are valuable but notoriously difficult to construct: your every decision must be geared toward making them easy to be used correctly and difficult to be used incorrectly. This book takes you through a progression of recommendations that will eliminate many of those downstream 'I wish I'd known that earlier' moments. I wish *I'd* read it earlier."

—Paul Besly, Principal Technologist, QA

"Not since Brooks' *The Mythical Man Month* has the major software maker of its time produced a book so full of relevant advice for the modern software developer. This book has a permanent place on my bookshelf and I consult it frequently."

—George Byrkit, Senior Software Engineer, Genomic Solutions

"Updated for the new language features of the .NET Framework 3.0 and 3.5, this book continues to be the definitive resource for .NET developers and architects who are designing class library frameworks. Some of the existing guidelines have been expanded with new annotations and more detail, and new guidance covering such features as extension methods and nullable types has also been included. The guidance will help any developer write clearer and more understandable code, while the annotations provide invaluable insight into some of the design decisions that made the .NET Framework what it is today."

—Scott Dorman, Microsoft MVP and President, Tampa Bay International Association of Software Architects

"Filled with information useful to developers and architects of all levels, this book provides practical guidelines and expert background information to get behind the rules. *Framework Design Guidelines* takes the already published guidelines to a higher level, and it is needed to write applications that integrate well in the .NET area."

—Cristof Falk, Software Engineer

"This book is an absolute must read for all .NET developers. It gives clear 'do' and 'don't' guidance on how to design class libraries for .NET. It also offers insight into the design and creation of .NET that really helps developers understand the reasons why things are the way they are. This information will aid developers designing their own class libraries and will also allow them to take advantage of the .NET class library more effectively."

—Jeffrey Richter, Author/Trainer/Consultant, Wintellect

"The second edition of *Framework Design Guidelines* gives you new, important insight into designing your own class libraries: Abrams and Cwalina frankly discuss the challenges of adding new features to shipping versions of their products with minimal impact on existing code. You'll find great examples of how to create version N+1 of your software by learning how the .NET class library team created versions 2.0, 3.0, and 3.5 of the .NET library. They were able to add generics, WCF, WPF, WF, and LINQ with minimal impact on the existing APIs, even providing capabilities for customers wanting to use only some of the new features, while still maintaining compatibility with the original library."

—Bill Wagner, Founder and Consultant, SRT Solutions,
author of *Effective C#* and *More Effective C#*

"This book is a must read for all architects and software developers thinking about frameworks. The book offers insight into some driving factors behind the design of the .NET Framework. It should be considered mandatory reading for anybody tasked with creating application frameworks."

—Peter Winkler, Sr. Software Engineer, Balance Technology Inc.

Framework Design Guidelines
Second Edition

Microsoft .NET Development Series

John Montgomery, *Series Advisor*
Don Box, *Series Advisor*
Brad Abrams, *Series Advisor*

The award-winning Microsoft .NET Development Series was established in 2002 to provide professional developers with the most comprehensive and practical coverage of the latest .NET technologies. It is supported and developed by the leaders and experts of Microsoft development technologies, including Microsoft architects, MVPs, and leading industry luminaries. Books in this series provide a core resource of information and understanding every developer needs to write effective applications.

Titles in the Series

Brad Abrams, *.NET Framework Standard Library Annotated Reference Volume 1: Base Class Library and Extended Numerics Library*, 978-0-321-15489-7

Brad Abrams and Tamara Abrams, *.NET Framework Standard Library Annotated Reference, Volume 2: Networking Library, Reflection Library, and XML Library*, 978-0-321-19445-9

Chris Anderson, *Essential Windows Presentation Foundation (WPF)*, 978-0-321-37447-9

Bob Beauchemin and Dan Sullivan, *A Developer's Guide to SQL Server 2005*, 978-0-321-38218-4

Adam Calderon, Joel Rumerman, *Advanced ASP.NET AJAX Server Controls: For .NET Framework 3.5*, 978-0-321-51444-8

Eric Carter and Eric Lippert, *Visual Studio Tools for Office: Using C# with Excel, Word, Outlook, and InfoPath*, 978-0-321-33488-6

Eric Carter and Eric Lippert, *Visual Studio Tools for Office: Using Visual Basic 2005 with Excel, Word, Outlook, and InfoPath*, 978-0-321-41175-4

Steve Cook, Gareth Jones, Stuart Kent, Alan Cameron Wills, *Domain-Specific Development with Visual Studio DSL Tools*, 978-0-321-39820-8

Krzysztof Cwalina and Brad Abrams, *Framework Design Guidelines: Conventions, Idioms, and Patterns for Reusable .NET Libraries*, Second Edition, 978-0-321-54561-9

Joe Duffy, *Concurrent Programming on Windows*, 978-0-321-43482-1

Sam Guckenheimer and Juan J. Perez, *Software Engineering with Microsoft Visual Studio Team System*, 978-0-321-27872-2

Anders Hejlsberg, Mads Torgersen, Scott Wiltamuth, Peter Golde, *The C# Programming Language*, Third Edition, 978-0-321-56299-9

Alex Homer and Dave Sussman, *ASP.NET 2.0 Illustrated*, 978-0-321-41834-0

Joe Kaplan and Ryan Dunn, *The .NET Developer's Guide to Directory Services Programming*, 978-0-321-35017-6

Mark Michaelis, *Essential C# 3.0: For .NET Framework 3.5*, 978-0-321-53392-0

James S. Miller and Susann Ragsdale, *The Common Language Infrastructure Annotated Standard*, 978-0-321-15493-4

Christian Nagel, *Enterprise Services with the .NET Framework: Developing Distributed Business Solutions with .NET Enterprise Services*, 978-0-321-24673-8

Brian Noyes, *Data Binding with Windows Forms 2.0: Programming Smart Client Data Applications with .NET*, 978-0-321-26892-1

Brian Noyes, *Smart Client Deployment with ClickOnce: Deploying Windows Forms Applications with ClickOnce*, 978-0-321-19769-6

Fritz Onion with Keith Brown, *Essential ASP.NET 2.0*, 978-0-321-23770-5

Steve Resnick, Richard Crane, Chris Bowen, *Essential Windows Communication Foundation: For .NET Framework 3.5*, 978-0-321-44006-8

Scott Roberts and Hagen Green, *Designing Forms for Microsoft Office InfoPath and Forms Services 2007*, 978-0-321-41059-7

Neil Roodyn, *eXtreme .NET: Introducing eXtreme Programming Techniques to .NET Developers*, 978-0-321-30363-9

Chris Sells and Michael Weinhardt, *Windows Forms 2.0 Programming*, 978-0-321-26796-2

Dharma Shukla and Bob Schmidt, *Essential Windows Workflow Foundation*, 978-0-321-39983-0

Guy Smith-Ferrier, *.NET Internationalization: The Developer's Guide to Building Global Windows and Web Applications*, 978-0-321-34138-9

Will Stott and James Newkirk, *Visual Studio Team System: Better Software Development for Agile Teams*, 978-0-321-41850-0

Paul Yao and David Durant, *.NET Compact Framework Programming with C#*, 978-0-321-17403-1

Paul Yao and David Durant, *.NET Compact Framework Programming with Visual Basic .NET*, 978-0-321-17404-8

For more information go to informit.com/msdotnetseries/

Framework Design Guidelines

Conventions, Idioms, and Patterns for Reusable .NET Libraries

Second Edition

- **Krzysztof Cwalina**
- **Brad Abrams**

Addison-Wesley

Upper Saddle River, NJ • Boston • Indianapolis • San Francisco
New York • Toronto • Montreal • London • Munich • Paris • Madrid
Capetown • Sydney • Tokyo • Singapore • Mexico City

The publisher offers excellent discounts on this book when ordered in quantity for bulk purchases or special sales, which may include electronic versions and/or custom covers and content particular to your business, training goals, marketing focus, and branding interests. For more information, please contact:

U.S. Corporate and Government Sales
(800) 382-3419
corpsales@pearsontechgroup.com

For sales outside the United States please contact:

International Sales
international@pearson.com

Visit us on the Web: informit.com/aw

Library of Congress Cataloging-in-Publication Data

Cwalina, Krzysztof.
 Framework design guidelines : conventions, idioms, and patterns for reusable .NET libraries / Krzysztof Cwalina, Brad Abrams. — 2nd ed.
  p. cm.
 Includes bibliographical references and index.
 ISBN 978-0-321-54561-9 (hardcover : alk. paper)
 1. Microsoft .NET Framework. 2. Application program interfaces (Computer software) I. Abrams, Brad. II. Title.

QA76.76.M52C87 2008
006.7'882—dc22

2008034905

ISBN-13: 978-0-321-54561-9
ISBN-10:   0-321-54561-3

Text printed in the United States on recycled paper at Donnelley in Crawfordsville, Indiana.
First printing, October 2008

To my wife, Ela,
for her support throughout the long process of writing this book,
and to my parents,
Jadwiga and Janusz, for their encouragement.
—Krzysztof Cwalina

To my wife, Tamara:
Your love and patience strengthen me.
—Brad Abrams

Contents

Figures

Tables

Foreword

When the .NET Framework was first published, I was fascinated by the technology. The benefits of the CLR (Common Language Runtime), its extensive APIs, and the C# language were immediately obvious. But underneath all the technology were a common design for the APIs and a set of conventions that were used everywhere. This was the .NET culture. Once you had learned a part of it, it was easy to translate this knowledge into other areas of the Framework.

For the past 16 years, I have been working on open source software. Since contributors span not only multiple backgrounds but multiple years, adhering to the same style and coding conventions has always been very important. Maintainers routinely rewrite or adapt contributions to software to ensure that code adheres to project coding standards and style. It is always better when contributors and people who join a software project follow conventions used in an existing project. The more information that can be conveyed through practices and standards, the simpler it becomes for future contributors to get up-to-speed on a project. This helps the project converge code, both old and new.

As both the .NET Framework and its developer community have grown, new practices, patterns, and conventions have been identified. Brad and Krzysztof have become the curators who turned all of this new knowledge into the present-day guidelines. They typically blog about a new convention, solicit feedback from the community, and keep track of these guidelines. In my opinion, their blogs are must-read documents for everyone who is interested in getting the most out of the .NET Framework.

The first edition of *Framework Design Guidelines* became an instant classic in the Mono community for two valuable reasons. First, it provided us a means of understanding why and how the various .NET APIs had been implemented. Second, we appreciated it for its invaluable guidelines that we too strived to follow in our own programs and libraries. This new edition not only builds on the success of the first but has been updated with new lessons that have since been learned. The annotations to the guidelines are provided by some of the lead .NET architects and great programmers who have helped shape these conventions.

In conclusion, this text goes beyond guidelines. It is a book that you will cherish as the "classic" that helped you become a better programmer, and there are only a select few of those in our industry.

Miguel de Icaza
Boston, MA

Foreword to the First Edition

In the early days of development of the .NET Framework, before it was even called that, I spent countless hours with members of the development teams reviewing designs to ensure that the final result would be a coherent platform. I have always felt that a key characteristic of a framework must be consistency. Once you understand one piece of the framework, the other pieces should be immediately familiar.

As you might expect from a large team of smart people, we had many differences of opinion—there is nothing like coding conventions to spark lively and heated debates. However, in the name of consistency, we gradually worked out our differences and codified the result into a common set of guidelines that allow programmers to understand and use the Framework easily.

Brad Abrams, and later Krzysztof Cwalina, helped capture these guidelines in a living document that has been continuously updated and refined during the past six years. The book you are holding is the result of their work.

The guidelines have served us well through three versions of the .NET Framework and numerous smaller projects, and they are guiding the development of the next generation of APIs for the Microsoft Windows operating system.

With this book, I hope and expect that you will also be successful in making your frameworks, class libraries, and components easy to understand and use.

Good luck and happy designing.

Anders Hejlsberg
Redmond, WA
June 2005

Preface

This book, *Framework Design Guidelines,* presents best practices for designing frameworks, which are reusable object-oriented libraries. The guidelines are applicable to frameworks in various sizes and scales of reuse, including the following:

- Large system frameworks, such as the .NET Framework, usually consisting of thousands of types and used by millions of developers.
- Medium-size reusable layers of large distributed applications or extensions to system frameworks, such as the Web Services Enhancements.
- Small components shared among several applications, such as a grid control library.

It is worth noting that this book focuses on design issues that directly affect the programmability of a framework (publicly accessible APIs[1]). As a result, we generally do not cover much in terms of implementation details. Just as a user interface design book doesn't cover the details of how to implement hit testing, this book does not describe how to implement a binary sort, for example. This scope allows us to provide a definitive guide for framework designers instead of being yet another book about programming.

---

1. This includes public types, and their public, protected, and explicitly implemented members of these types.

These guidelines were created in the early days of .NET Framework development. They started as a small set of naming and design conventions but have been enhanced, scrutinized, and refined to a point where they are generally considered the canonical way to design frameworks at Microsoft. They carry the experience and cumulative wisdom of thousands of developer hours over three versions of the .NET Framework. We tried to avoid basing the text purely on some idealistic design philosophies, and we think its day-to-day use by development teams at Microsoft has made it an intensely pragmatic book.

The book contains many annotations that explain trade-offs, explain history, amplify, or provide critiquing views on the guidelines. These annotations are written by experienced framework designers, industry experts, and users. They are the stories from the trenches that add color and setting for many of the guidelines presented.

To make them more easily distinguished in text, namespace names, classes, interfaces, methods, properties, and types are set in monospace font.

The book assumes basic familiarity with .NET Framework programming. A few guidelines assume familiarity with features introduced in version 3.5 of the Framework. If you are looking for a good introduction to Framework programming, there are some excellent suggestions in the Suggested Reading List at the end of the book.

Guideline Presentation

The guidelines are organized as simple recommendations using **Do**, **Consider**, **Avoid**, and **Do not**. Each guideline describes either a good or bad practice, and all have a consistent presentation. Good practices have a ✓ in front of them, and bad practices have an ✗ in front of them. The wording of each guideline also indicates how strong the recommendation is. For example, a **Do** guideline is one that should always[2] be followed (all examples are from this book):

---

2. *Always* might be a bit too strong a word. There are guidelines that should literally be always followed, but they are extremely rare. On the other hand, you probably need to have a really unusual case for breaking a **Do** guideline and still have it be beneficial to the users of the framework.

✓ **DO** name custom attribute classes with the suffix "Attribute."

```
public class ObsoleteAttribute : Attribute { ... }
```

On the other hand, **Consider** guidelines should generally be followed, but if you fully understand the reasoning behind a guideline and have a good reason to not follow it anyway, you should not feel bad about breaking the rules:

✓ **CONSIDER** defining a struct instead of a class if instances of the type are small and commonly short-lived or are commonly embedded in other objects.

Similarly, **Do not** guidelines indicate something you should almost never do:

✗ **DO NOT** assign instances of mutable types to read-only fields.

Less strong, **Avoid** guidelines indicate that something is generally not a good idea, but there are known cases where breaking the rule makes sense:

✗ **AVOID** using ICollection<T> or ICollection as a parameter just to access the Count property.

Some more complex guidelines are followed by additional background information, illustrative code samples, and rationale:

✓ **DO** implement IEquatable<T> on value types.

The Object.Equals method on value types causes boxing and its default implementation is not very efficient because it uses reflection. IEquatable<T>.Equals can offer much better performance and can be implemented so it does not cause boxing.

```
public struct Int32 : IEquatable<Int32> {
    public bool Equals(Int32 other){ ... }
}
```

Language Choice and Code Examples

One of the goals of the Common Language Runtime (CLR) is to support a variety of programming languages: those with implementations provided by Microsoft, such as C++, VB, C#, F#, Python, and Ruby, as well as third-party languages such as Eiffel, COBOL, Fortran, and others. Therefore, this book was written to be applicable to a broad set of languages that can be used to develop and consume modern frameworks.

To reinforce the message of multilanguage framework design, we considered writing code examples using several different programming languages. However, we decided against this. We felt that using different languages would help to carry the philosophical message, but it could force readers to learn several new languages, which is not the objective of this book.

We decided to choose a single language that is most likely to be readable to the broadest range of developers. We picked C#, because it is a simple language from the C family of languages (C, C++, Java, and C#), a family with a rich history in framework development.

Choice of language is close to the hearts of many developers, and we offer apologies to those who are uncomfortable with our choice.

About This Book

This book offers guidelines for framework design from the top down.

Chapter 1, "Introduction," is a brief orientation to the book, describing the general philosophy of framework design. This is the only chapter without guidelines.

Chapter 2, "Framework Design Fundamentals," offers principles and guidelines that are fundamental to overall framework design.

Chapter 3, "Naming Guidelines," contains common design idioms and naming guidelines for various parts of a framework, such as namespaces, types, and members.

Chapter 4, "Type Design Guidelines," provides guidelines for the general design of types.

Chapter 5, "Member Design," takes a further step and presents guidelines for the design of members of types.

Chapter 6, "Designing for Extensibility," presents issues and guidelines that are important to ensure appropriate extensibility in your framework.

Chapter 7, "Exceptions," presents guidelines for working with exceptions, the preferred error reporting mechanisms.

Chapter 8, "Usage Guidelines," contains guidelines for extending and using types that commonly appear in frameworks.

Chapter 9, "Common Design Patterns," offers guidelines and examples of common framework design patterns.

Appendix A, "C# Coding Style Conventions," contains a short description of coding conventions used in this book.

Appendix B, "Using FxCop to Enforce the Framework Design Guidelines," describes a tool called FxCop. The tool can be used to analyze framework binaries for compliance with the guidelines described in this book. A link to the tool is included on the DVD that accompanies this book.

Appendix C, "Sample API Specification," is a sample of an API specification that framework designers within Microsoft create when designing APIs.

Included with the book is a DVD that contains several hours of video presentations covering topics presented in this book by the authors, a sample API specification, and other useful resources.

Acknowledgments

This book, by its nature, is the collected wisdom of many hundreds of people, and we are deeply grateful to all of them.

Many people within Microsoft have worked long and hard, over a period of years, proposing, debating, and finally, writing many of these guidelines. Although it is impossible to name everyone who has been involved, a few deserve special mention: Chris Anderson, Erik Christensen, Jason Clark, Joe Duffy, Patrick Dussud, Anders Hejlsberg, Jim Miller, Michael Murray, Lance Olson, Eric Gunnerson, Dare Obasanjo, Steve Starck, Kit George, Mike Hillberg, Greg Schecter, Mark Boulter, Asad Jawahar, Justin Van Patten, and Mircea Trofin.

We'd also like to thank the annotators: Mark Alcazar, Chris Anderson, Christopher Brumme, Pablo Castro, Jason Clark, Steven Clarke, Joe Duffy, Patrick Dussud, Mike Fanning, Kit George, Jan Gray, Brian Grunkemeyer, Eric Gunnerson, Phil Haack, Anders Hejlsberg, David Kean, Rico Mariani, Anthony Moore, Vance Morrison, Christophe Nasarre, Dare Obasanjo, Brian Pepin, Jon Pincus, Jeff Prosise, Brent Rector, Jeffrey Richter, Greg Schechter, Chris Sells, Steve Starck, Herb Sutter, Clemens Szyperski, Mircea Trofin, and Paul Vick.

Their insights provide much needed commentary, color, humor, and history that add tremendous value to this book.

Sheridan Harrison and David Kean actually wrote and edited Appendix B on FxCop, which would not have been done without their skill and passion for this tool.

For all of the help, reviews, and support, both technical and moral, we thank Martin Heller. And for their insightful and helpful comments, we appreciate Pierre Nallet, George Byrkit, Khristof Falk, Paul Besley, Bill Wagner, and Peter Winkler.

We would also like to give special thanks to Susann Ragsdale, who turned this book from a semi-random collection of disconnected thoughts into seamlessly flowing prose. Her flawless writing, patience, and fabulous sense of humor made the process of writing this book so much easier.

About the Authors

Brad Abrams was a founding member of the Common Language Runtime and .NET Framework teams at Microsoft Corporation. He has been designing parts of the .NET Framework since 1998 and is currently Group Program Manager of the .NET Framework team. Brad started his framework design career building the Base Class Library (BCL) that ships as a core part of the .NET Framework. Brad was also the lead editor on the Common Language Specification (CLS), the .NET Framework Design Guidelines, and the libraries in the ECMA\ISO CLI Standard. Brad has authored and coauthored multiple publications, including *Programming in the .NET Environment* and *.NET Framework Standard Library Annotated Reference*, Volumes 1 and 2. Brad graduated from North Carolina State University with a B.S. in computer science. You can find his most recent musings on his blog at http://blogs.msdn.com/BradA.

Krzysztof Cwalina is a program manager on the .NET Framework team at Microsoft. He was a founding member of the .NET Framework team and throughout his career has designed many .NET Framework APIs and framework development tools, such as FxCop. He is currently leading a companywide effort to develop, promote, and apply framework design and architectural guidelines to the .NET Framework. He is also leading the team responsible for delivering core .NET Framework APIs. Krzysztof graduated with a B.S. and an M.S. in computer science from the University of Iowa. You can find his blog at http://blogs.msdn.com/kcwalina.

About the Annotators

Mark Alcazar wanted to be a famous sportsman. After discovering he had no hand-eye coordination or athletic ability, however, he decided a better career might be computers. Mark has been at Microsoft for the last nine years, where he's worked on the HTML rendering engine in Internet Explorer and has been a member of the Windows Presentation Foundation team since its inception. Mark is a big fan of consistent white space, peach-nectarine Talking Rain, and spicy food. He has a B.Sc. from the University of the West Indies and an M.Sc. from the University of Pennsylvania.

Chris Anderson is an architect at Microsoft in the Connected Systems Division. Chris's primary focus is on the design and architecture of .NET technologies used to implement the next generation of applications and services. From 2002 until recently he was the lead architect of the WPF team. Chris has written numerous articles and white papers, and he has presented and been a keynote speaker at numerous conferences (Microsoft Professional Developers Conference, Microsoft TechEd, WinDev, DevCon, etc.) worldwide. He has a very popular blog at www.simplegeek.com.

Christopher Brumme joined Microsoft in 1997, when the Common Language Runtime (CLR) team was being formed. Since then, he has contributed to the execution engine portions of the codebase and more broadly to the design. He is currently focused on concurrency issues in managed code. Prior to joining the CLR team, Chris was an architect at Borland and Oracle.

Pablo Castro is a technical lead in the SQL Server team. He has contributed extensively to several areas of SQL Server and the .NET Framework, including SQL-CLR integration, type-system extensibility, the TDS client-server protocol, and the ADO.NET API. Pablo is currently involved with the development of the ADO.NET Entity Framework and also leads the ADO.NET Data Services project, which is looking at how to bring data and Web technologies together. Before joining Microsoft, Pablo worked in various companies on a broad set of topics that range from distributed inference systems for credit scoring/risk analysis to collaboration and groupware applications.

Jason Clark works as a software architect for Microsoft. His Microsoft software engineering credits include three versions of Windows, three releases of the .NET Framework, and WCF. In 2000 he published his first book on software development and continues to contribute to magazines and other publications. He is currently responsible for the Visual Studio Team System Database Edition. Jason's only other passions are his wife and kids, with whom he happily lives in the Seattle area.

Steven Clarke has been a user experience researcher in the Developer Division at Microsoft since 1999. His main interests are observing, understanding, and modeling the experiences that developers have with APIs in order to help design APIs that provide an optimal experience to their users.

Joe Duffy is the development lead for parallel extensions to .NET at Microsoft. He codes heavily, manages a team of developers, and defines the team's long-term vision and strategy. Joe previously worked on concurrency in the CLR team and was a software engineer at EMC. While not geeking out, Joe spends his time playing guitar, studying music theory, and blogging at www.bluebytesoftware.com.

Patrick Dussud is a Technical Fellow at Microsoft, where he serves as the chief architect of both the CLR and the .NET Framework architecture groups. He works on .NET Framework issues across the company, helping development teams best utilize the CLR. He specifically focuses on taking advantage of the abstractions the CLR provides to optimize program execution.

Michael Fanning is the current development lead for Expression Web at Microsoft. He was an early member of the team that produced FxCop for internal use and ultimately added it to Visual Studio 2005 for release to the general public.

Kit George is a program manager on the .NET Framework team at Microsoft. He graduated in 1995 with a B.A. in psychology, philosophy, and mathematics from Victoria University of Wellington (New Zealand). Prior to joining Microsoft, he worked as a technical trainer, primarily in Visual Basic. He participated in the design and implementation of the first two releases of the Framework for the last two years.

Jan Gray is a software architect at Microsoft who now works on concurrency programming models and infrastructure. He was previously a CLR performance architect, and in the 1990s he helped write the early MS C++ compilers (e.g., semantics, runtime object model, precompiled headers, PDBs, incremental compilation, and linking) and Microsoft Transaction Server. Jan's interests include building custom multiprocessors in FPGAs.

Brian Grunkemeyer has been a software design engineer on the .NET Framework team at Microsoft since 1998. He implemented a large portion of the Framework Class Libraries and contributed to the details of the classes in the ECMA/ISO CLI standard. Brian is currently working on future versions of the .NET Framework, including areas such as generics, managed code reliability, versioning, contracts in code, and improving the developer experience. He has a B.S. in computer science with a double major in cognitive science from Carnegie Mellon University.

Eric Gunnerson found himself at Microsoft in 1994 after working in the aerospace and going-out-of-business industries. He has worked on the C++ compiler team, as a member of the C# language design team, and as an early thought follower on the DevDiv community effort. He worked on the Windows DVD Maker UI during Vista and joined the Microsoft HealthVault team in early 2007. He spends his free time cycling, skiing, cracking ribs, building decks, blogging, and writing about himself in the third person.

Phil Haack is a program manager with the ASP.NET team working on the ASP.NET MVC Framework, which is being developed in a community-driven transparent manner. The Framework driving goal is to embody and encourage certain principles of good software design: separation of concerns, testability, and the single responsibility principle, among others. Phil is also a code junkie and loves to both write software as well as write about software development on his blog.

Anders Hejlsberg is a technical fellow in the Developer Division at Microsoft. He is the chief designer of the C# programming language and a key participant in the development of the .NET Framework. Before joining Microsoft in 1996, Anders was a principal engineer at Borland International. As one of the first employees of Borland, he was the original author of Turbo Pascal and later worked as the chief architect of the Delphi product line. Anders studied engineering at the Technical University of Denmark.

David Kean is a developer on the .NET Framework team at Microsoft, where he works on the Managed Extensibility Framework (MEF), a set of building blocks for developing extensible and dynamic applications. He worked earlier on the often well-loved but also greatly misunderstood tool FxCop and its related sibling, Visual Studio Code Analysis. He graduated with a B.CS. from Deakin University in Melbourne, Australia, and is now based in Seattle with his wife, Lucy, and two children, Jack and Sarah.

Rico Mariani began his career at Microsoft in 1988, working on language products, beginning with Microsoft C version 6.0, and he contributed there until the release of the Microsoft Visual C++ version 5.0 development system. In 1995, Rico became development manager for what was to become the "Sidewalk" project, which started his seven years of platform work on various MSN technologies. In the summer of 2002, Rico returned to the Developer Division as a performance architect on the CLR team. His performance work led to his most recent assignment as chief architect of Visual Studio. Rico's interests include compilers and language theory, databases, 3D art, and good fiction.

Anthony Moore is a development lead for the Connected Systems Division. He was the development lead for the Base Class Libraries of the CLR from 2001 to 2007, spanning FX V1.0 to FX 3.5. Anthony joined Microsoft in 1999 and initially worked on Visual Basic and ASP.NET. Before that he worked as a corporate developer for eight years in his native Australia, including a three-year period working in the snack food industry.

Vance Morrison is a performance architect for the .NET Runtime at Microsoft. He involves himself with most aspects of runtime performance, with current attention devoted to improving startup time. He has been involved in designs of components of the .NET runtime since its inception. He previously drove the design of the .NET Intermediate Language (IL) and has been the development lead for the JIT compiler for the runtime.

Christophe Nasarre is a software architect and development lead for Business Objects, a multinational software company from SAP that is focused on business intelligence solutions. During his spare time, Christophe writes articles for *MSDN Magazine*, MSDN, and ASPToday. Since 1996, he has also worked as a technical editor on numerous books on Win32, COM, MFC, .NET, and WPF. In 2007, he wrote his first book, *Windows via C/C++* from Microsoft Press.

Dare Obasanjo is a program manager on the MSN Communication Services Platform team at Microsoft. He brings his love of solving problems with XML to building the server infrastructure utilized by the MSN Messenger, MSN Hotmail, and MSN Spaces teams. He was previously a program manager on the XML team responsible for the core XML application programming interfaces and W3C XML Schema-related technologies in the .NET Framework.

Brian Pepin is a software architect at Microsoft and is currently working on the WPF and Silverlight designers for Visual Studio. He's been involved in developer tools and frameworks for 14 years and has provided input on the design of Visual Basic 5, Visual J++, the .NET Framework, WPF, Silverlight, and more than one unfortunate experiment that luckily never made it to market.

Jonathan Pincus was a senior researcher in the Systems and Networking Group at Microsoft Research, where he focused on the security, privacy, and reliability of software and software-based systems. He was previously founder and CTO of Intrinsa and worked in design automation (placement and routing for ICs and CAD frameworks) at GE Calma and EDA Systems.

Jeff Prosise is a cofounder of Wintellect (www.wintellect.com). His most recent book, *Programming Microsoft .NET*, was published by Microsoft Press in 2002, and his writings appear regularly in *MSDN Magazine* and other developer magazines. Jeff's professional life revolves around ASP.NET, ASP.NET AJAX, and Silverlight. A reformed engineer who discovered after college that there's more to life than computing loads on mounting brackets, Jeff is known to go out of his way to get wet in some of the world's best dive spots and to spend way too much time building and flying R/C aircraft.

Brent Rector is a program manager at Microsoft on a technical strategy incubation effort. He has more than 30 years of experience in the software development industry in the production of programming language compilers, operating systems, ISV applications, and other products. Brent is the author and coauthor of numerous Windows software development books, including *ATL Internals, Win32 Programming* (both Addison-Wesley), and *Introducing WinFX* (Microsoft Press). Prior to joining Microsoft, Brent was the president and founder of Wise Owl Consulting, Inc. and chief architect of its premier .NET obfuscator, Demeanor for .NET.

Jeffrey Richter is a cofounder of Wintellect (www.Wintellect.com), a training, debugging, and consulting firm dedicated to helping companies build better software faster. He is the author of several best-selling .NET and Win32 programming books, including *Applied Microsoft .NET Framework Programming* (Microsoft Press). Jeffrey is also a contributing editor at *MSDN Magazine*, where he writes the "Concurrent Affairs" column. Jeff has been consulting with Microsoft's .NET Framework team since 1999 and was also a consultant on Microsoft's Web Services and Messaging Team.

Greg Schechter has been working on API implementation and API design for over 20 years, primarily in the 2D and 3D graphics realm, but also in media, imaging, general user interface systems, and asynchronous programming. Greg is currently an architect on the Windows Presentation Foundation and Silverlight teams at Microsoft. Prior to coming to Microsoft in 1994, Greg was at Sun Microsystems for six years. Beyond all of that, Greg also loves to write about himself in the third person.

Chris Sells is a program manager for the Connected Systems Division at Microsoft. He's written several books, including *Programming WPF, Windows Forms 2.0 Programming*, and *ATL Internals*. In his free time, Chris hosts various conferences and makes a pest of himself on Microsoft internal product team discussion lists.

Steve Starck is a technical lead on the ADO.NET team at Microsoft, where he has been developing and designing data access technologies, including ODBC, OLE DB, and ADO.NET, for the past ten years.

Herb Sutter is a leading authority on software development. During his career, Herb has been the creator and principal designer of several major commercial technologies, including the PeerDirect peer replication system for heterogeneous distributed databases, the C++/CLI language extensions to C++ for .NET programming, and most recently the Concur concurrent programming model. Currently a software architect at Microsoft, he also serves as chair of the ISO C++ standards committee and is the author of four acclaimed books and hundreds of technical papers and articles on software development topics.

Clemens Szyperski joined Microsoft Research as a software architect in 1999. He focuses on leveraging component software to effectively build new kinds of software. Clemens is cofounder of Oberon Microsystems and its spin-off, Esmertec, and he was an associate professor at the School of Computer Science, Queensland University of Technology, Australia, where he retains an adjunct professorship. He is the author of the Jolt award-winning *Component Software* (Addison-Wesley) and the coauthor of *Software Ecosystem* (MIT Press). He has a Ph.D. in computer science from the Swiss Federal Institute of Technology in Zurich and an M.S. in electrical engineering/computer engineering from the Aachen University of Technology.

Mircea Trofin is a program manager with the .NET Application Framework Core group at Microsoft. He is primarily responsible for driving the effort for ensuring and improving the architecture of the .NET Framework. He is also responsible for a number of upcoming features in .NET in the area of component-based programming. He received his B.A.Sc. in computer engineering from University of Waterloo, and his Ph.D. in computer science from University College Dublin.

Paul Vick is the language architect for Visual Basic, leading the language design team. Paul originally began his career working at Microsoft in 1992 on the Microsoft Access team, shipping versions 1.0 through 97 of Access. In 1998, he moved to the Visual Basic team, participating in the design and implementation of the Visual Basic compiler and driving the redesign of the language for the .NET Framework. He is the author of the Visual Basic .NET Language Specification and the Addison-Wesley book *The Visual Basic .NET Language*. His weblog can be found at www.panopticoncentral.net.

1

Introduction

IF YOU COULD STAND over the shoulder of every developer who is using your framework to write code and explain how it is supposed to be used, guidelines would not be necessary. The guidelines presented in this book give you, as the framework author, a palette of tools that allow you to create a common language between framework authors and the developers who will use the frameworks. For example, exposing an operation as a property instead of exposing it as a method conveys vital information about how that operation is to be used.

In the early days of the PC era, the main tools for developing applications were a programming language compiler, a very small set of standard libraries, and the raw operating system application programming interfaces (APIs)—a very basic set of low-level programming tools.

Even as developers were building applications using such basic tools, they were discovering an increasing amount of code that was repetitive and could be abstracted away through higher-level APIs. Operating system vendors noticed that they could make it cheaper for developers to create applications for their systems if they provided them with such higher-level APIs. The number of applications that could run on the system would increase, which would then make the system more appealing to end users who demanded a variety of applications. Also, independent tool and component vendors quickly recognized the business opportunities offered by raising the API abstraction level.

In parallel, the industry slowly began to accept object-oriented design and its emphasis on extensibility and reusability.[1] When reusable library vendors adopted object-oriented programming (OOP) for the development of their high-level APIs, the concept of what we consider a *framework* was born. Application developers were no longer expected to write most of the application from scratch. The framework would provide most of the needed pieces, which would then be customized and connected[2] to form applications.

As more vendors started to provide components that could be reused by stitching them together into a single application, developers noticed that some of the components did not fit together well. Their applications looked and worked like a house built by different contractors who never talked to each other. Likewise, as a larger percentage of application source code became constructed of API calls rather than standard language constructs, developers started to complain that they now had to read and write multiple languages: one programming language and several "languages" of the components they wanted to reuse. This had significant negative impact on developer productivity, and productivity is one of the main factors in the success of a framework. It became clear that there was a need for common rules that would ensure consistency and seamless integration of reusable components.

Most of today's application development platforms spell out some kind of design conventions to be used when designing frameworks for the platform. Frameworks that do not follow such conventions, and so do not integrate well with the platform, are either a source of constant frustration to those trying to use them, or are at a competitive disadvantage

---

1. Object-oriented languages are not the only languages well suited for developing extensible and reusable libraries, but they played a key role in popularizing the concepts of reusability and extensibility. Extensibility and reusability are a large part of the philosophy of object-oriented programming (OOP), and the adoption of OOP contributed to increased awareness of their benefits.

2. There has been a great deal of recent criticism of object-oriented (OO) design, which claims that the promise of reusability never materialized. OO design is not a guarantee of reusability (especially without testing), but we are not sure that it was ever promised. On the other hand, OO design provides natural constructs to express units of reusability (types), to communicate and control extensibility points (virtual members), and to facilitate decoupling (abstractions).

and ultimately fail in the marketplace. The ones that succeed are often described as self-consistent, making sense, and well-designed.

1.1 Qualities of a Well-Designed Framework

The question is, then, what defines a well-designed framework, and how do you get there? There are many factors, such as performance, reliability, security, dependency management, and so on, that affect software quality. Frameworks, of course, must adhere to these same quality standards. The difference between frameworks and other kinds of software is that frameworks are made up of reusable APIs, which presents a set of special considerations in designing quality frameworks.

1.1.1 Well-Designed Frameworks Are Simple

Most frameworks do not lack power, because more features are reasonably easy to add as requirements become clearer. On the other hand, simplicity often gets sacrificed when schedule pressure, feature creep, or the desire to satisfy every little corner-case scenario takes over the development process. However, simplicity is a must-have feature of every framework. If you have any second thoughts about the complexity of a design, it is almost always much better to cut the feature from the current release and spend more time to get the design right for the next release. As framework designers often say, "You can always add; you cannot ever remove." If the design does not feel right, and you ship it anyway, you are likely to regret having done so.

> ■ **CHRIS SELLS** As a test of whether an API is "simple," I like to submit it to a test I call "client-first programming." If you say what your library does and ask a developer to write a program against what he or she expects such a library to look like (without actually looking at your library), does the developer come up with something substantially similar to what you've produced? Do this with a few developers. If the majority of them write similar things without matching what you've produced, they're right, you're wrong, and your library should be updated appropriately.
>
> I find this technique so useful that I often design library APIs by writing the client code I wish I could write and then just implement the library to match that. Of course, you have to balance simplicity with the intrinsic complexity of the functionality you're trying to provide, but that's what your computer science degree is for!

Many of the guidelines described in this book are motivated by the desire to strike the right balance between power and simplicity. In particular, Chapter 2 talks extensively about some basic techniques used by the most successful framework designers to design the right level of simplicity and power.

1.1.2 Well-Designed Frameworks Are Expensive to Design

Good framework design does not happen magically. It is hard work that consumes lots of time and resources. If you are not willing to invest real money in the design, you should not expect to create a well-designed framework.

Framework design should be an explicit and distinct part of the development process;[3] it must be explicit because it needs to be appropriately planned, staffed, and executed, and it must be distinct because it cannot just be a side effect of the implementation process. It is too often the case that the framework is whatever types and members happen to remain public after the implementation process ends.

The best framework designs are done either by people whose explicit responsibility is framework design, or by people who can put the framework designer's hat on at the right time in the development process. Mixing the responsibilities is a mistake and leads to designs that expose implementation details, which should not be visible to the end user of the framework. [4]

---

3. Do not misunderstand this as an endorsement of heavy up-front design processes. In fact, heavy API design processes lead to waste, because APIs often need to be tweaked after they are implemented. However, the API design process has to be separate from the implementation process and has to be incorporated in every part of the product cycle: the planning phase (what are the APIs our customers need?), the design process (what are the functionality trade-offs we are willing to make to get the right framework APIs?), the development process (have we allocated time to try to use the framework to see how the end result feels?), the beta process (have we allocated time for the costly API redesign?), and maintenance (are we decreasing the design quality as we evolve the framework?).

4. Prototyping is one of the most important parts of the framework design process, but prototyping is very different from implementation.

1.1.3 Well-Designed Frameworks Are Full of Trade-Offs

There is no such thing as the perfect design. Design is all about making trade-offs, and to make the right decisions, you need to understand the options, their benefits, and their drawbacks. If you find yourself thinking you have a design without trade-offs, you are probably missing something big instead of finding the silver bullet.

The practices described in this book are presented as guidelines, rather than rules, precisely because framework design requires managing trade-offs. Some of the guidelines discuss the trade-offs involved and even provide alternatives that need to be considered in specific situations.

1.1.4 Well-Designed Frameworks Borrow from the Past

Most successful frameworks borrow from and build on top of existing proven designs. It is possible—and often desirable—to introduce completely novel solutions into framework design, but it should be done with the utmost caution. As the number of new concepts increases, the probability that the overall design will be right goes down.

> ■ **CHRIS SELLS**   Please don't innovate in library design. Make the API to your library as boring as possible. You want the functionality to be interesting, not the API.

The guidelines contained in this book are based on the experiences we gained while designing the .NET Framework; they encourage borrowing from things that worked and withstood the test of time, and warn about ones that did not. We encourage you to use these good practices as a starting point, and to improve on them. Chapter 9 talks extensively about common design approaches that worked.

1.1.5 Well-Designed Frameworks Are Designed to Evolve

Thinking about how to evolve your framework in the future has some trade-offs. On the one hand, a framework designer can certainly take more time and painstaking effort in the design process, and occasionally additional complexity can be introduced "just in case." But, on the other hand, careful consideration can also save you from shipping something that will degrade over time, or even worse, something that will not be able to preserve backward compatibility.[5] As a general rule, it is better to move a complete feature to the next release than to do it halfway in the current release.

Whenever you make a design trade-off, you should determine how the decision will affect your ability to evolve the framework in the future. The guidelines presented in this book take this important concern into account.

1.1.6 Well-Designed Frameworks Are Integrated

Modern frameworks need to be designed to integrate well with a large ecosystem of different development tools, programming languages, application models, and so on. Distributed computing means that the era of frameworks designed for specific application models is over. This is also true of frameworks designed without thinking about proper tool support or integration with programming languages used by the developer community.

1.1.7 Well-Designed Frameworks Are Consistent

Consistency is the key characteristic of a well-designed framework. It is one of the most important factors affecting productivity. A consistent framework allows for transfer of knowledge between the parts of the framework that a developer knows to parts that the developer is trying to learn. Consistency also helps developers to quickly recognize which parts of the design are truly unique to the particular feature area and so require special attention, and which are just the same old common design patterns and idioms.

Consistency is probably the main theme of this book. Almost every single guideline is partially motivated by consistency, but Chapters 3 to 5 are probably the most important ones, because they describe the core consistency guidelines.

---

5. Backward compatibility is not discussed in detail in this book, but it should be considered one of the basics of framework design, together with reliability, security, and performance.

We offer these guidelines to help you make your framework successful. The next chapter presents guidelines for general library design.

> ■ **PHIL HAACK**   I would add one more point to this list, which is that "Well-Designed Frameworks Are Testable." And by "testable" I don't just mean that the framework itself can be unit tested, though that is important as well.
>
> One hard lesson we learned from our customers as we released early previews of the ASP.NET MVC framework is that unit test coverage of a framework is not sufficient to calling it "testable."
>
> While we could easily test our framework, we needed to go further and strive to make sure that applications built *using our framework* are themselves testable.
>
> This usually falls out naturally by following solid design principles such as Separation of Concerns, Orthogonality, Composition, and DRY (Don't Repeat Yourself). Most importantly, we put ourselves in our customers' shoes and built apps using our framework in a test-driven manner. This app building effort improved the design of the Framework immensely.

◼ 2 ◼
Framework Design Fundamentals

A SUCCESSFUL GENERAL-PURPOSE framework must be designed for a broad range of developers with different requirements, skills, and backgrounds. One of the biggest challenges facing framework designers is to offer both power and simplicity to this diverse group of customers.

Another important goal of a managed framework designer must be to offer a unified programming model regardless of the kind of application[1] a developer writes or the programming language the developer uses.

By using widely accepted general software design principles and following the guidelines described in this chapter, you can create a framework that offers consistent functionality that is appropriate for a broad range of developers who are building different kinds of applications using a variety of programming languages.

✓ **DO** design frameworks that are both powerful and easy to use.

A well-designed framework makes implementing simple scenarios easy. At the same time, it does not prohibit implementing more advanced scenarios, though these might be more difficult. As Alan Kay said, "Simple things should be simple and complex things should be possible."

---

1. For example, a framework component should have the same programming model whether it is used in a console, Windows Forms, or ASP.NET application, if at all possible.

This guideline is also related to the 80/20 rule, which says that in any situation, 20 percent will be important, and 80 percent will be trivial. When designing a framework, concentrate on the important 20 percent of scenarios and APIs. In other words, invest in the design of the most commonly used parts of the framework.

✓ **DO** understand and explicitly design for a broad range of developers with different programming styles, requirements, and skill levels.

> ▪▪ **PAUL VICK**   There is no magic bullet when designing frameworks for Visual Basic developers. Our users run the gamut from people who are picking up a programming tool for the first time to industry veterans building large-scale commercial applications. The key to designing a framework that appeals to Visual Basic developers is to focus on allowing them to get the job done with the minimum amount of fuss and bother. Designing a framework that uses the minimum number of concepts is a good idea, not because VB developers can't handle concepts, but because having to stop and think about concepts extraneous to the task at hand interrupts workflow. The goal of a VB developer usually is not to learn some interesting or exciting new concept or to be impressed with the intellectual purity and simplicity of your design but to get the job done and move on.

> ▪▪ **KRZYSZTOF CWALINA**   It is easy to design for users who are like you, and very difficult to design for somebody unlike you. There are too many APIs that are designed by domain experts and, frankly, they are only good for domain experts. The problem is that most developers are not, will never be, and do not need to be experts in all technologies used in modern applications.

> ▪▪ **BRAD ABRAMS**   Although the famous Hewlett-Packard motto "Build for the engineer at the next bench" is useful for driving quality and completeness into software projects, it is misleading for API design. For example, the developers on the Microsoft Word team have a clear understanding that they are not the target customers for Word. My mom is much more the target customer. Therefore the Word team puts in many more features that my mom might find helpful rather than the features the development team finds helpful. Although that is obvious in the case of applications such as Word, we often tend to miss the principle when designing APIs. We tend to design APIs only for ourselves instead of thinking clearly about the customer scenarios.

✓ **DO** understand and design for the broad variety of programming languages.

There are many programming language implementations supporting the Common Language Runtime (CLR) and the .NET Framework. Some of these languages might be very different from the language you are using to implement your APIs. Often special care needs to be taken to ensure that your APIs can work well with a variety of languages.

For example, developers using dynamically typed languages (such as Python, Ruby, and others) might have problems using APIs that require them to create a strongly typed type or apply an attribute to a type. Such APIs usually have *Generic*[2] parameters or `System.Type` parameters and require the user to pass a custom type as the argument.

Other special considerations for various programming languages are described throughout the book.

2.1 Progressive Frameworks

Designing a single framework for a broad range of developers, scenarios, and languages is a difficult and costly enterprise. Historically, framework vendors offered several products targeted at specific developer groups for specific scenarios. For example, Microsoft was providing Visual Basic libraries optimized for simplicity and a relatively narrow set of scenarios, and Win32 libraries optimized for power and flexibility, even if it meant sacrificing ease of use. Other frameworks, such as MFC and ATL, were also targeted at specific developer groups and scenarios.

Although this multiframework approach has proven to be successful in providing APIs that were powerful and easy for specific developer groups, it has significant drawbacks. The main drawback[3] is that the multitude of frameworks makes it difficult for developers using one of the frameworks to transfer their knowledge to the next skill level or scenario (which often requires a different framework). For example, when there is a need to

---

2. Parameters of Generic Types or Generic Members.
3. Other drawbacks include slower time to market for frameworks that are wrappers on top of other frameworks, duplication of effort, and lack of common tools.

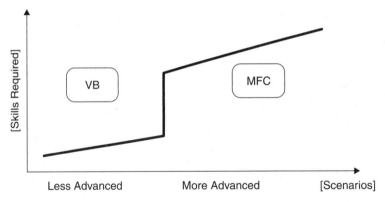

FIGURE 2-1: Learning curve of a multiframework platform

implement a different application that requires more powerful functional-ity, developers hit a very steep learning curve, because they have to learn a completely different way of programming, as shown in Figure 2-1.

ANDERS HEJLSBERG   In the good old days of early Windows, you had the Windows API. To write apps you fired up your C compiler, #included windows.h, created a winproc, and handled your windows messages—basically the old Petzold style of Windows programming. Although this worked, it was neither particularly productive nor particularly easy.

Over time, various programming models on top of the Windows API have emerged. VB embraced Rapid Application Development (RAD). With VB you could instantiate a form, drag components onto the form, and write event handlers; through delegation, your code executes.

In the world of C++, we had MFC and ATL taking a different view. The key concept here is subclassing. Developers would subclass from an existing monolithic, object-oriented framework. Although this gives you more power and expressiveness, it doesn't really match the ease or productivity of VB's composition model.

With ASP and the Web, we've seen the emergence of the ASP model, where you write stateless code that's embedded in HTML pages.

If you look at this picture, one of the problems is that your choice of programming model also necessarily becomes your choice of programming language. This is an unfortunate situation. If you're a skilled MFC developer and you need to write some code in an ASP page, your skills don't translate. Likewise, if you know a lot about VB, there's not much that transfers to MFC.

There is also not a consistent availability of APIs. Each of these models has dreamed up its own solutions to a number of problems that are actually core and common to all of the models; for example, how do I deal with file I/O, how do I do string formatting, how do I do security, threading, and so on?

What the .NET Framework does is unify all of these models. It gives you a consistent API that is available everywhere regardless of what language you use or what programming model you are targeting.

PAUL VICK   It's also worth noting that this unification comes at a cost. There is an unresolvable tension between writing frameworks that expose a great amount of power and allow a developer a great deal of control over behavior and writing frameworks that expose a more limited functionality in an extremely conceptually simple way. In most cases, there is no silver bullet, and trade-offs inevitably have to be made between power on the one hand and simplicity on the other. An enormous amount of effort went into the .NET Framework to ensure that it achieved the best possible balance between these two, but it is something that I think we continue to work on to this day.

A much better approach is to provide a *progressive framework*, which is a single framework targeted at a broad range of developers that allows for transfer of knowledge from less advanced to more advanced scenarios.

The .NET Framework is a progressive framework and provides such a gradual learning curve (see Figure 2-2).

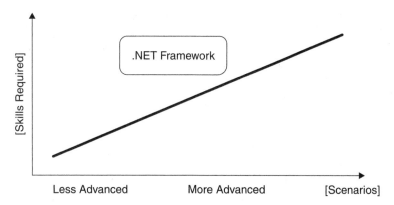

FIGURE 2-2: Learning curve of a progressive framework platform

Achieving a gradual learning curve with a low entry point is difficult but not impossible. It is difficult because it requires a new approach to the process of framework design, demands much greater design discipline, and has a higher design cost.

Fortunately, the guidelines described in this chapter and throughout the book are meant to guide you through the difficult design process and ultimately help you design a great progressive framework.

You should also keep in mind that the developer community is vast. It ranges from office workers recording macros to authors of low-level device drivers. Any framework that attempts to serve all of these users could end up being a mess that could not satisfy any of them. The goal of a progressive framework is to scale through a broad range of developers, but not every possible developer. This clearly means that those developers who fall outside this target will need specialty APIs.

2.2 Fundamental Principles of Framework Design

Providing a development platform that is both powerful and easy to use is one of the main goals of the .NET Framework, and it should be one of your goals if you are extending it. The first version of the Framework indeed presented a powerful set of APIs, but some developers found parts of the Framework too difficult to use.

> ■ **RICO MARIANI**   The flip side of this is that it must not only be easy to use the API; it must also be easy to use the API in the best possible way. Think carefully about what patterns you offer and be sure that the most natural way to use your system gives results that are correct, is secure against attacks, and has great performance. Make it hard to do things the wrong way. A few years ago I wrote:
>
> **The Pit of Success**
> In stark contrast to a summit, a peak, or a journey across a desert to find victory through many trials and surprises, we want our customers to simply fall into winning practices by using our platform and frameworks. To the extent that we make it easy to get into trouble we fail.
>
> True productivity comes from being able to easily create great products—not from being able to easily create junk. Build a pit of success.

Customer feedback and usability studies have shown that a large segment of the VB developer group had problems learning VB.NET. Part of the problem lay simply in the fact that the Framework is different from VB 6.0 libraries, but there were also several major usability problems related to API design. Fixing these problems became a high priority for Microsoft in the Framework 2.0 time frame.

The principles described in this section were developed to address the problems just mentioned and are meant to help framework designers avoid the most severe design mistakes reported in many usability studies and in customer feedback. We believe that these principles are central to the design of any general-purpose framework. Some of the principles and recommendations overlap, which is probably a testimony to their validity.

2.2.1 The Principle of Scenario-Driven Design

Frameworks often contain a very large set of APIs. This is necessary to enable advanced scenarios that require power and expressiveness. However, most development revolves around a small set of common scenarios that use a relatively small subset of the full framework. To optimize the overall productivity of the developers using a framework, it is crucial to invest heavily in the design of APIs that are used in the most common scenarios.

Therefore, framework design should be focused around a set of common scenarios to the point where the whole design process is scenario-driven. We recommend that framework designers first write code that the users of the framework will have to write in main scenarios, and then design the object model to support these code samples.[4]

Framework Design Principle

Frameworks must be designed starting from a set of usage scenarios and code samples implementing these scenarios.

---

4. This is similar to processes based on test-driven development (TDD) or on use cases. There are some differences, though. TDD is more heavyweight because it has other objectives beyond driving the design of APIs. Use cases are describing scenarios on a higher level than individual API calls.

> ■ **KRZYSZTOF CWALINA**   I would like to add "There is simply no other way to design a great framework" to the principle just spelled out. If I had to choose only one design principle to be included in the book, this would be it. If I could not write a book but only a short article on what's important in API design, I would choose this principle.

Framework designers often make the mistake of starting with the design of the object model (using various design methodologies) and then writing code samples based on the resulting API. The problem is that most design methodologies (including most commonly used object-oriented design methodologies) are optimized for the maintainability of the resulting implementation, not for the usability of the resulting APIs. They are best suited for internal architecture designs—not for designs of the public API layer of a large framework.

When designing a framework, you should start with producing a scenario-driven API specification (see Appendix C). This specification can be either separate from the functional specification or part of a larger specification document. In the latter case, the API specification should precede the functional one in location and time.

The specification should contain a scenario section listing the top five to ten scenarios for a given technology area and should show code samples that implement these scenarios. The code samples should be in at least two programming languages. This is very important, because sometimes code written using those languages differs significantly.

It is also important that these scenarios be written using different coding styles that are common among users of the particular language (using language-specific features). The samples should be written using language-specific casing. For example, VB.NET is case insensitive, so samples should reflect that. C# code should follow the standard casing described in Chapter 3.

✓ **DO** make sure that the API design specification is the central part of the design of any feature that includes a publicly accessible API.

Appendix C contains an example of such a specification.

✓ **DO** define top usage scenarios for each major feature area.

The API specification should include a section that describes the main scenarios and shows code samples implementing these scenarios. The section should appear immediately after the executive overview section. The average feature area (such as file I/O) should have five to ten main scenarios.

✓ **DO** ensure that the scenarios correspond to an appropriate abstraction level. They should roughly correspond to the end-user use cases.

For example, reading from a file is a good scenario. Opening a file, reading a line of text from a file, or closing a file are not good scenarios; they are too granular.

✓ **DO** design APIs by first writing code samples for the main scenarios and then defining the object model to support the code samples.

For example, when designing an API to measure elapsed time, you might write the following scenario code samples:

```
// scenario #1 : measure time elapsed
Stopwatch watch = Stopwatch.StartNew();
DoSomething();
Console.WriteLine(watch.Elapsed);

// scenario #2 : reuse stopwatch
Dim watch As Stopwatch = Stopwatch.StartNew()
DoSomething();
Console.WriteLine(watch.ElapsedMilliseconds)

watch.Reset()
watch.Start()
DoSomething()
Console.WriteLine(watch.Elapsed)
```

These code samples lead to the following object model:

```
public class Stopwatch {
    public static Stopwatch StartNew();

    public void Start();
    public void Reset();

    public TimeSpan Elapsed            { get; }
    public long     ElapsedMilliseconds { get; }
    ...
}
```

> **JOE DUFFY**   As software developers, we enjoy creating fun and power-ful new capabilities, and sharing them with other developers. That's one of the reasons API design is so enjoyable. But it's also incredibly difficult to step back and objectively assess whether some new capability that you're particularly passionate about has utility in the real world. Using scenarios is the best way I know of to identify the need for and ideal usage of new capa-bilities. Developing scenarios is in fact incredibly *hard*, for good reason: It requires a unique combination of technical skill and customer understand-ing. When you're finished, you could make a series of decisions based only on gut feel and intuition, and perhaps deliver some useful APIs, but the risk that you will make a decision you will later regret is far greater. When in doubt, it's best to leave a feature out and decide to add it later when a com-pelling need is better understood.

✓ **DO** write main scenario code samples in at least two different language families (e.g., VB.NET and C++).

It is best to ensure that the languages chosen have significantly differ-ent syntax, style, and capabilities.

> **PAUL VICK**   If you are writing a framework to be used by multiple lan-guages, it is helpful to actually know more than one programming language (and knowing more than one C-style language doesn't count). We've found that sometimes an API works well only in one language, and that's because the person designing the API (and testing the API) only really knew that one language. Learn several .NET languages and really work with them the way they were designed to be used. Expecting the whole world to speak your language does not work well on a multilanguage platform like the .NET Framework.

✓ **CONSIDER** writing main scenario code samples using a dynamically typed language such as Python or Ruby.

It is easy to design APIs that don't work well with dynamically typed languages. Such languages often have problems dealing with some generic methods, APIs that rely on applying attributes or creating strongly typed types.

✗ **DO NOT** rely solely on standard design methodologies when designing the public API layer of a framework.

Standard design methodologies (including object-oriented design methodologies) are optimized for the maintainability of the resulting implementation, not for the usability of the resulting APIs. Scenario-driven design together with prototyping, usability studies, and some amount of iteration is a much better approach.

▪▪ **CHRIS ANDERSON**   Each developer has his or her own methodology, and although there isn't anything fundamentally wrong with using other modeling approaches, the problem generally is the output. Starting by writing the code you want a developer to write is almost always the best approach—think of it as a form of test-driven development. You write the perfect code and then work backwards to figure out the object model that you would want.

2.2.1.1 Usability Studies

Usability studies of a framework prototype conducted with a wide range of developers are the key to scenario-driven design. The APIs for the top scenarios might seem simple to their authors, but they might not actually be simple to other developers.

Understanding the way developers approach each of the main scenarios provides useful insight into the design of the framework and how well it meets the needs of all target developers. Because of this fact, conducting usability studies, either formally or informally, is a very important part of the framework design process.

If you discover during usability studies that the majority of developers cannot implement one of the scenarios, or if the approach they take is significantly different from what the designer expected, the API should be redesigned.

■ **KRZYSZTOF CWALINA** We did not test the usability of the types in the `System.IO` namespace before shipping version 1.0 of the Framework. Soon after shipping, we received negative customer feedback about `System.IO` usability. We were quite surprised, and we decided to conduct usability studies with eight average VB developers. Eight out of eight failed to read text from a file in the 30 minutes we allocated for the task. We believe this was due in part to problems with the documentation search engine and insufficient sample coverage; however, it is clear that the API itself had several usability problems. If we had conducted the studies before shipping the product, we could have eliminated a significant source of customer dissatisfaction and avoided the cost of trying to fix the API of a major feature area without introducing breaking changes.

■ **BRAD ABRAMS** There is no more powerful experience to give an API designer a visceral understanding of the usability of his or her API than sitting behind a one-way mirror watching developer after developer get frustrated with an API he or she designed and ultimately fail to complete the task. I personally went through a full range of emotions while watching the usability studies for `System.IO` that we did right after shipping version 1.0. As developer after developer failed to complete the simple task, my emotions moved from arrogance to disbelief, then to frustration, and finally to stringent resolve to fix the problem in the API.

■ **CHRIS SELLS** Usability studies can be formal, if you've got that kind of time and money, but you'll get 80 percent of the feedback you need by just running your proposed API by a few developers close to the target audience for your library. Don't let the term "usability study" scare you into doing nothing—think of it as a "hey, look at this" study instead.

The API usability studies should ideally be performed using the actual development environment, code editors, and the documentation most widely used by the targeted developer group. However, it is best to run usability studies early rather than late in the product cycle, so don't postpone organizing a study just because the whole product is not ready yet.

Also, formal usability studies are often impractical for small development teams and frameworks that target a relatively small set of customers. In such cases, an informal study can be conducted. Giving a prototype library to somebody not familiar with the design, asking them to spend 30 minutes writing a simple program, and observing how they deal with the design is a great way to find the most troublesome API design issues.

✓ **DO** organize usability studies to test APIs in main scenarios.

> The studies should be organized early in the development cycle, because the most severe usability problems often require substantial design changes. Most developers should be able to write code for the main scenarios without major problems; if they cannot, you need to redesign the API. Although redesign is a costly practice, we found that it actually saves resources in the long run because the cost of fixing an unusable API without introducing changes that break existing code is enormous.

The next section describes the importance of designing APIs so that the initial encounter is not discouraging. This is called the principle of low barrier to entry.

2.2.2 The Principle of Low Barrier to Entry

Today, many developers expect to learn the basics of new frameworks very quickly. They want to do it by experimenting with parts of the framework on an ad hoc basis, and only take the time to fully understand the whole architecture if they find a particular feature interesting or if they need to move beyond the simple scenarios. The initial encounter with a badly designed API can leave a lasting impression of complexity and discourage some from using the framework. This is why it is very important for frameworks to provide a very low barrier for developers who just want to experiment with the framework.

Framework Design Principle

Frameworks must offer a low barrier to entry for nonexpert users through ease of experimentation.

Many developers want to experiment with an API to discover what it does and then adjust their code slowly to get their program to do what they really want. The huge demand for the Edit & Continue feature is a manifestation of this preference.

■■ **PAUL VICK** Most developers, regardless of the language that they work in, learn by doing. Documentation can help give the initial idea of what's supposed to happen, but we all know that you never really learn how something works until you get down into it and start fiddling around, trying to do something useful. Visual Basic, in particular, encourages this kind of experimental approach to programming. Although we never eschew forethought and advance planning, we try to make the process of learning and programming a continuous flow. Writing APIs that are self-evident and do not require a complex knowledge of the interaction of multiple objects or APIs encourages this flow. (In fact, this seems to apply across most languages, not just Visual Basic.)

Some APIs lend themselves to experimentation and some do not. To be easy to experiment with, an API must do the following:

- Allow easy identification of the right set of types and members for common programming tasks. A namespace intended to hold common scenario APIs that contains 500 types, out of which only a handful are actually important in common scenarios, is not easy to experiment with. The same applies to mainline scenario types with many members that are intended only for very advanced scenarios.

■■ **CHRIS ANDERSON** In the early days of the Windows Presentation Foundation (WPF) project, we ran into this exact issue. We had a common base type named `Visual` from which almost all of our elements were derived. The problem was that it introduced members that directly conflicted with the object model of the more derived elements, specifically around children. `Visual` had a single hierarchy of child visuals for rendering, but our elements wanted to introduce domain-specific children (like a `TabControl` only accepting `TabPages`). Our solution was to create a `VisualOperations` class that had static members that worked on a `Visual` instead of complicating the object model of every element.

- Allow a developer to use it immediately, whether or not it does what the developer ultimately wants it to do or not. A framework that requires an extensive initialization or an instantiating of several types and then hooking them together is not easy to experiment with. Similarly, APIs with no convenience overloads (overloaded members with short parameter lists) or bad defaults for properties pose a high barrier for developers who just want to experiment with the APIs.

> **CHRIS ANDERSON** Think of the object model as a map—you have to put clear signs about how to get from one place to another. You want a property to clearly point people to what it does, what values it takes, and what will happen if you set it. Pointing to an abstract base type with no obvious derivations is a bad, bad thing. An example of this being broken is how animations were exposed in WPF: The type for animations was `Timeline`, but nothing in the namespace ended in the word "Timeline." It turns out that `Animation` derived from `Timeline` and there were lots of `DoubleAnimation`, `ColorAnimation`, and so on, but there was no connection between the property type and the valid items with which to fill the property.

- Allow for easy finding and fixing of mistakes caused by incorrect usage of an API. For example, APIs should throw exceptions that clearly describe what needs to be done to fix the problem.

> **CHRIS SELLS** In my own programming, I dearly love error messages that say what I did wrong and how to fix it. All too often, all I get is the former, when all I really care about is the latter.

The following guidelines will help you ensure that your framework is well suited for developers who want to learn by experimenting.

✓ **DO** ensure that each main feature area namespace contains only types that are used in the most common scenarios. Types used in advanced scenarios should be placed in subnamespaces.

For example, the `System.Net` namespace provides networking mainline-scenario APIs. The more advanced socket APIs are placed in the `System.Net.Sockets` subnamespace.

> ■▪ **ANTHONY MOORE** The converse of this is also true, which could be stated as, "Don't bury a commonly used type in a namespace with much less commonly used types." `StringBuilder` is an example of something we later wished we had included in the `System` namespace. It lives in `System.Text` but is much more commonly used than the other types in there and is not closely related to them.
>
> That being said, this is the only thing in the `System` namespace that suffers from the converse of this rule. For the most part, we suffered from having too many infrequently used types in there.

✓ **DO** provide simple overloads of constructors and methods. A simple overload has a very small number of parameters, and all parameters are primitives.

✗ **DO NOT** have members intended for advanced scenarios on types intended for mainline scenarios.

> ■▪ **BRAD ABRAMS** One of the important principles in designing the .NET Framework was the notion of addition through subtraction. That is, by removing features from (or never adding them to) the framework, we could actually make developers more productive because there would be fewer concepts to deal with. Leaving out multiple inheritance is a classic example of addition through subtraction at the CLR level.

✗ **DO NOT** require users to explicitly instantiate more than one type in the most basic scenarios.

> ■▪ **KRZYSZTOF CWALINA** Book publishers say that the number of copies a book will sell is inversely proportional to the number of equations in the book. The framework designer version of this law is this: The number of customers who will use your framework is inversely proportional to the number of explicit constructor invocations required to implement the top ten simple scenarios.

✗ **DO NOT** require that users perform any extensive initialization before they can start programming basic scenarios.

Mainline-scenario APIs should be designed to require minimal initialization. Ideally, a default constructor or a constructor with one simple parameter should be sufficient to start working with a type designed for the basic scenarios.

```
var zipCodes = new Dictionary<string,int>();
zipCodes.Add("Redmond",98052);
zipCodes.Add("Sammamish",98074);
```

If some initialization is necessary, the exception that results from not performing the initialization should clearly explain what needs to be done.

> ■ **STEVEN CLARKE** Since the first edition of this book was published, we have done significant usability studies in this area. Time and time again we observe that types that require extensive initialization significantly raise the barrier to entry. The consequences of this are that some developers will decide not to use those types and will look for something else that might do the job instead, some developers will end up using the type incorrectly, and only a few developers will eventually figure out how to use the type correctly.

ADO.NET is an example of a feature area that our customers found difficult to use because of the extensive initialization it requires. Even in the simplest scenarios, users are expected to understand complex interactions and dependencies between several types. To use this feature, even in simple scenarios, users must instantiate and hook up several objects (instances of DataSet, DataAdapter, SqlConnection, and SqlCommand). Note that many of these problems were addressed in the .NET Framework 2.0 through the addition of helper classes, which greatly simplified basic scenarios.

✓ **DO** provide good defaults for all properties and parameters (using convenience overloads), if possible.

`System.Messaging.MessageQueue` is a good illustration of this concept. The component can send messages after passing just a path string to the constructor and calling the `Send` method. The message priority, encryption algorithms, and other message properties can be customized by adding code to the simple scenario.

```
var ordersQueue = new MessageQueue(path);
ordersQueue.Send(order); // uses default priority, encryption, etc.
```

These recommendations cannot be applied blindly. Framework designers should avoid providing defaults if the default can lead the user astray. For example, a default should never result in a security hole or horribly performing code.

✓ **DO** communicate incorrect usage of APIs using exceptions.

The exceptions should clearly describe their cause and the way the developer should modify the code to get rid of the problem. For example, the `EventLog` component requires the `Source` property to be set before events can be written. If the `Source` is not set before `WriteEntry` is called, an exception is thrown that states, "`Source` property was not set before writing to the event log."

> ◾ **STEVEN CLARKE** We've observed many developers in our usability studies who consider exceptions like these to be the best kind of documentation an API can provide. The guidance provided is always in the context of what the developer is trying to achieve, and it really supports the learning-by-doing approach favored by many developers.

The next section describes the importance of making the object model as self-documenting as possible.

2.2.3 The Principle of Self-Documenting Object Models

Many frameworks consist of hundreds, if not thousands, of types and significantly more members and parameters. Developers using such frameworks require a great deal of guidance and frequent reminders of the purpose and proper usage of the APIs. Reference documentation by itself cannot meet the demand. If it is necessary to refer to the documentation to answer the simplest questions, doing so is likely to be time-consuming and break the developer's workflow. Moreover, as noted earlier, many developers prefer to code by trial and error, and they resort to reading documentation only when intuition fails them.

Therefore, it is very important to design APIs that do not require that developers read documentation every time they want to perform a simple task. We found that following a simple set of guidelines can help in producing intuitive APIs that are relatively self-documenting.

Framework Design Principle

In simple scenarios, frameworks must be usable without the need for documentation.

■ CHRIS SELLS Never underestimate the power of Intellisense when anticipating how a developer will learn to use your framework. If your API is intuitive, Intellisense is 80 percent of all a new developer will need to be happy and successful with your library. Optimize for Intellisense.

■ KRZYSZTOF CWALINA Reference documentation is still a very important part of the framework. It is impossible to design a completely self-documenting API. Different people, depending on their skills and past experiences, will find different areas of your framework to be self-explanatory. Also, the documentation remains critically important for many users who do take the time to understand the overall design of the framework up front. For those users, informative, concise, and complete documentation is as crucial as self-explanatory object models.

✓ **DO** ensure that APIs are intuitive and can be successfully used in basic scenarios without referring to the reference documentation.

✓ **DO** provide great documentation with all APIs.

Not all APIs can be self-explanatory, and there are developers who want to thoroughly understand APIs before they start using them.

To make a framework self-documenting, care must be taken when choosing names, types, designing exceptions, and so on. The following sections describe some of the most important considerations related to the design of self-documenting APIs.

2.2.3.1 Naming

The simplest but also the most often missed opportunity for making frameworks self-documenting is to reserve simple and intuitive names for types that developers are expected to use (instantiate) in the most common scenarios. Framework designers often "burn" the best names for less commonly used types, with which most users do not have to be concerned.

For example, naming the abstract base class `File` and then providing a concrete type `NtfsFile` works well if the expectation is that all users will understand the inheritance hierarchy before they start using the APIs. If the users do not understand the hierarchy, the first thing they will try to use, most often unsuccessfully, is the `File` type. Although this naming works well in the object-oriented design sense (after all, `NtfsFile` is a kind of `File`), it fails the usability test, because `File` is the name most developers would intuitively think to program against.

> ■■ **KRZYSZTOF CWALINA**   The designers of the .NET Framework spent a lot of time discussing naming alternatives for main types. The majority of the identifiers in the Framework have well-chosen names. The cases in which the name choices are not so fortunate resulted from focusing on concepts and abstractions instead of the top scenarios.

Another recommendation is to use descriptive identifier names that clearly state what each method does and what each type and parameter represents. Framework designers should not be afraid to be quite verbose when choosing identifier names. For example, `EventLog.DeleteEventSource( string source, string machineName)` might be seen as rather verbose, but we think it has a positive net usability value.

Descriptive method names are only possible for methods that have simple and clear semantics. This is another reason avoiding complex semantics is a great general design principle to follow.

The overall point is that the names of identifiers need to be chosen extremely carefully. Name choices are one of the most important design choices a framework designer has to make. It is extremely difficult and costly to make changes to identifier names after the API has shipped.

✓ **DO** make the discussion about identifier naming choices a significant part of specification reviews.

What are the types most scenarios start with? What are the names most people will think of first when trying to implement this scenario? Are the names of the common types what users will think of first? For example, because "File" is the name most people think of when dealing with file I/O scenarios, the main type for accessing files should be named `File`.

Also, you should discuss the most commonly used methods of the most commonly used types and all of their parameters. Can anybody familiar with your technology, but not this specific design, recognize and call those methods quickly, correctly, and easily?

✗ **DO NOT** be afraid to use verbose identifier names.

Most identifier names should clearly state what each method does and what each type and parameter represents.

> ■ **BRENT RECTOR** Developers read identifier names hundreds, if not thousands, of times more than they type them. Modern editors even make the typing chore minimal. Longer names allow developers to find the right type or member via Intellisense more quickly. Additionally, code using types with well-chosen identifier names is more understandable and maintainable over the long term.
>
> A note to C-based language developers especially: Free yourselves from the shackles of reduced productivity induced by cryptic identifier naming habits.

✓ **CONSIDER** involving user education experts early in the design process. They can be a great resource for spotting designs with bad name choices and designs that would be difficult to explain to the customer.

✓ **CONSIDER** reserving the best type names for the most commonly used types.

If you believe you will add more high-level APIs in a future version, don't be afraid to reserve the best name in the first version of your framework for future APIs.

> ■■ **ANTHONY MOORE**   There are other reasons to avoid names that are too general even if you never anticipate using the name later. More specific names help to make the API more understandable and readable. If someone sees a general name in code, that person is likely to assume that it has a very general application, so it is misleading to use a general name for something more specialized. A more descriptive name can also help identify what scenario or technology a type is associated with.

2.2.3.2 Exceptions

Exceptions play a crucial role in designing self-documenting frameworks. They should communicate the correct usage to the developer through the exception message. For example, the following sample code should throw an exception with a message "Source property was not set before writing to the event log."

```
// C#
var log = new EventLog();
// The log source is not set yet.
log.WriteEntry("Hello World");
```

✓ **DO** use exception messages to communicate framework usage mistakes to the developer. For example, if a user forgets to set the Source property on an EventLog component, any calls to a method that requires the source to be set should state this clearly in the exception message. See more about the design of exceptions and exception messages in Chapter 7.

2.2.3.3 Strong Typing

Strong typing is probably the single most important factor in determining how intuitive APIs are. Clearly, calling Customer.Name is easier than calling

`Customer.Properties["Name"]`. Also, a `Name` property returning the name as a `String` is more usable than if the property returned an `Object`.

There are cases where property bags, late-bound calls, and other loosely typed APIs are necessary, but they should be an exception to the rule rather than common practice. Moreover, designers should consider providing strongly typed helpers for the most common operations that the user would perform on the nonstrongly typed API layer. For example, the `Customer` type may have a property bag but in addition provide strongly typed APIs for most common properties like `Name`, `Address`, and so on.

✓ **DO** provide strongly typed APIs if at all possible.

Do not rely exclusively on weakly typed APIs such as property bags. In cases in which a property bag is required, provide strongly typed properties for the most common properties in the bag.

■ **VANCE MORRISON** The strong typing (and thus much better Intellisense) is a crucial reason why .NET frameworks are easier to "learn by programming" than your typical COM API. From time to time, I still need to use functionality exposed through COM, and as long as it stays strongly typed, I do fine, but all too often APIs return or take a generic object or string parameter or passed DWORD when an enumeration is needed, and it takes me ten times longer to discover what exactly needs to be passed.

2.2.3.4 Consistency

Consistency with existing APIs that are already familiar to the user is yet another powerful technique for designing self-documenting frameworks. This includes consistency with other APIs in the .NET Framework as well as some legacy APIs. Having said that, you should not use legacy APIs or badly designed Framework APIs as an excuse to avoid following any guidelines described in this book, but you should also not change good established patterns and designs arbitrarily without having a reason to do so.

✓ **DO** ensure consistency with the .NET Framework and other frameworks your customers are likely to use.

Consistency is great for general usability. If a user is familiar with some part of a framework that your API is similar to, he or she will see your design as natural and intuitive. Your API should differ from other .NET Framework APIs only in places where there is something unique about your particular API.

2.2.3.5 Limiting Abstractions

Common scenario APIs should not use many abstractions but should instead correspond to physical or well-known logical parts of the system.

As noted before, standard object-oriented design methodologies are aimed at producing designs that are optimized for maintainability of the code base. This makes sense, because the maintenance cost is the largest chunk of the overall expense of developing a software product. One way of improving maintainability is through the use of abstractions. Because of that, modern design methodologies tend to produce a lot of them.

The problem is that frameworks with many abstractions force users to become experts in the framework architecture before starting to implement even the simplest scenarios. However, most developers don't have the desire or business justification to become experts in all of the APIs that such frameworks provide. For simple scenarios, developers demand that APIs be simple enough to be used without their having to understand how the entire feature areas fit together. This is something that the standard design methodologies are not optimized for and never claimed to be optimized for.

Of course, abstractions have their place in framework design. For example, abstractions can be extremely useful in improving testability and general extensibility of frameworks. Such extensibility is often possible because of well-designed abstractions. Chapter 6 talks about designing extensible APIs and should help you strike the right balance between too much and too little extensibility.

✗ **AVOID** many abstractions in mainline scenario APIs.

> ▪▪ **KRZYSZTOF CWALINA** Abstractions are almost always necessary, but too many abstractions indicate overengineered systems. Framework designers should be careful to design for customers, not for their own intellectual pleasure.

■ **JEFF PROSISE**   A design with too many abstractions can impact performance, too. I once worked with a customer who reengineered its product to incorporate a heavily OO design. They modeled *everything* as a class and ended up with some ridiculously deeply nested object hierarchies. Part of the intent of the redesign was to improve performance, but the "improved" software ran four times slower than the original!

■ **VANCE MORRISON**   Anyone who has had the "pleasure" of debugging through the C++ STL libraries knows that abstraction is a double-edged sword. Too much abstraction and code gets very difficult to understand, because you have to remember what all the abstract names really mean in your scenario. Going overboard with generics or inheritance are common symptoms that you may have overgeneralized.

■ **CHRIS SELLS**   It's often said that any problem in computer science can be solved by adding a layer of abstraction. Unfortunately, problems of developer education are often caused by them.

2.2.4 The Principle of Layered Architecture

Not all developers are required to solve the same kinds of problems. Different developers often require and expect different levels of abstraction and different amounts of control from the frameworks they use. Some developers who typically use C++ or C# value APIs that are expressive and powerful. We refer to APIs of this type as low-level APIs because they often offer a low level of abstraction. On the other hand, some developers who typically use C# or VB.NET value APIs that optimize for productivity and simplicity. We refer to these APIs as high-level APIs because they offer a higher level of abstraction. By using a layered design it is possible to build a single framework that meets these diverse needs.

Framework Design Principle

Layered design makes it possible to provide both power and ease of use in a single framework.

PAUL VICK   Part of the reason for moving Visual Basic to the .NET platform was the fact that many VB developers ran into problems when they needed to use low-level APIs to access specific functionality that was not available in the high-level APIs that we provided. The fact that VB developers might spend much of their initial time rapidly developing their applications using high-level APIs doesn't change the fact that sooner or later most developers need to tweak or fine-tune their applications, and doing that usually involves working with lower-level APIs to achieve those extra bits of functionality. So the design for low-level APIs should very much take VB developers into consideration.

The general guideline for building a single framework that targets the breadth of developers is to factor your API set into low-level types that expose all the richness and power and into high-level types that wrap the lower layer with convenience APIs.

This is a very powerful simplification technique. In a single-layer API, you are often forced to decide between having a more complex design and not supporting some scenarios. Having a low-level power layer provides the freedom to scope the high-level API to truly mainline scenarios.

Note that in some cases one of the layers might not be needed. For example, some feature areas might expose only the low-level APIs.

ASP.NET (the `System.Web` namespace) is an example of such a layered design. For the power and expressiveness crowd, ASP.NET offers a low-level HTTP layer that allows developers to code against the raw requests coming to the Web server, with very little abstraction provided. However, ASP.NET also offers a rich set of Web Controls that allows developers to code against high-level concepts with properties and methods without worrying about the Web protocols. In this way, ASP.NET offers a single framework that is consistently available but has layers that target different scenarios and developer audiences.

There are two main namespace factoring approaches for the API layers:

- Expose layers in separate namespaces.
- Expose layers in the same namespace.

> ■ **JEFF PROSISE** In addition to providing a fine example of layered architecture, ASP.NET also serves as a model for modular architecture. Many of the key services and features of ASP.NET are implemented in the form of HTTP handlers and HTTP modules. You can extend (or modify) ASP.NET's HTTP runtime by writing HTTP handlers and HTTP modules of your own. Moreover, the same handler and module architecture can be used to extend IIS 7.

2.2.4.1 **Exposing Layers in Separate Namespaces**

One way to factor a framework is to put the high-level and low-level types in different but related namespaces. This has the advantage of hiding the low-level types from the mainstream scenarios without putting them too far out of reach when developers need to implement more complex scenarios.

ASP.NET is factored this way. The low-level `HttpRuntime` APIs are in a different namespace than the high-level page framework and controls, which are in the `System.Web.UI` namespace. The page framework is built on top of the low-level functionality (the `Page` class implements `IHttpHandler`) and provides the programming model for 99 percent of scenarios.

The large majority of frameworks should follow this namespace-factoring approach.

2.2.4.2 **Exposing Layers in the Same Namespace**

The other way to factor a framework is to put the high-level and low-level types in the same namespace. This has the advantage of providing a more automatic fall-back to the more complex functionality when it is needed. The downside is that having the complex types in the namespace makes some scenarios more difficult, even if the more complex types are not used.

This factorization works best for simple features. For example, the `System.Net` namespace includes both low-level types such as `Dns` as well as the higher-level `WebClient` class. It should be noted that the even lower-level socket classes are factored out to the `System.Net.Sockets` namespace.

> ■■ **STEVEN CLARKE**   Also take care to think about the runtime behavior of a layered API. For example, make sure that if the developer is working at one layer, he or she isn't expected to catch exceptions thrown from a different layer. You want to make sure that, in writing, reading, and understanding code, developers only ever need to really concern themselves with what is going on in one layer and that they can safely consider other layers as a black box.

✓ **CONSIDER** using a layered framework with high-level APIs optimized for productivity, and using low-level APIs optimized for power and expressiveness.

✗ **AVOID** mixing low-level and high-level APIs in a single namespace if the low-level APIs are very complex (i.e., they contain many types).

✓ **DO** ensure that layers of a single feature area are well integrated. Developers should be able to start programming using one of the layers and then change their code to use the other layer without rewriting the whole application.

SUMMARY

In designing a framework, it is very important to be aware that the audience is very diverse, in terms of both needs and skill levels. Following the principles described in this chapter ensures that your framework is usable for a diverse group of developers.

3
Naming Guidelines

FOLLOWING A CONSISTENT set of naming conventions in the development of a framework can be a major contribution to the framework's usability. It allows the framework to be used by many developers on widely separated projects. Beyond consistency of form, names of framework elements must be easily understood and must convey the function of each element.

The goal of this chapter is to provide a consistent set of naming conventions that results in names that make immediate sense to developers.

Most of the naming guidelines are simply conventions that have no technical rationale. However, following these naming guidelines will ensure that the names are understandable and consistent.

Although adopting these naming conventions as general code development guidelines would result in more consistent naming throughout your code, you are required only to apply them to APIs that are publicly exposed (public or protected types and members, and explicitly implemented interfaces).

> ■ **KRZYSZTOF CWALINA** The team that develops the .NET Framework Base Class Library spends an enormous amount of time on naming and considers it to be a crucial part of framework development.

This chapter describes general naming guidelines, including how to use capitalization, mechanics, and certain specific terms. It also provides specific guidelines for naming namespaces, types, members, parameters, assemblies, and resources.

3.1 Capitalization Conventions

Because the CLR supports many languages that might or might not be case sensitive, case alone should not be used to differentiate names. However, the importance of case in enhancing the readability of names cannot be overemphasized. The guidelines in this chapter lay out a simple method for using case that, when applied consistently, make identifiers for types, members, and parameters easy to read.

3.1.1 Capitalization Rules for Identifiers

To differentiate words in an identifier, capitalize the first letter of each word in the identifier. Do not use underscores to differentiate words, or for that matter, anywhere in identifiers. There are two appropriate ways to capitalize identifiers, depending on the use of the identifier:

- PascalCasing
- camelCasing

> **■▪ BRAD ABRAMS**   In the initial design of the Framework, we had hundreds of hours of debate about the naming style. To facilitate these debates, we coined a number of terms. With Anders Hejlsberg, the original designer of Turbo Pascal, and a key member of the design team, it is no wonder that we chose the term PascalCasing for the casing style popularized by the Pascal programming language. We were somewhat cute in using the term camelCasing for the casing style that looks something like the hump on a camel. We used the term SCREAMING_CAPS to indicate an all-uppercase style. Luckily, this style (and name) did not survive in the final guideline.

The PascalCasing convention, used for all identifiers except parameter names, capitalizes the first character of each word (including acronyms over two letters in length), as shown in the following examples:

```
PropertyDescriptor
HtmlTag
```

A special case is made for two-letter acronyms in which both letters are capitalized, as shown in the following identifier:

```
IOStream
```

The camelCasing convention, used only for parameter names, capitalizes the first character of each word except the first word, as shown in the following examples. As the example also shows, two-letter acronyms that begin a camel-cased identifier are both lowercase.

```
propertyDescriptor
ioStream
htmlTag
```

The following are two basic capitalization guidelines for identifiers:

✓ **DO** use PascalCasing for namespace, type, and member names consisting of multiple words.

For example, use `TextColor` rather than `Textcolor` or `Text_color`. Single words, such as `Button`, simply have initial capitals. Compound words that are always written as a single word, like endpoint, are treated as single words and have initial capitals only. More information on compound words is given in section 3.1.3.

✓ **DO** use camelCasing for parameter names.

Table 3-1 describes the capitalization rules for different types of identifiers.

> ■ **BRAD ABRAMS**   An early version of this table included a convention for instance field names. We later adopted the guideline that you should almost never use publicly exposed instance fields and should use properties instead. Thus, the guideline for publicly exposed instance fields was no longer needed. For the record, the convention was camelCasing.

TABLE 3-1: Capitalization Rules for Different Types of Identifiers

Identifier	Casing	Example
Namespace	Pascal	`namespace System.Security { ... }`
Type	Pascal	`public class StreamReader { ... }`
Interface	Pascal	`public interface IEnumerable { ... }`

Method	Pascal	`public class Object {`
		`    public virtual string ToString();`
		`}`

Property	Pascal	`public class String {`
		`    public int Length { get; }`
		`}`

Event	Pascal	`public class Process {`
		`    public event EventHandler Exited;`
		`}`

Field	Pascal	`public class MessageQueue {`
		`    public static readonly TimeSpan`
		`InfiniteTimeout;`
		`}`
		`public struct UInt32 {`
		`    public const Min = 0;`
		`}`

Enum value	Pascal	`public enum FileMode {`
		`    Append,`
		`    ...`
		`}`

Parameter	Camel	`public class Convert {`
		`    public static int ToInt32(string`
		`value);`
		`}`

3.1.2 Capitalizing Acronyms

In general, it is important to avoid using acronyms in identifier names unless they are in common usage and are immediately understandable to anyone who might use the framework. For example, HTML, XML, and IO are all well understood, but less well-known acronyms should definitely be avoided.

> ▪ **KRZYSZTOF CWALINA** Acronyms are distinct from abbreviations, which should never be used in identifiers. An acronym is a word made from the initial letters of a phrase, whereas an abbreviation simply shortens a word.

By definition, an acronym must be at least two characters. Acronyms of three or more characters follow the guidelines of any other word. Only the first letter is capitalized, unless it is the first word in a camel-cased parameter name, which is all lowercase.

As mentioned in the preceding section, two-character acronyms (e.g., IO) are treated differently, primarily to avoid confusion. Both characters should be capitalized unless the two-character acronym is the first word in a camel-cased parameter name, in which case both characters are lowercase. The following examples illustrate all of these cases:

```
public void StartIO(Stream ioStream, bool closeIOStream);
public void ProcessHtmlTag(string htmlTag)
```

✔ **DO** capitalize both characters of two-character acronyms, except the first word of a camel-cased identifier.

```
System.IO
public void StartIO(Stream ioStream)
```

✔ **DO** capitalize only the first character of acronyms with three or more characters, except the first word of a camel-cased identifier.

```
System.Xml
public void ProcessHtmlTag(string htmlTag)
```

✔ **DO NOT** capitalize any of the characters of any acronyms, whatever their length, at the beginning of a camel-cased identifier.

> ▪ **BRAD ABRAMS** In my time working on the .NET Framework, I have heard every possible excuse for violating these naming guidelines. Many teams feel that they have some special reason to use case differently in their identifiers than in the rest of the Framework. These excuses include consistency with other platforms (MFC, HTML, etc.), avoiding geopolitical issues

(casing of some country names), honoring the dead (abbreviation names that came up with some crypto algorithm), and the list goes on and on. For the most part, our customers have seen the places in which we have diverged from these guidelines (for even the best excuse) as warts in the Framework. The only time I think it really makes sense to violate these guidelines is when using a trademark as an identifier. However, I suggest not using trademarks, because they tend to change faster than APIs do.

■ **BRAD ABRAMS** Here is an example of putting these naming guidelines to the test. We have the class shown here in the Framework today. It successfully follows the guidelines for casing and uses `Argb` rather than `ARGB`. But we have actually gotten bug reports along the lines of "How do you convert a color from an ARGB value—all I see are methods to convert 'from argument b.'?"

```
public struct Color {
    ...
    public static Color FromArgb(int alpha, Color baseColor);
    public static Color FromArgb(int alpha, int red, int green, int blue);
    public static Color FromArgb(int argb);
    public static Color FromArgb(int red, int green, int blue);
    ...
}
```

In retrospect, should this have been a place where we violated the guidelines and used `FromARGB`? I do not think so. It turns out that this is a case of overabbreviation. RGB is a well-recognized acronym for red-green-blue values. An ARGB value is a relatively uncommon abbreviation that includes the alpha channel. It would have been clearer to name these `AlphaRgb` and would have been more consistent in naming with the rest of the Framework.

```
public struct Color {
    ...
    public static Color FromAlphaRgb(int alpha, Color baseColor);
    public static Color FromAlphaRgb(int alpha, int red, int green, int blue);
    public static Color FromAlphaRgb(int argb);
    public static Color FromAlphaRgb(int red, int green, int blue);
    ...
}
```

3.1.3 Capitalizing Compound Words and Common Terms

Most compound terms are treated as single words for purposes of capitalization.

✗ **DO NOT** capitalize each word in so-called closed-form compound words.

These are compound words written as a single word, such as endpoint. For the purpose of casing guidelines, treat a closed-form compound word as a single word. Use a current dictionary to determine if a compound word is written in closed form.

Table 3-2 shows capitalization for some of the most commonly used compound words and common terms.

TABLE 3-2: Capitalization and Spelling for Common Compound Words and Common Terms

Pascal	Camel	Not
BitFlag	bitFlag	Bitflag
Callback	callback	CallBack
Canceled	canceled	Cancelled
DoNot	doNot	Don't
Email	email	EMail
Endpoint	endpoint	EndPoint
FileName	fileName	Filename
Gridline	gridline	GridLine
Hashtable	hashtable	HashTable
Id	id	ID
Indexes	indexes	Indices
LogOff	logOff	LogOut

Continues

TABLE 3.2: Continued

Pascal	Camel	Not
LogOn	logOn	LogIn
Metadata	metadata	MetaData, metaData
Multipanel	multipanel	MultiPanel
Multiview	multiview	MultiView
Namespace	namespace	NameSpace
Ok	ok	OK
Pi	pi	PI
Placeholder	placeholder	PlaceHolder
SignIn	signIn	SignOn
SignOut	signOut	SignOff
UserName	userName	Username
WhiteSpace	whiteSpace	Whitespace
Writable	writable	Writeable

Two other terms that are in common usage are in a category by themselves, because they are common slang abbreviations. The two words *Ok* and *Id* (and they should be cased as shown) are the exceptions to the guideline that no abbreviations should be used in names.

BRAD ABRAMS Table 3-2 presents specific examples found in the development of the .NET Framework. You might find it useful to create your own appendix to this table for compound words and other terms commonly used in your domain.

> **BRAD ABRAMS** One abbreviation commonly used in COM interface names was Ex (for interfaces that were extended versions of previously existing interfaces). This abbreviation should be avoided in reusable libraries. Use instead a meaningful name that describes the new functionality. For example, rather than `IDispatchEx`, consider `IDynamicDispatch`.

3.1.4 Case Sensitivity

Languages that can run on the CLR are not required to support case sensitivity, although some do. Even if your language supports it, other languages that might access your framework do not. Any APIs that are externally accessible, therefore, cannot rely on case alone to distinguish between two names in the same context.

> **PAUL VICK** When it came to the question of case sensitivity, there was no question in the minds of the Visual Basic team that the CLR had to support case insensitivity as well as case sensitivity. Visual Basic has been case insensitive for a very long time, and the shock of trying to move VB developers (including myself) into a case-sensitive world would have made any of the other challenges we faced pale in comparison. Add to that the fact that COM is case insensitive, and the matter seemed pretty clear. The CLR would have to take case insensitivity into account.

> **JEFFREY RICHTER** To be clear, the CLR is actually case sensitive. Some programming languages, like Visual Basic, are case insensitive. When the VB compiler is trying to resolve a method call to a type defined in a case-sensitive language like C#, the compiler (not the CLR) figures out the actual case of the method's name and embeds it in metadata. The CLR knows nothing about this. Now if you are using reflection to bind to a method, the reflection APIs do offer the ability to do case-insensitive lookups. This is the extent to which the CLR supports case insensitivity.

There is really only one guideline for case sensitivity, albeit an important one.

✗ **DO NOT** assume that all programming languages are case sensitive. They are not. Names cannot differ by case alone.

3.2 General Naming Conventions

This section describes general naming conventions that relate to word choice, guidelines on using abbreviations and acronyms, and recommendations on how to avoid using language-specific names.

3.2.1 Word Choice

It is important that names of framework identifiers make sense on first reading. Identifier names should clearly state what each member does and what each type and parameter represents. To this end, it is more important that the name be clear than that it be short. Names should correspond to scenarios, logical or physical parts of the system, and well-known concepts rather than to technologies or architecture.

✓ **DO** choose easily readable identifier names.

For example, a property named `HorizontalAlignment` is more English-readable than `AlignmentHorizontal`.

✓ **DO** favor readability over brevity. The property name `CanScroll-Horizontally` is better than `ScrollableX` (an obscure reference to the X-axis).

✗ **DO NOT** use underscores, hyphens, or any other non-alphanumeric characters.

✗ **DO NOT** use Hungarian notation.

> ■ **BRENT RECTOR** It might be useful here to define what Hungarian notation is. It is the convention of prefixing a variable name with some lowercase encoding of its data type. For example, the variable `uiCount` would be an unsigned integer. Another common convention also adds a prefix indicating the scope of the variable in addition to or in place of the type (see Jeffrey's later example of static and member variable-scope prefixes).

One downside of Hungarian notation is that developers frequently change the type of variables during early coding, which requires the name of the variable to also change. Additionally, while commonly used fundamental data types (integers, characters, etc.) had well-recognized and standard prefixes, developers frequently fail to use a meaningful and consistent prefix for their custom data types.

■ **KRZYSZTOF CWALINA** There have always been both positive and negative effects of using the Hungarian naming convention, and they still exist today. Positives include better readability (if used correctly). Negatives include cost of maintenance, confusion if maintenance was not done properly, and finally, Hungarian makes the API more cryptic (less approachable) to some developers. In the world of procedural languages (e.g., C) and the separation of the System APIs for advanced developers from framework libraries for a much wider developer group, the positives seemed to be greater than the negatives. Today, with System APIs designed to be approachable to more developers, and with object-oriented languages, the trade-off seems to be pulling in the other direction. OO encapsulation brings variable declaration and usage points closer together, OO style favors short, well-factored methods, and abstractions often make the exact type less important or even meaningless.

■ **JEFFREY RICHTER** I'll admit it; I miss Hungarian notation. Although in many editors, like Visual Studio, you can hover the mouse over a variable and the editor pops up the type, this does not work when reading source code in a book chapter or magazine article. Fortunately, in OOP, variables tend have a short scope, so that you only need to scan a few lines to find the definition of a variable. However, this is not true for a type's static and instance fields. Personally, I make all my fields private, and I now prefix my instance fields with "m_" and my static fields with "s_" so that I can easily spot fields in my methods. Luckily, this does not conflict with the guidelines described in this chapter, because they only cover publicly exposed members. This helps me a lot, but I still can't tell what type a variable represents. I rely on my editor's tool tips for this.

■ **ANTHONY MOORE**   While most coding guidelines in use at Microsoft do not promote the use of "m_" and "s_" described above, I believe that practice is worth consideration. For the most part, the consistency of use of a coding guideline is more important than its details. However, in this case I've seen a few bugs caused by confusion between local variables and member fields that this practice could prevent. Similarly, static fields are a dangerous construct, because for a library you generally need to make them—as well as any instances transitively hanging off them—threadsafe. Making them look different from regular members makes it easier to find thread-safety errors when reviewing code.

✗ **AVOID** using identifiers that conflict with keywords of widely used programming languages.

According to Rule 4 of the Common Language Specification (CLS), all compliant languages must provide a mechanism that allows access to named items that use a keyword of that language as an identifier. C#, for example, uses the @ sign as an escape mechanism in this case. However, it is still a good idea to avoid common keywords because it is much more difficult to use a method with the escape sequence than one without it.

■ **JEFFREY RICHTER**   When I was porting my *Applied Microsoft .NET Framework Programming* book from C# to Visual Basic, I ran into this situation a lot. For example, the class library has `Delegate`, `Module`, and `Assembly` classes, and Visual Basic uses these same terms for keywords. This problem is exacerbated by the fact that VB is a case-insensitive language. Visual Basic, like C#, has a way to escape the keywords to disambiguate the situation to the compiler (using square brackets), but I was surprised that the VB team selected keywords that conflict with so many class library names.

3.2.2 Using Abbreviations and Acronyms

In general, do not use abbreviations or acronyms in identifiers. As stated earlier, it is more important for names to be readable than it is for them to be brief. It is equally important not to use abbreviations and acronyms that are not generally understood—that is, do not use anything that the large majority of people who are not experts in a given field would not know the meaning of immediately.

✗ DO NOT use abbreviations or contractions as part of identifier names.

For example, use `GetWindow` rather than `GetWin`.

✗ DO NOT use any acronyms that are not widely accepted, and even if they are, only when necessary.

For example, UI is used for User Interface and HTML is used for Hyper Text Markup Language. Although many framework designers feel that some recent acronym will soon be widely accepted, it is bad practice to use it in framework identifiers.

For acronym capitalization rules, see section 3.1.2.

> ■■ **BRAD ABRAMS** We continually debate about whether a given acronym is well known or not. A good divining rod is what I call the grep test. Simply use some search engine to grep the Web for the acronym. If the first few results returned are indeed the meaning you intend, it is likely that your acronym qualifies as well known; if you don't get those search results, think harder about the name. If you fail the test, don't just spell out the acronym but consider how you can be descriptive in the name.

3.2.3 Avoiding Language-Specific Names

Programming languages that target the CLR often have their own names (aliases) for the so-called primitive types. For example, `int` is a C# alias for `System.Int32`. To ensure that your framework can take full advantage of the cross-language interoperation that is one of the core features of the CLR, it is important to avoid the use of these language-specific type names in identifiers.

> ■. **JEFFREY RICHTER**   Personally, I take this a step further and never use the language's alias names. I find that the alias adds nothing of value and introduces enormous confusion. For example, I'm frequently asked what the difference is between `String` and `string` in C#. I've even heard people say that strings (lowercase "S") are allocated on the stack while Strings (uppercase "S") are allocated on the heap. In my book *CLR via C#*, I give several reasons in addition to the one offered here for avoiding the alias names. Another example of a class library/language mismatch is the `NullReferenceException` class, which can be thrown by VB code. But VB uses `Nothing`, not `null`.

✓ **DO** use semantically interesting names rather than language-specific keywords for type names.

For example, `GetLength` is a better name than `GetInt`.

✓ **DO** use a generic CLR type name, rather than a language-specific name, in the rare cases when an identifier has no semantic meaning beyond its type.

For example, a method converting to `System.Int64` should be named `ToInt64`, not `ToLong` (because `System.Int64` is a CLR name for the C#-specific alias `long`). Table 3-3 presents several base data types using the CLR type names (as well as the corresponding type names for C#, Visual Basic, and C++).

TABLE 3-3: CLR Type Names for Language-Specific Type Names

C#	Visual Basic	C++	CLR
sbyte	SByte	char	SByte
byte	Byte	unsigned char	Byte
short	Short	short	Int16
ushort	UInt16	unsigned short	UInt16
int	Integer	int	Int32

C#	Visual Basic	C++	CLR
uint	UInt32	unsigned int	UInt32
long	Long	__int64	Int64
ulong	UInt64	unsigned __int64	UInt64
float	Single	float	Single
double	Double	double	Double
bool	Boolean	bool	Boolean
char	Char	wchar_t	Char
string	String	String	String
object	Object	Object	Object

✓ **DO** use a common name, such as *value* or *item*, rather than repeating the type name, in the rare cases when an identifier has no semantic meaning and the type of the parameter is not important.

The following is a good example of methods of a class that supports writing a variety of data types into a stream:

```
void Write(double value);
void Write(float value);
void Write(short value);
```

3.2.4 Naming New Versions of Existing APIs

Sometimes a new feature cannot be added to an existing type even though the type's name implies that it is the best place for the new feature. In such a case, a new type needs to be added, which often leaves the framework designer with the difficult task of finding a good new name for the new type. Similarly, an existing member often cannot be extended or overloaded to provide additional functionality, and so a member with a new name needs to be added. The guidelines that follow describe how to choose names for new types and members that supersede or replace existing types or members.

✓ **DO** use a name similar to the old API when creating new versions of an existing API.

This helps to highlight the relationship between the APIs.

```
class AppDomain {
    [Obsolete("AppDomain.SetCachePath has been deprecated. Please use
AppDomainSetup.CachePath instead.")]
    public void SetCachePath(String path) { ... }
}

class AppDomainSetup {
    public string CachePath { get { ... }; set  { ... }; }
}
```

✓ **DO** prefer adding a suffix rather than a prefix to indicate a new version of an existing API.

> ▪▫ **VANCE MORRISON**   We did exactly this when we added a faster (but not completely backward-compatible) version of `ReaderWriterLock`. We called it `ReaderWriterLockSlim`. There was debate whether we should call it `SlimReaderWriterLock` (following the guideline that you write it like you say it in English), but decided the discoverability (and the fact that lexical sorting would put them close to each other) was more important.

This will assist discovery when browsing documentation, or using Intellisense. The old version of the API will be organized close to the new APIs, because most browsers and Intellisense show identifiers in alphabetical order.

✓ **CONSIDER** using a brand new, but meaningful identifier, instead of adding a suffix or a prefix.

✓ **DO** use a numeric suffix to indicate a new version of an existing API, particularly if the existing name of the API is the only name that makes sense (i.e., if it is an industry standard) and if adding any meaningful suffix (or changing the name) is not an appropriate option.

```
// old API
[Obsolete("This type is obsolete. Please use the new version of the same
class, X509Certificate2.")]
public class X509Certificate { ... }
// new API
public class X509Certificate2 { ... }
```

■ **KRZYSZTOF CWALINA** I would use numeric suffixes as the very last resort. A much better approach is to use a new name or a meaningful suffix.

The BCL team shipped a new type named `TimeZone2` in one of the early prereleases of the .NET Framework 3.5. The name immediately became the center of a controversy in the blogging community. After a set of lengthy discussions, the team decided to rename the type to `TimeZoneInfo`, which is not a great name but is much better than `TimeZone2`.

It's interesting to note that nobody dislikes X509Certificate2. My interpretation of this fact is that programmers are more willing to accept the ugly numeric suffix on rarely used library types somewhere in the corner of the Framework than on a core type in the System namespace.

✗ DO NOT use the "Ex" (or a similar) suffix for an identifier to distinguish it from an earlier version of the same API.

```
[Obsolete("This type is obsolete. ...")]
public class Car   { ... }

// new API
public class CarEx       { ... }    // the wrong way
public class CarNew      { ... }    // the wrong way
public class Car2        { ... }    // the right way
public class Automobile { ... }    // the right way
```

✓ DO use the "64" suffix when introducing versions of APIs that operate on a 64-bit integer (a long integer) instead of a 32-bit integer. You only need to take this approach when the existing 32-bit API exists; don't do it for brand new APIs with only a 64-bit version.

For example, various APIs on `System.Diagnostics.Process` return `Int32` values representing memory sizes, such as `PagedMemorySize` or

PeakWorkingSet. To appropriately support these APIs on 64-bit systems, APIs have been added that have the same name but a "64" suffix.

```
public class Process {
  // old APIs
  public int PeakWorkingSet { get; }
  public int PagedMemorySize { get; }
  // ...
  // new APIs
  public long PeakWorkingSet64 { get; }
  public long PagedMemorySize64 { get; }
}
```

■■ **KIT GEORGE**   Note that this guideline applies only to retrofitting APIs that have already shipped. When designing a brand new API, use the most appropriate type and name for the API that will work on all platforms, and avoid using both "32" and "64" suffixes. Consider using overloading.

3.3 Names of Assemblies and DLLs

An assembly is the unit of deployment and identity for managed code programs. Although assemblies can span one or more files, typically an assembly maps one-to-one with a DLL. Therefore, this section describes only DLL naming conventions, which then can be mapped to assembly naming conventions.

■■ **JEFFREY RICHTER**   Multifile assemblies are rarely used, and Visual Studio has no built-in support for them.

Keep in mind that namespaces are distinct from DLL and assembly names. Namespaces represent logical groupings for developers, whereas DLLs and assemblies represent packaging and deployment boundaries. DLLs can contain multiple namespaces for product factoring and other reasons. Because namespace factoring is different than DLL factoring, you should design them independently. For example, if you decide to name your DLL MyCompany.MyTechnology, it does not mean that the DLL has to contain a namespace named MyCompany.MyTechnology, though it can.

◼ **JEFFREY RICHTER** Programmers are frequently confused by the fact that the CLR does not enforce a relationship between namespaces and assembly file names. For example, `System.IO.FileStream` is in `MSCorLib.dll`, and `System.IO.FileSystemWatcher` is in `System.dll`. As you can see, types in a single namespace can span multiple files. Also notice that the .NET Framework doesn't ship with a `System.IO.dll` file at all.

◼ **BRAD ABRAMS** We decided early in the design of the CLR to separate the developer view of the platform (namespaces) from the packaging and deployment view of the platform (assemblies). This separation allows each to be optimized independently based on its own criteria. For example, we are free to factor namespaces to group types that are functionally related (e.g., all the I/O stuff is in `System.IO`), but the assemblies can be factored for performance (load time), deployment, servicing, or versioning reasons.

✓ **DO** choose names for your assembly DLLs that suggest large chunks of functionality, such as `System.Data`.

Assembly and DLL names don't have to correspond to namespace names, but it is reasonable to follow the namespace name when naming assemblies. A good rule of thumb is to name the DLL based on the common prefix of the assemblies contained in the assembly. For example, an assembly with two namespaces, `MyCompany.MyTechnology.FirstFeature` and `MyCompany.MyTechnology.SecondFeature`, could be called `MyCompany.MyTechnology.dll`.

✓ **CONSIDER** naming DLLs according to the following pattern:

```
<Company>.<Component>.dll
```

where `<Component>` contains one or more dot-separated clauses. For example:

```
Microsoft.VisualBasic.dll
Microsoft.VisualBasic.Vsa.dll
Fabrikam.Security.dll
Litware.Controls.dll
```

3.4 **Names of Namespaces**

As with other naming guidelines, the goal when naming namespaces is creating sufficient clarity for the programmer using the framework to immediately know what the content of the namespace is likely to be. The following template specifies the general rule for naming namespaces:

```
<Company>.(<Product>|<Technology>)[.<Feature>][.<Subnamespace>]
```

The following are examples:

```
Microsoft.VisualStudio
Microsoft.VisualStudio.Design
Fabrikam.Math
Litware.Security
```

✓ **DO** prefix namespace names with a company name to prevent namespaces from different companies from having the same name.

For example, the Microsoft Office automation APIs provided by Microsoft should be in the namespace `Microsoft.Office`.

> ■■ **BRAD ABRAMS**   It is important to use the official name of your company or organization when choosing the first part of your namespace name to avoid possible conflicts. For example, if Microsoft had chosen to use MS as its root namespace, it might have been confusing to developers at other companies that use MS as an abbreviation.

✓ **DO** use a stable, version-independent product name at the second level of a namespace name.

> ■■ **BRAD ABRAMS**   This means staying away from the latest cool and catchy name that the marketing folks have come up with. It is fine to tweak the branding of a product from release to release, but the namespace name is going to be burned into your client's code forever. Therefore, choose something that is technically sound and not subject to the marketing whims of the day.

✗ **DO NOT** use organizational hierarchies as the basis for names in namespace hierarchies, because group names within corporations tend to be short-lived. Organize the hierarchy of namespaces around groups of related technologies.

> ■ **BRAD ABRAMS** We added a set of controls to ASP.NET late in the ship cycle for V1.0 of the .NET Framework that rendered for mobile devices. Because these controls came from a team in a different division, our immediate reaction was to put them in a different namespace (`System.Web.MobileControls`). Then, after a couple of reorganizations and .NET Framework versions, we realized a better engineering trade-off was to fold that functionality into the existing controls in `System.Web.Controls`. In retrospect, we let internal organizational differences affect the public exposure of the APIs, and we came to regret that later. Avoid this type of mistake in your designs.

✓ **DO** use PascalCasing, and separate namespace components with periods (e.g., `Microsoft.Office.PowerPoint`). If your brand employs nontraditional casing, you should follow the casing defined by your brand, even if it deviates from normal namespace casing.

✓ **CONSIDER** using plural namespace names where appropriate.

For example, use `System.Collections` instead of `System.Collection`. Brand names and acronyms are exceptions to this rule, however. For example, use `System.IO` instead of `System.IOs`.

✗ **DO NOT** use the same name for a namespace and a type in that namespace.

For example, do not use `Debug` as a namespace name and then also provide a class named `Debug` in the same namespace. Several compilers require such types to be fully qualified.

These guidelines cover general namespace naming guidelines, but the next section provides specific guidelines for certain special subnamespaces.

3.4.1 Namespaces and Type Name Conflicts

Namespaces are used to organize types into a logical and easy-to-explore hierarchy. They are also indispensable in resolving type name ambiguities that might arise when importing multiple namespaces. However, that fact should not be used as an excuse to introduce known ambiguities between types in different namespaces that are commonly used together. Developers should not be required to qualify type names in common scenarios.

✗ **DO NOT** introduce generic type names such as `Element`, `Node`, `Log`, and `Message`.

There is a very high probability that doing so will lead to type name conflicts in common scenarios. You should qualify the generic type names (`FormElement`, `XmlNode`, `EventLog`, `SoapMessage`).

There are specific guidelines for avoiding type name conflicts for different categories of namespaces. Namespaces can be divided into the following categories:

- Application model namespaces
- Infrastructure namespaces
- Core namespaces
- Technology namespace groups

3.4.1.1 Application Model Namespaces

Namespaces belonging to a single application model are very often used together, but they are almost never used with namespaces of other application models. For example, the `System.Windows.Forms` namespace is very rarely used together with the `System.Web.UI` namespace. The following is a list of well-known application model namespace groups:

```
System.Windows*
System.Web.UI*
```

✗ **DO NOT** give the same name to types in namespaces within a single application model.

For example, do not add a type named Page to the System.Web.UI.Adapters namespace, because the System.Web.UI namespace already contains a type named Page.

3.4.1.2 **Infrastructure Namespaces**

This group contains namespaces that are rarely imported during development of common applications. For example, .Design namespaces are mainly used when developing programming tools. Avoiding conflicts with types in these namespaces is not critical.

```
System.Windows.Forms.Design
*.Design
*.Permissions
```

3.4.1.3 **Core Namespaces**

Core namespaces include all System namespaces, excluding namespaces of the application models and the Infrastructure namespaces. Core namespaces include, among others, System, System.IO, System.Xml, and System.Net.

✗ **DO NOT** give types names that would conflict with any type in the Core namespaces.

For example, never use Stream as a type name. It would conflict with System.IO.Stream, a very commonly used type.

By the same token, do not add a type named EventLog to the System.Diagnostics.Events namespace, because the System.Diagnostics namespace already contains a type named EventLog.

3.4.1.4 **Technology Namespace Groups**

This category includes all namespaces with the same first two namespace nodes (<Company>.<Technology>*), such as Microsoft.Build.Utilities and `Microsoft.Build.Tasks`. It is important that types belonging to a single technology do not conflict with each other.

✗ **DO NOT** assign type names that would conflict with other types within a single technology.

✗ **DO NOT** introduce type name conflicts between types in technology namespaces and an application model namespace (unless the technology is not intended to be used with the application model).

For example, one would not add a type named `Binding` to the `Microsoft.VisualBasic` namespace because the `System.Windows.Forms` namespace already contains that type name.

3.5 **Names of Classes, Structs, and Interfaces**

In general, class and struct names should be nouns or noun phrases, because they represent entities of the system. A good rule of thumb is that if you are not able to come up with a noun or a noun phrase name for a class or a struct, you probably should rethink the general design of the type. Interfaces representing roots of a hierarchy (e.g., `IList<T>`) should also use nouns or noun phrases. Interfaces representing capabilities should use adjectives and adjective phrases (e.g., `IComparable<T>`, `IFormattable`).

Another important consideration is that the most easily recognizable names should be used for the most commonly used types, even if the name fits some other less-used type better in the purely technical sense. For example, a type used in mainline scenarios to submit print jobs to print queues should be named `Printer`, rather than `PrintQueue`. Even though technically the type represents a print queue and not the physical device (printer), from the scenario point of view, `Printer` is the ideal name because most people are interested in submitting print jobs and not in other operations related to the physical printer device (e.g., configuring the printer). If you need to provide another type that corresponds, for example, to the physical printer to be used in configuration scenarios, the type could be called `PrinterConfiguration` or `PrinterManager`.

■ **KRZYSZTOF CWALINA**   I know this goes against the technical precision that is one of the core character traits of most software engineers, but I really do think it's more important to have better names from the point of view of the most common scenario, even if it results in slightly inconsistent or even wrong type names from a purely technical point of view. Advanced users will be able to understand slightly inconsistent naming. Most users are usually not concerned with technicalities and will not even notice the inconsistency, but they *will* appreciate the names guiding them to the most important APIs.

Similarly, names of the most commonly used types should reflect usage scenarios, not inheritance hierarchy. Most users use the leaves of an inheritance hierarchy almost exclusively, and they are rarely concerned with the structure of the hierarchy. Yet API designers often see the inheritance hierarchy as the most important criterion for type name selection. For example, `Stream`, `StreamReader`, `TextReader`, `StringReader`, and `FileStream` all describe the place of each of the types in the inheritance hierarchy quite well, but they obscure the most important information for the majority of users: the type that they need to instantiate to read text from a file.

The naming guidelines that follow apply to general type naming.

✓ **DO** name classes and structs with nouns or noun phrases, using PascalCasing.

This distinguishes type names from methods, which are named with verb phrases.

✓ **DO** name interfaces with adjective phrases, or occasionally with nouns or noun phrases.

Nouns and noun phrases should be used rarely and they might indicate that the type should be an abstract class, and not an interface. See section 4.3 for details about deciding how to choose between abstract classes and interfaces.

✗ **DO NOT** give class names a prefix (e.g., "C").

KRZYSZTOF CWALINA   One of the few prefixes used is "I" for interfaces (as in ICollection), but that is for historical reasons. In retrospect, I think it would have been better to use regular type names. In a majority of the cases, developers don't care that something is an interface and not an abstract class, for example.

BRAD ABRAMS   On the other hand, the "I" prefix on interfaces is a clear recognition of the influence of COM (and Java) on the .NET Framework. COM popularized, even institutionalized, the notation that interfaces begin with "I." Although we discussed diverging from this historic pattern, we decided to carry forward the pattern because so many of our users were already familiar with COM.

JEFFREY RICHTER   Personally, I like the "I" prefix, and I wish we had more stuff like this. Little one-character prefixes go a long way toward keeping code terse and yet descriptive. As I said earlier, I use prefixes for my private type fields because I find this very useful.

BRENT RECTOR   Note: This is really another application of Hungarian notation (though one without the disadvantages of the notation's use in variable names).

✓ **CONSIDER** ending the name of derived classes with the name of the base class.

This is very readable and explains the relationship clearly. Some examples of this in code are: ArgumentOutOfRangeException, which is a kind of Exception, and SerializableAttribute, which is a kind of Attribute. However, it is important to use reasonable judgment in applying this guideline; for example, the Button class is a kind of

Control event, although Control doesn't appear in its name. The following are examples of correctly named classes:

```
public class FileStream : Stream {...}
public class Button : Control {...}
```

✓ **DO** prefix interface names with the letter *I*, to indicate that the type is an interface.

For example, IComponent (descriptive noun), ICustomAttribute-Provider (noun phrase), and IPersistable (adjective) are appropriate interface names. As with other type names, avoid abbreviations.

> ▪ **JEFFREY RICHTER** There is one interface I'm aware of that doesn't follow this guideline: System._AppDomain. It is very disconcerting to me when I see this type used without the uppercase *I*. Please don't make this same mistake in your code.

✓ **DO** ensure that the names differ only by the "I" prefix on the interface name when you are defining a class–interface pair where the class is a standard implementation of the interface.

The following example illustrates this guideline for the interface IComponent and its standard implementation, the class Component:

```
public interface IComponent { ... }
public class Component : IComponent { ... }
```

> ▪ **PHIL HAACK** One place where the Framework violates this convention is the class HttpSessionState, which you would suspect implements IHttpSessionState, but you'd be wrong, as I was.
> This inconsistency nearly bit us when we were developing our HttpContextBase abstraction of HttpContext, because it seemed we could expose the Session property as the IHttpSessionState interface, which turned out to not be the case.

3.5.1 Names of Generic Type Parameters

Generics were added to .NET Framework 2.0. The feature introduced a new kind of identifier called *type parameter*. The following guidelines describe naming conventions related to naming such type parameters:

✓ **DO** name generic type parameters with descriptive names unless a single-letter name is completely self-explanatory and a descriptive name would not add value.

```
public interface ISessionChannel<TSession> { ... }
public delegate TOutput Converter<TInput,TOutput>(TInput from);
public class Nullable<T> { ... }
public class List<T> { ... }
```

✓ **CONSIDER** using T as the type parameter name for types with one single-letter type parameter.

```
public int IComparer<T> { ... }
public delegate bool Predicate<T>(T item);
public struct Nullable<T> where T:struct { ... }
```

✓ **DO** prefix descriptive type parameter names with T.

```
public interface ISessionChannel<TSession> where TSession : ISession{
    TSession Session { get; }
}
```

✓ **CONSIDER** indicating constraints placed on a type parameter in the name of the parameter.

For example, a parameter constrained to ISession might be called TSession.

3.5.2 Names of Common Types

If you are deriving from or implementing types contained in the .NET Framework, it is important to follow the guidelines in this section.

✓ **DO** follow the guidelines described in Table 3-4 when naming types derived from or implementing certain .NET Framework types.

These suffixing guidelines apply to the whole hierarchy of the specified base type. For example, it is not just types derived directly from System. Exception that need the suffixes, but those derived from Exception subclasses as well.

These suffixes should be reserved for the named types. Types derived from or implementing other types should not use these suffixes. For example, the following represent incorrect naming:

```
public class ElementStream : Object { ... }
public class WindowsAttribute : Control { ... }
```

TABLE 3-4: Name Rules for Types Derived from or Implementing Certain Core Types

Base Type	Derived/Implementing Type Guideline
System.Attribute	✔ **DO** add the suffix "Attribute" to names of custom attribute classes.
System.Delegate	✔ **DO** add the suffix "EventHandler" to names of delegates that are used in events. ✔ **DO** add the suffix "Callback" to names of delegates other than those used as event handlers. ✗ **DO NOT** add the suffix "Delegate" to a delegate.
System.EventArgs	✔ **DO** add the suffix "EventArgs."
System.Enum	✗ **DO NOT** derive from this class; use the keyword supported by your language instead; for example, in C#, use the enum keyword. ✗ **DO NOT** add the suffix "Enum" or "Flag."
System.Exception	✔ **DO** add the suffix "Exception."
IDictionary IDictionary<TKey,TValue>	✔ **DO** add the suffix "Dictionary." Note that IDictionary is a specific type of collection, but this guideline takes precedence over the more general collections guideline that follows.

Continues

TABLE 3.4: Continued

Base Type	Derived/Implementing Type Guideline
IEnumerable ICollection IList IEnumerable<T> ICollection<T> IList<T>	✓ **DO** add the suffix "Collection."
System.IO.Stream	✓ **DO** add the suffix "Stream."
CodeAccessPermission IPermission	✓ **DO** add the suffix "Permission."

3.5.3 **Naming Enumerations**

Names of enumeration types (also called enums) in general should follow the standard type-naming rules (PascalCasing, etc.). However, there are additional guidelines that apply specifically to enums.

✓ **DO** use a singular type name for an enumeration unless its values are bit fields.

```
public enum ConsoleColor {
    Black,
    Blue,
    Cyan,
    ...
}
```

✓ **DO** use a plural type name for an enumeration with bit fields as values, also called flags enum.

```
[Flags]
public enum ConsoleModifiers {
    Alt,
    Control,
    Shift
}
```

✗ **DO NOT** use an "Enum" suffix in enum type names.

For example, the following enum is badly named:

```
// Bad naming
public enum ColorEnum {
   ...
}
```

✗ **DO NOT** use "Flag" or "Flags" suffixes in enum type names.

For example, the following enum is badly named:

```
// Bad naming
[Flags]
public enum ColorFlags {
   ...
}
```

✗ **DO NOT** use a prefix on enumeration value names (e.g., "ad" for ADO enums, "rtf" for rich text enums, etc.).

```
public enum ImageMode {
   ImageModeBitmap = 0, // ImageMode prefix is not necessary
   ImageModeGrayscale = 1,
   ImageModeIndexed = 2,
   ImageModeRgb = 3,
}
```

The following naming scheme would be better:

```
public enum ImageMode {
   Bitmap = 0,
   Grayscale = 1,
   Indexed = 2,
   Rgb = 3,
}
```

▪ **BRAD ABRAMS** Notice that this guideline is the exact opposite of common usage in C++ programming. It is important in C++ to fully qualify each enum member because they can be accessed outside of the scope of the enum name. However, in the managed world, enum members are only accessed through the scope of the enum name.

3.6 Names of Type Members

Types are made of members: methods, properties, events, constructors, and fields. The following sections describe guidelines for naming type members.

3.6.1 Names of Methods

Because methods are the means of taking action, the design guidelines require that method names be verbs or verb phrases. Following this guideline also serves to distinguish method names from property and type names, which are noun or adjective phrases.

> ■ **STEVEN CLARKE** Do your best to name methods according to the task that they enable, not according to some implementation detail. In a usability study on the System.Xml APIs, participants were asked to write code that would perform a query over an instance of an XPathDocument. To do this, participants needed to call the CreateXPathNavigator method from XPath-Document. This returns an instance of an XPathNavigator that is used to iterate over the document data returned by a query. However, no participants expected or realized that they would have to do this. Instead, they expected to be able to call some method named Query or Select on the document itself. Such a method could just as easily return an instance of XPathNavigator in the same way that CreateXPathNavigator does. By tying the name of the method more directly to the task it enables, rather than to the implementation details, it is more likely that developers using your API will be able to find the correct method to accomplish a task.

✓ **DO** give methods names that are verbs or verb phrases.

```
public class String {
    public int CompareTo(...);
    public string[] Split(...);
    public string Trim();
}
```

3.6.2 Names of Properties

Unlike other members, properties should be given noun phrase or adjective names. That is because a property refers to data, and the name of the property reflects that. PascalCasing is always used for property names.

✔ **DO** name properties using a noun, noun phrase, or adjective.

```
public class String {
    public int Length { get; }
}
```

✗ **DO NOT** have properties that match the name of "Get" methods as in the following example:

```
public string TextWriter { get {...} set {...} }
public string GetTextWriter(int value) { ... }
```

This pattern typically indicates that the property should really be a method. See section 5.1.3 for additional information.

✔ **DO** name collection properties with a plural phrase describing the items in the collection instead of using a singular phrase followed by "List" or "Collection."

```
public class ListView {
    // good naming
    public ItemCollection Items { get; }

    // bad naming
    public ItemCollection ItemCollection { get; }
}
```

✔ **DO** name Boolean properties with an affirmative phrase (`CanSeek` instead of `CantSeek`). Optionally, you can also prefix Boolean properties with "Is," "Can," or "Has," but only where it adds value.

For example, `CanRead` is more understandable than `Readable`. However, `Created` is actually more readable than `IsCreated`. Having the prefix is often too verbose and unnecessary, particularly in the face of Intellisense in the code editors. It is just as clear to type `MyObject.Enabled =` and have Intellisense give you the choice of true or false as it is to have `MyObject.IsEnabled =`, and the second one is more verbose.

> ▪▪ **KRZYSZTOF CWALINA**   In selecting names for Boolean properties and functions, consider testing out the common uses of the API in an if-statement. Such a usage test will highlight whether the word choices and grammar of the API name (e.g., active versus passive voice, singular versus plural) make sense as English phrases. For example, both of the following
>
> ```
> if(collection.Contains(item))
> if(regularExpression.Matches(text))
> ```
>
> read more naturally than
>
> ```
> if(collection.IsContained(item))
> if(regularExpression.Match(text))
> ```
>
> Also, all else being equal, you should prefer the active voice to the passive voice:
>
> ```
> if(stream.CanSeek) // better than ..
> if(stream.IsSeekable)
> ```

✓ **CONSIDER** giving a property the same name as its type.

For example, the following property correctly gets and sets an enum value named `Color`, so the property is named `Color`:

```
public enum Color {...}
public class Control {
    public Color Color { get {...} set {...} }
}
```

3.6.3 Names of Events

Events always refer to some action, either one that is happening or one that has occurred. Therefore, as with methods, events are named with verbs, and verb tense is used to indicate the time when the event is raised.

✓ **DO** name events with a verb or a verb phrase.

Examples include `Clicked`, `Painting`, `DroppedDown`, and so on.

✓ **DO** give events names with a concept of before and after, using the present and past tenses.

For example, a close event that is raised before a window is closed would be called `Closing`, and one that is raised after the window is closed would be called `Closed`.

✗ **DO NOT** use "Before" or "After" prefixes or postfixes to indicate pre- and post-events. Use present and past tenses as just described.

✓ **DO** name event handlers (delegates used as types of events) with the "EventHandler" suffix, as shown in the following example:

```
public delegate void ClickedEventHandler(object sender, ClickedEventArgs e);
```

Note that you should create custom event handlers very rarely. Instead, most APIs should simply use `EventHandler<T>`. Section 5.4.1 talks about event design in more detail.

> ■ **JASON CLARK**   Today, it is the rare case where you would need to define your own "EventHandler" delegate. Instead, you should use the `EventHandler<TEventArgs>` delegate type, where `TEventArgs` is either `EventArgs` or your own `EventArgs` derived class. This reduces type definitions in the system and ensures that your event follows the pattern described in the preceding bullet.

✓ **DO** use two parameters named *sender* and *e* in event handlers.

The sender parameter represents the object that raised the event. The sender parameter is typically of type `object`, even if it is possible to employ a more specific type. The pattern is used consistently across the Framework and is described in more detail in section 5.4.

```
public delegate void <EventName>EventHandler(object sender,
                                    <EventName>EventArgs e);
```

✓ **DO** name event argument classes with the "EventArgs" suffix, as shown in the following example:

```
public class ClickedEventArgs : EventArgs {
    int x;
    int y;
```

```
    public ClickedEventArgs (int x, int y) {
      this.x = x;
      this.y = y;
    }
    public int X { get { return x; } }
    public int Y { get { return y; } }
  }
```

3.6.4 **Naming Fields**

The field-naming guidelines apply to static public and protected fields. Internal and private fields are not covered by guidelines, and public or protected instance fields are not allowed by the member design guidelines, which are described in Chapter 5.

✓ **DO** use PascalCasing in field names.

```
    public class String {
       public static readonly string Empty ="";
    }
    public struct UInt32 {
       public const Min = 0;
    }
```

✓ **DO** name fields using a noun, noun phrase, or adjective.

✗ **DO NOT** use a prefix for field names.

For example, do not use "g_" or "s_" to indicate static fields. Publicly accessible fields (the subject of this section) are very similar to properties from the API design point of view; therefore, they should follow the same naming conventions as properties.

> ■■ **BRAD ABRAMS** Notice that, as with just about all the guidelines in this book, this guideline is meant to apply only to publicly exposed fields. In this case, it's important that the names be clean and simple so the masses of consumers can easily understand them. As many have noted, there are very good reasons to use some sort of convention for private fields and local variables.

> ■ **JEFF PROSISE**   As a matter of personal preference, I typically prefix the names of private fields with an underscore (for example, `_connection`). When I read the code back after a time away, this makes it obvious to me which fields are not intended for public consumption. This convention is used quite a lot in the .NET Framework—for example, in `System.Net.HttpWebRequest` and `System.Web.HttpContext`—but it is not used throughout.

3.7 **Naming Parameters**

Beyond the obvious reason of readability, it is important to follow the guidelines for parameter names because parameters are displayed in documentation and in the designer when visual design tools provide Intellisense and class browsing functionality.

✔ **DO** use camelCasing in parameter names.

```
public class String {
    public bool Contains(string value);
    public string Remove(int startIndex, int count);
}
```

✔ **DO** use descriptive parameter names.

Parameter names should be descriptive enough to use with their types to determine their meaning in most scenarios.

✔ **CONSIDER** using names based on a parameter's meaning rather than the parameter's type.

Development tools must provide useful information about the type, so the parameter name can be put to better use describing semantics rather than the type. Occasional use of type-based parameter names is entirely appropriate—but it is not ever appropriate under these guidelines to revert to the Hungarian naming convention.

3.7.1 **Naming Operator Overload Parameters**

This section talks about naming parameters of operator overloads.

✓ **DO** use *left* and *right* for binary operator overload parameter names if there is no meaning to the parameters.

```
public static TimeSpan operator-(DateTimeOffset left,
                                 DateTimeOffset right)
public static bool operator==(DateTimeOffset left,
                              DateTimeOffset right)
```

✓ **DO** use *value* for unary operator overload parameter names if there is no meaning to the parameters.

```
public static BigInteger operator-(BigInteger value);
```

✓ **CONSIDER** meaningful names for operator overload parameters if doing so adds significant value.

```
public static BigInteger Divide(BigInteger dividend,
                                BigInteger divisor);
```

✗ **DO NOT** use abbreviations or numeric indices for operator overload parameter names.

```
// incorrect parameter naming
public static bool operator ==(DateTimeOffset d1,
                               DateTimeOffset d2);
```

3.8 **Naming Resources**

Because localizable resources can be referenced via certain objects as if they were properties, the naming guidelines for resources are similar to property guidelines.

✓ **DO** use PascalCasing in resource keys.

✓ **DO** provide descriptive rather than short identifiers.

Keep them concise where possible, but do not sacrifice readability for space.

✗ **DO NOT** use language-specific keywords of the main CLR languages.

✓ **DO** use only alphanumeric characters and underscores in naming resources.

✓ **DO** use the following naming convention for exception message resources.

The resource identifier should be the exception type name plus a short identifier of the exception:

```
ArgumentExceptionIllegalCharacters
ArgumentExceptionInvalidName
ArgumentExceptionFileNameIsMalformed
```

SUMMARY

The naming guidelines described in this chapter, if followed, provide a consistent scheme that will make it easy for users of a framework to identify the function of elements of the framework. The guidelines provide naming consistency across frameworks developed by different organizations or companies.

The next chapter provides general guidelines for implementing types.

4

Type Design Guidelines

From the CLR perspective, there are only two categories of types—reference types and value types—but for the purpose of a discussion about framework design, we divide types into more logical groups, each with its own specific design rules. Figure 4-1 shows these logical groups.

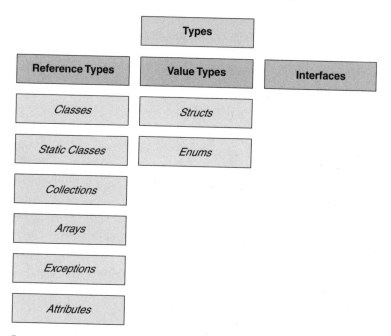

FIGURE 4-1: The logical grouping of types

Classes are the general case of reference types. They make up the bulk of types in the majority of frameworks. Classes owe their popularity to the rich set of object-oriented features they support and to their general applicability. Base classes and abstract classes are special logical groups related to extensibility. Extensibility and base classes are covered in Chapter 6.

Interfaces are types that can be implemented by both reference types and value types. They can thus serve as roots of polymorphic hierarchies of reference types and value types. In addition, interfaces can be used to simulate multiple inheritance, which is not natively supported by the CLR.

Structs are the general case of value types and should be reserved for small, simple types, similar to language primitives.

Enums are a special case of value types used to define short sets of values, such as days of the week, console colors, and so on.

Static classes are types intended to be containers for static members. They are commonly used to provide shortcuts to other operations.

Delegates, exceptions, attributes, arrays, and collections are all special cases of reference types intended for specific uses, and guidelines for their design and usage are discussed elsewhere in this book.

✔ **DO** ensure that each type is a well-defined set of related members, not just a random collection of unrelated functionality.

It is important that a type can be described in one simple sentence. A good definition should also rule out functionality that is only tangentially related.

> **■ BRAD ABRAMS**   If you have ever managed a team of people, you know that they don't do well without a crisp set of responsibilities. Well, types work the same way. I have noticed that types without a firm and focused scope tend to be magnets for more random functionality, which over time makes a small problem a lot worse. It becomes more difficult to justify why the next member with even more random functionality does not belong in the type. As the focus of the members in a type blurs, the developer's ability to predict where to find a given functionality is impaired, and therefore so is productivity.

■ RICO MARIANI   Good types are like good diagrams: What has been omitted is as important to clarity and usability as what has been included. Every additional member you add to a type starts at a net negative value and only by proven usefulness does it go from there to positive. If you add too much in an attempt to make the type more useful to some, you are just as likely to make the type useless to everyone.

■ JEFFREY RICHTER   When I was learning OOP back in the early 1980s, I was taught a mantra that I still honor today: If things get too complicated, make more types. Sometimes I find that I am thinking really hard trying to define a good set of methods for a type. When I start to feel that I'm spending too much time on this or when things just don't seem to fit together well, I remember my mantra and I define more, smaller types where each type has well-defined functionality. This has worked extremely well for me over the years. On the flip side, sometimes types do end up being dumping grounds for various loosely related functions. The .NET Framework offers several types like this, such as `Marshal`, `GC`, `Console`, `Math`, and `Application`. You will note that all members of these types are static and so it is not possible to create any instances of these types. Programmers seem to be OK with this. Fortunately, these types' methods are separated a bit into separate types. It would be awful if all these methods were defined in just one type!

4.1 Types and Namespaces

You should decide how to factor your functionality into a set of functional areas represented by namespaces before you design a large framework. This kind of top-down architectural design is important because it ensures a coherent set of namespaces containing types that are well integrated, don't collide, and are not repetitive. The namespace design process is iterative, of course, and it should be expected that the design will have to be tweaked as types are added to the namespaces over the course of several releases. This philosophy leads to the following guidelines.

✓ **DO** use namespaces to organize types into a hierarchy of related feature areas.

The hierarchy should be optimized for developers browsing the framework for desired APIs.

> ■ **KRZYSZTOF CWALINA** This is an important guideline. Contrary to popular belief, the main purpose of namespaces is not to help in resolving naming conflicts between types with the same name. As the guideline states, the main purpose of namespaces is to organize types in a hierarchy that is coherent, easy to navigate, and easy to understand.
>
> I consider type-name conflicts in a single framework to indicate sloppy design. Types with identical names should either be merged to allow for better integration between parts of the library or be renamed to improve code readability and searchability.

✗ **AVOID** very deep namespace hierarchies. Such hierarchies are difficult to browse because the user has to backtrack often.

✗ **AVOID** having too many namespaces.

Users of a framework should not have to import many namespaces in most common scenarios. Types that are used together in common scenarios should reside in a single namespace if at all possible.

> ■ **JEFFREY RICHTER** As an example of a problem, the runtime serializer types are defined under the `System.Runtime.Serialization` namespace and its subnamespaces. However, the `Serializable` and `NonSerialized` attributes are incorrectly defined in the `System` namespace. Because these types are not in the same namespace, developers don't realize that they are closely related. In fact, I have run into many developers who apply the `Serializable` attribute to a class that they are serializing with the `System.Xml.Serialization`'s `XmlSerializer` type. However, the `XmlSerializer` completely ignores the `Serializable` attribute; applying the attribute gives no value and just bloats your assembly's metadata.

✗ **AVOID** having types designed for advanced scenarios in the same namespace as types intended for common programming tasks.

This makes it easier to understand the basics of the framework and to use the framework in the common scenarios.

BRAD ABRAMS One of the best features of Visual Studio is Intellisense, which provides a drop-down for your likely next type or member usage. The benefit of this feature is inversely proportional to the number of options. That is, if there are too many items in the list it takes longer to find the one you are looking for. Following this guideline to split out advanced functionality into a separate namespace enables developers to see the smallest number of types possible in the common case.

BRIAN PEPIN One thing we've learned is that most programmers live or die by Intellisense. If something isn't listed in the drop-down, most programmers won't believe it exists. But, as Brad says, too much of a good thing can be bad, and having too much stuff in the drop-down list dilutes its value. If you have functionality that should be in the same namespace but you don't think it needs to be shown all the time to users, you can use the EditorBrowsable attribute. Put this attribute on a class or member and you can instruct Intellisense to only show the class or member for advanced scenarios.

RICO MARIANI Don't go crazy adding members for every exotic thing someone might want to do with your type. You'll make fatter, uglier assemblies that are hard to grasp. Provide good primitives with understandable limitations. A great example of this is the urge people get to duplicate functionality that is already easy to use via Interop to native. Interop is there for a reason—it's not an unwanted stepchild. When wrapping anything, be sure you are adding plenty of value. Otherwise, the value added by not implementing the type and therefore being smaller would make your assembly more helpful to more people.

JEFFREY RICHTER I agree with this guideline, but I'd like to further add that the more advanced classes should be in a namespace that is under the namespace that contains the simple types. For example, the simple types might be in System.Mail, and the more advanced types should be in System.Mail.Advanced.

✗ **DO NOT** define types without specifying their namespaces.

This organizes related types in a hierarchy and can help to resolve potential type name collisions. Please note that the fact that namespaces can help to resolve name collisions does not mean that such collisions should be introduced. See section 3.4.1 for details.

▪▫ **BRAD ABRAMS**   It is important to realize that namespaces cannot actually prevent naming collisions; however, they can significantly reduce them. I could define a class called `MyNamespace.MyType` in an assembly called `MyAssembly` and define a class with precisely the same name in another assembly. I could then build an application that uses both of these assemblies and types. The CLR would not get confused because the type identity in the CLR is based on the strong name (which includes the fully qualified assembly name) rather than just the namespace and type name. This fact can be seen by looking at the C# and ILASM of code creating an instance of `MyType`.

```
C#:
new MyType();
```

```
IL:
IL_0000: newobj instance void [MyAssembly]MyNamespace.MyType::.ctor()
```

Notice that the C# compiler adds a reference to the assembly that defines the type, of the form `[MyAssembly]`, so the runtime always has a disambiguated, fully qualified name to work with.

▪▫ **JEFFREY RICHTER**   Although what Brad says is true, the C# compiler doesn't let you specify in source code which assembly to pull a type out of, so if you have code that wants to use a type called `MyNamespace.MyType` that exists in two or more assemblies, there is no easy way to do this in C# source code. Prior to C# 2.0, distinguishing between the two types was impossible. However, with C# 2.0, it is now possible using the new extern aliases and namespace qualifier features.

> **■ RICO MARIANI**   Namespaces are a language thing. The CLR doesn't know anything about them really. As far as the CLR is concerned, the name of the class really is something like `MyNameSpace.MyOtherNameSpace.MyAmazingType`. The compilers give you syntax (e.g., "using") so that you don't have to type those long class names all the time. So the CLR is never confused about class names because everything is always fully qualified.

4.1.1 Standard Subnamespace Names

Types that are rarely used should be placed in subnamespaces to avoid cluttering the main namespaces. We have identified several groups of types that should be separated from their main namespaces.

4.1.1.1 The `.Design` Subnamespace

Design-time-only types should reside in a subnamespace named `.Design`. For example, `System.Windows.Forms.Design` contains `Designers` and related classes used to do design of applications based on `System.Windows.Forms`.

```
System.Windows.Forms.Design
System.Messaging.Design
System.Diagnostics.Design
```

✓ **DO** use a namespace with the ".Design" suffix to contain types that provide design-time functionality for a base namespace.

4.1.1.2 The `.Permissions` Subnamespace

Permission types should reside in a subnamespace named `.Permissions`.

✓ **DO** use a namespace with the ".Permissions" suffix to contain types that provide custom permissions for a base namespace.

> **■ KRZYSZTOF CWALINA**   In the initial design of the .NET Framework namespaces, all types related to a given feature area were in the same namespace. Prior to the first release, we moved design-related types to sub-namespaces with the ".Design" suffix. Unfortunately, we did not have time to do it for the `Permission` types. This is a problem in several parts of the Framework. For example, a large portion of the types in the `System.Diagnostics` namespace are types needed for the security infrastructure and very rarely used by the end users of the API.

4.1.1.3 The .Interop Subnamespace

Many frameworks need to support interoperability with legacy components. Due diligence should be used in designing interoperability from the ground up. However, the nature of the problem often requires that the shape and style of such interoperability APIs are often quite different from good managed framework design. Thus, it makes sense to put functionality related to interoperation with legacy components in a subnamespace.

You should not put types that completely abstract unmanaged concepts into the Interop subnamespace and expose them as managed. It is often the case that managed APIs are implemented by calling out to unmanaged code. For example, the System.IO.FileStream class calls out to Win32 CreateFile. This is perfectly acceptable and does not imply that the FileStream class needs to be in the System.IO.Interop namespace because FileStream completely abstracts the Win32 concepts and publicly exposes a nice managed abstraction.

✔ **DO** use a namespace with the ".Interop" suffix to contain types that provide interop functionality for a base namespace.

✔ **DO** use a namespace with the ".Interop" suffix for all code in a Primary Interop Assembly (PIA).

4.2 Choosing Between Class and Struct

One of the basic design decisions every framework designer faces is whether to design a type as a class (a reference type) or as a struct (a value type). Good understanding of the differences in the behavior of reference types and value types is crucial in making this choice.

The first difference between reference types and value types we will consider is that reference types are allocated on the heap and garbage-collected, whereas value types are allocated either on the stack or inline in containing types and deallocated when the stack unwinds or when their containing type gets deallocated. Therefore, allocations and deallocations of value types are in general cheaper than allocations and deallocations of reference types.

Next, arrays of reference types are allocated out-of-line, meaning the array elements are just references to instances of the reference type residing on the heap. Value type arrays are allocated inline, meaning that the array elements are the actual instances of the value type. Therefore, allocations and deallocations of value type arrays are much cheaper than allocations and deallocations of reference type arrays. In addition, in a majority of cases value type arrays exhibit much better locality of reference.

> **RICO MARIANI** The preceding is often true, but it's a very broad generalization that I would be very careful about. Whether or not you get better locality of reference when value types get boxed when cast to an array of value types will depend on how much of the value type you use, how much searching you have to do, how much data reuse there could have been with equivalent array members (sharing a pointer), the typical array access patterns, and probably other factors I can't think of at the moment. Your mileage might vary, but value type arrays are a great tool for your toolbox.

> **CHRIS SELLS** I find the restrictions of value types to be painful and therefore prefer reference types. Custom value types are often used for performance improvements, so I would recommend profiling large-scale anticipated usage of your library and changing reference types to value types based on actual data instead of on some anticipated problem that may never manifest itself in real-world conditions.

The next difference is related to memory usage. Value types get boxed when cast to a reference type or one of the interfaces they implement. They get unboxed when cast back to the value type. Because boxes are objects that are allocated on the heap and are garbage-collected, too much boxing and unboxing can have a negative impact on the heap, the garbage collector, and ultimately the performance of the application. In contrast, no such boxing occurs as reference types are cast.

Next, reference type assignments copy the reference, whereas value type assignments copy the entire value. Therefore, assignments of large reference types are cheaper than assignments of large value types.

Finally, reference types are passed by reference, whereas value types are passed by value. Changes to an instance of a reference type affect all references pointing to the instance. Value type instances are copied when they are passed by value. When an instance of a value type is changed, it of course does not affect any of its copies. Because the copies are not created explicitly by the user but are implicitly created when arguments are passed or return values are returned, value types that can be changed can be confusing to many users. Therefore, value types should be immutable.[1]

■ RICO MARIANI If you make your value type mutable, you will find that you end up having to pass it by reference a lot to get the semantics you want (using, for example, "out" syntax in C#). This might be important in cases in which the value type is expected to be embedded in a variety of other objects that are themselves reference types or embedded in arrays. The biggest trouble from having mutable value types is where they look like independent entities like complex numbers. Value types that have a mission in life of being an accumulator of sorts or a piece of a reference type have fewer pitfalls for mutability.

■ VANCE MORRISON Today all reference types have an overhead of 8 bytes (16 on 64 bit) per object. Thus if your application memory usage is dominated by a large number (> 1M) of small objects (< 16 bytes), you will "waste" a large fraction of your memory on object overhead. You can avoid this by putting these objects into a value type array instead (which has 0 per object overhead).

You can even refer to these elements inside the array as if they were normal objects by making "smart pointer" value types. These types have two fields; the first is to the large array, and the second is to the index within the array. From a user's point of view, using these "smart pointers" is just like using normal reference types, but you have saved large amounts of memory.

The downside to this technique is that you don't get garbage collection on elements in your array. Thus, this technique should be used only when that is not an issue (e.g., when you have a large read-only array of small structures).

---

1. Immutable types are types that don't have any public members that can modify this instance. For example, System.String is immutable. Its members, such as ToUpper, do not modify the string on which they are called but return a new modified string instead and leave the original string unchanged.

As a rule of thumb, the majority of types in a framework should be classes. There are, however, some situations in which the characteristics of a value type make it more appropriate to use structs.

✓ **CONSIDER** defining a struct instead of a class if instances of the type are small and commonly short-lived or are commonly embedded in other objects.

✗ **AVOID** defining a struct unless the type has all of the following characteristics:

- It logically represents a single value, similar to primitive types (int, double, etc.).
- It has an instance size under 16 bytes.
- It is immutable.
- It will not have to be boxed frequently.

In all other cases, you should define your types as classes.

■ **JEFFREY RICHTER**   In my opinion, a value type should be defined for types that have approximately 16 bytes or less. Value types can be more than 16 bytes if you don't intend to pass them to other methods or copy them to and from a collection class (like an array). I would also define a value type if you expect instances of the type to be used for short periods of time (usually they are created in a method and no longer needed after a method returns). I used to discourage defining value types if you thought that instances of them would be placed in a collection due to all the boxing that would have to be done. But, fortunately, newer versions of the CLR, C#, and other languages support generics so that boxing is no longer necessary when putting value type instances in a collection.

■ **ERIC GUNNERSON**   Rather than avoiding all value types that are bigger than 16 bytes in size, use this guideline as a trigger to do more investigation. Figure out how your type is used and do some benchmarking to understand what implications a bigger value type might have.

Also consider a value type if it is part of a set of types where all the others are value types. Having one reference type in such a group will likely be confusing.

> **■ JOE DUFFY** I frequently struggle with the reference versus value type decision. Although these rules are very black-and-white, there is a fairly large cliff you jump off of when you decide to implement a reference type. This decision means you will pay the cost of heap allocation for each instance—which can impact scalability on multiprocessor machines due to the shared heap and cost of collections—in addition to at least a pointer of overhead (due to the object header) and a level of indirection to each access (due to the need to go through an object reference). That said, my experience has shown that whenever I attempt to be clever and break any of these rules, it usually comes back to bite me.

4.3 Choosing Between Class and Interface

In general, classes are the preferred construct for exposing abstractions.

The main drawback of interfaces is that they are much less flexible than classes when it comes to allowing for evolution of APIs. After you ship an interface, the set of its members is fixed forever. Any additions to the interface would break existing types that implement the interface.

A class offers much more flexibility. You can add members to classes that have already shipped. As long as the method is not abstract (i.e., as long as you provide a default implementation of the method), any existing derived classes continue to function unchanged.

Let's illustrate the concept with a real example from the .NET Framework. The `System.IO.Stream` abstract class shipped in version 1.0 of the Framework without any support for timing out pending I/O operations. In version 2.0, several members were added to `Stream` to allow subclasses to support timeout-related operations, even when accessed through their base class APIs.

```
public abstract class Stream {
   public virtual bool CanTimeout {
      get { return false; }
   }
   public virtual int ReadTimeout{
      get{
         throw new InvalidOperationException(...);
      }
```

```
        set {
            throw new InvalidOperationException(...);
        }
    }
}

public class FileStream : Stream {
    public override bool CanTimeout {
        get { return true; }
    }
    public override int ReadTimeout{
        get{
            ...
        }
        set {
            ...
        }
    }
}
```

The only way to evolve interface-based APIs is to add a new interface with the additional members. This might seem like a good option, but it suffers from several problems. Let's illustrate this on a hypothetical IStream interface. Let's assume we had shipped the following APIs in version 1.0 of the Framework.

```
public interface IStream {
    ...
}

public class FileStream : IStream {
    ...
}
```

If we wanted to add support for timeouts to streams in version 2.0, we would have to do something like the following:

```
public interface ITimeoutEnabledStream : IStream  {
    int ReadTimeout{ get; set; }
}

public class FileStream : ITimeoutEnabledStream {
    public int ReadTimeout{
        get{
            ...
```

```
        {
        set {
            ...
        }
    }
}
```

But now we would have a problem with all the existing APIs that consume and return `IStream`. For example, `StreamReader` has several constructor overloads and a property typed as `Stream`.

```
public class StreamReader {
    public StreamReader(IStream stream){ ... }
    public IStream BaseStream { get { ... } }
}
```

How would we add support for `ITimeoutEnabledStream` to `Stream-Reader`? We would have several options, each with substantial development cost and usability issues:

- Leave the `StreamReader` as is, and ask users who want to access the timeout-related APIs on the instance returned from `BaseStream` property to use a dynamic cast and query for the `ITimeout-EnabledStream` interface.

```
StreamReader reader = GetSomeReader();
ITimeoutEnabledStream stream = reader.BaseStream as ITimeoutEnabledStream;
if(stream != null){
    stream.ReadTimeout = 100;
}
```

Unfortunately, this option does not perform well in usability studies. The fact that some streams can now support the new operations is not immediately apparent to the users of `StreamReader` APIs. Also, some developers have difficulty understanding and using dynamic casts.

- Add a new property to `StreamReader` that would return `ITimeout-EnabledStream` if one is passed to the constructor or `null` if `IStream` is passed.

```
StreamReader reader = GetSomeReader();
ITimeoutEnabledStream stream = reader.TimeoutEnabledBaseStream;
if(stream!= null){
    stream.ReadTimeout = 100;
}
```

Such APIs are only marginally better in terms of usability. It's really not obvious to the user that the TimeoutEnabledBaseStream property getter might return null, which results in confusing and often unexpected NullReferenceExceptions.

- Add a new type called TimeoutEnabledStreamReader that would take ITimeoutEnabledStream parameters to the constructor over-loads and return ITimeoutEnabledStream from the BaseStream property.

The problem with this approach is that every additional type in the framework adds complexity for the users. What's worse, the solution usually creates more problems like the one it is trying to solve. StreamReader itself is used in other APIs. These other APIs will now need new versions that can operate on the new TimeoutEnabledStreamReader.

The Framework streaming APIs are based on an abstract class. This allowed for an addition of timeout functionality in version 2.0 of the Framework. The addition is straightforward, discoverable, and had little impact on other parts of the Framework.

```
StreamReader reader = GetSomeReader();
if(reader.BaseStream.CanTimeout){
    reader.BaseStream.ReadTimeout = 100;
}
```

One of the most common arguments in favor of interfaces is that they allow separating contract from the implementation. However, the argument incorrectly assumes that you cannot separate contracts from implementation using classes. Abstract classes residing in a separate assembly from their concrete implementations are a great way to achieve such separation. For example, the contract of IList<T> says that when an item is added to a collection, the `Count` property is incremented by one. Such a simple contract can be expressed and, what's more important, locked for all subtypes, using the following abstract class:

```
public abstract class CollectionContract<T> : IList<T> {

    public void Add(T item){
        AddCore(item);
        this.count++;
    }
    public int Count {
        get { return this.count; }
    }
    protected abstract void AddCore(T item);
    private int count;
}
```

> ■ **KRZYSZTOF CWALINA** I often hear people saying that interfaces specify contracts. I believe this is a dangerous myth. Interfaces, by themselves, do not specify much beyond the syntax required to use an object. The interface-as-contract myth causes people to do the wrong thing when trying to separate contracts from implementation, which is a great engineering practice. Interfaces separate syntax from implementation, which is not that useful, and the myth provides a false sense of doing the right engineering. In reality, the contract is semantics, and these can actually be nicely expressed with some implementation.

COM exposed APIs exclusively through interfaces, but you should not assume that COM did this because interfaces were superior. COM did it because COM is an interface standard that was intended to be supported on many execution environments. CLR is an execution standard, and it provides a great benefit for libraries that rely on portable implementation.

✓ **DO** favor defining classes over interfaces.

Class-based APIs can be evolved with much greater ease than interface-based APIs because it is possible to add members to a class without breaking existing code.

KRZYSZTOF CWALINA   Over the course of the three versions of the .NET Framework, I have talked about this guideline with quite a few developers on our team. Many of them, including those who initially disagreed with the guideline, have said that they regret having shipped some API as an interface. I have not heard of even one case in which somebody regretted that they shipped a class.

JEFFREY RICHTER   I agree with Krzysztof in general. However, you do need to think about some other things. There are some special base classes, such as `MarshalByRefObject`. If your library type provides an abstract base class that isn't itself derived from `MarshalByRefObject`, then types that derive from your abstract base class cannot live in a different `AppDomain`.

✓ **DO** use abstract classes instead of interfaces to decouple the contract from implementations.

Abstract classes, if designed correctly, allow for the same degree of decoupling between contract and implementation.

CHRIS ANDERSON   Here is one instance in which the design guideline, if followed too strictly, can paint you into a corner. Abstract types do version much better, and allow for future extensibility, but they also burn your one and only one base type. Interfaces are appropriate when you are really defining a contract between two objects that is invariant over time. Abstract base types are better for defining a common base for a family of types. When we did .NET, there was somewhat of a backlash against the complexity and strictness of COM—interfaces, GUIDs, variants, and IDL were all seen as bad things. I believe today that we have a more balanced view of this. All of these COM-isms have their place, and in fact you can see interfaces coming back as a core concept in Indigo.

BRIAN PEPIN One thing I've started doing is to actually bake as much contract into my abstract class as possible. For example, I might want to have four overloads to a method where each overload offers an increasingly complex set of parameters. The best way to do this is to provide a nonvirtual implementation of these methods on the abstract class and have the implementations all route to a protected abstract method that provides the actual implementation. By doing this, you can write all the boring argument-checking logic once. Developers who want to implement your class will thank you.

✓ **DO** define an interface if you need to provide a polymorphic hierarchy of value types.

Value types cannot inherit from other types, but they can implement interfaces. For example, `IComparable`, `IFormattable`, and `IConvertible` are all interfaces, so value types such as `Int32`, `Int64`, and other primitives can all be comparable, formattable, and convertible.

```
public struct Int32 : IComparable, IFormattable, IConvertible {
    ...
}
public struct Int64 : IComparable, IFormattable, IConvertible {
    ...
}
```

RICO MARIANI Good interface candidates often have this "mix in" feel to them. All sorts of objects can be `IFormattable`—it isn't restricted to a certain subtype. It's more like a type attribute. Other times we have interfaces that look more like they should be classes—`IFormatProvider` springs to mind. The fact that the interface's name ended in "er" speaks volumes.

BRIAN PEPIN Another sign that you've got a well-defined interface is that the interface does exactly one thing. If you have an interface that has a grab bag of functionality, that's a warning sign. You'll end up regretting it because in the next version of your product you'll want to add new functionality to this rich interface, but you can't.

✓ **CONSIDER** defining interfaces to achieve a similar effect to that of multiple inheritance.

For example, `System.IDisposable` and `System.ICloneable` are both interfaces, so types, like `System.Drawing.Image`, can be both disposable and cloneable yet still inherit from the `System.MarshalByRefObject` class.

```
public class Image : MarshalByRefObject, IDisposable, ICloneable {
   ...
}
```

> ■ **JEFFREY RICHTER**   When a class is derived from a base class, I say that the derived class has an "is a" relationship with the base. For example, a `FileStream` "is a" `Stream`. However, when a class implements an interface, I say that the implementing class has a "can-do" relationship with the interface. For example, a `FileStream` "can-do" disposing because it implements the `IDisposable`.

4.4 Abstract Class Design

✗ **DO NOT** define public or protected internal constructors in abstract types.

Constructors should be public only if users will need to create instances of the type. Because you cannot create instances of an abstract type, an abstract type with a public constructor is incorrectly designed and misleading to the users.[2]

```
// bad design
public abstract class Claim {
   public Claim() {
   }
}
// good design
public abstract class Claim {
   protected Claim() {
   }
}
```

---

2. This also applies to protected internal constructors.

✓ **DO** define a protected or an internal constructor in abstract classes.

A protected constructor is more common and simply allows the base class to do its own initialization when subtypes are created.

```
public abstract class Claim {
    protected Claim() {
        ...
    }
}
```

An internal constructor can be used to limit concrete implementations of the abstract class to the assembly defining the class.

```
public abstract class Claim {
    internal Claim() {
        ...
    }
}
```

■ **BRAD ABRAMS** Many languages (such as C#) will insert a protected constructor if you do not. It is a good practice to define the constructor explicitly in the source so that it can be more easily documented and maintained over time.

✓ **DO** provide at least one concrete type that inherits from each abstract class that you ship.

Doing this helps to validate the design of the abstract class. For example, `System.IO.FileStream` is an implementation of the `System.IO.Stream` abstract class.

■ **BRAD ABRAMS** I have seen countless examples of a "well-designed" base class or interface where the designers spent hundreds of hours debating and tweaking the design only to have it blown out of the water when the first real-world client came to use the design. Far too often these real-world clients come too late in the product cycle to allow time for the correct fix. Forcing yourself to provide at least one concrete implementation reduces the chances of finding a new problem late in the product cycle.

> **CHRIS SELLS** My rule of thumb for testing a type or set of types is to have three people write three apps against it based on scenarios you hope to support. If the client code is pretty in all three cases, you've done a good job. Otherwise, you should consider refactoring until pretty happens.

4.5 Static Class Design

A static class is defined as a class that contains only static members (of course besides the instance members inherited from `System.Object` and possibly a private constructor). Some languages provide built-in support for static classes. In C# 2.0 and later, when a class is declared to be static, it is sealed, abstract, and no instance members can be overridden or declared.

```
public static class File {
    ...
}
```

If your language does not have built-in support for static classes, you can declare such classes manually as shown in the following C++ example:

```
public class File abstract sealed {
    ...
}
```

Static classes are a compromise between pure object-oriented design and simplicity. They are commonly used to provide shortcuts to other operations (such as `System.IO.File`), holders of extension methods, or functionality for which a full object-oriented wrapper is unwarranted (such as `System.Environment`).

✓ **DO** use static classes sparingly.

Static classes should be used only as supporting classes for the object-oriented core of the framework.

✗ **DO NOT** treat static classes as a miscellaneous bucket.

There should be a clear charter for the class.

✗ **DO NOT** declare or override instance members in static classes.

✓ **DO** declare static classes as sealed, abstract, and add a private instance constructor if your programming language does not have built-in support for static classes.

■ **BRIAN GRUNKEMEYER**   In the .NET Framework 1.0, I wrote the code for the `System.Environment` class, which is an excellent example of a static class. I messed up and accidentally added a property to this class that wasn't static (`HasShutdownStarted`). Because it was an instance method on a class that could never be instantiated, no one could call it. We didn't discover the problem early enough in the product cycle to fix it before releasing version 1.0.

If I were inventing a new language, I would explicitly add the concept of a static class into the language to help people avoid falling into this trap. And in fact, C# 2.0 did add support for static classes!

■ **JEFFREY RICHTER**   Make sure that you do not attempt to define a static structure, because structures (value types) can always be instantiated, no matter what. Only classes can be static.

4.6 Interface Design

Although most APIs are best modeled using classes and structs, there are cases in which interfaces are more appropriate or are the only option.

The CLR does not support multiple inheritance (i.e., CLR classes cannot inherit from more than one base class), but it does allow types to implement one or more interfaces in addition to inheriting from a base class. Therefore, interfaces are often used to achieve the effect of multiple inheritance. For example, `IDisposable` is an interface that allows types to support disposability independent of any other inheritance hierarchy in which they want to participate.

```
public class Component : MarshalByRefObject, IDisposable, IComponent {
    ...
}
```

The other situation in which defining an interface is appropriate is in creating a common interface that can be supported by several types, including some value types. Value types cannot inherit from types other than System.ValueType, but they can implement interfaces, so using an interface is the only option in order to provide a common base type.

```
public struct Boolean : IComparable {
   ...
}
public class String: IComparable {
   ...
}
```

✔ **DO** define an interface if you need some common API to be supported by a set of types that includes value types.

✔ **CONSIDER** defining an interface if you need to support its functionality on types that already inherit from some other type.

✘ **AVOID** using marker interfaces (interfaces with no members).

If you need to mark a class as having a specific characteristic (marker), in general, use a custom attribute rather than an interface.

```
// Avoid
public interface IImmutable {} // empty interface

public class Key: IImmutable {
   ...
}

// Consider
[Immutable]
public class Key {
   ...
}
```

Methods can be implemented to reject parameters that are not marked with a specific attribute, as follows:

```
public void Add(Key key, object value){
   if(!key.GetType().IsDefined(typeof(ImmutableAttribute), false)){
      throw new ArgumentException("The parameter must be immutable","key");
   }
   ...
}
```

> **RICO MARIANI** Of course any kind of marking like this has a cost. Attribute testing is a lot more costly than type checking. You might find that it's necessary to use the marker interface approach for performance reasons—measure and see. My own experience is that true markers (with no members) don't come up very often. Most of the time, you need a no-kidding-around interface with actual functionality to do the job, in which case there is no choice to make.

The problem with this approach is that the check for the custom attribute can occur only at runtime. Sometimes it is very important that the check for the marker be done at compile-time. For example, a method that can serialize objects of any type might be more concerned with verifying the presence of the marker than with type verification at compile-time. Using marker interfaces might be acceptable in such situations. The following example illustrates this design approach:

```
public interface ITextSerializable {} // empty interface
public void Serialize(ITextSerializable item){
   // use reflection to serialize all public properties
   ...
}
```

✓ **DO** provide at least one type that is an implementation of an interface.

Doing this helps to validate the design of the interface. For example, `System.Collections.Generic.List<T>` is an implementation of the `System.Collections.Generic.IList<T>` interface.

✓ **DO** provide at least one API that consumes each interface you define (a method taking the interface as a parameter or a property typed as the interface).

Doing this helps to validate the interface design. For example, `List<T>.Sort` consumes the `IComparer<T>` interface.

✗ **DO NOT** add members to an interface that has previously shipped.

Doing so would break implementations of the interface. You should create a new interface in order to avoid versioning problems.

Except for the situations described in these guidelines, you should, in general, choose classes rather than interfaces in designing managed code reusable libraries.

4.7 Struct Design

The general-purpose value type is most often referred to as a struct, its C# keyword. This section provides guidelines for general struct design. Section 4.8 presents guidelines for the design of a special case of value type, the enum.

✗ DO NOT provide a default constructor for a struct.

Following this guideline allows arrays of structs to be created without having to run the constructor on each item of the array. Notice that C# does not allow structs to have default constructors.

✗ DO NOT define mutable value types.

Mutable value types have several problems. For example, when a property getter returns a value type, the caller receives a copy. Because the copy is created implicitly, developers might not be aware that they are mutating the copy, and not the original value. Also, some languages (dynamic languages, in particular) have problems using mutable value types because even local variables, when dereferenced, cause a copy to be made.

```
// bad design
public struct ZipCode {
   int fiveDigitCode;
   int plusFourExtension;

   public int FiveDigitCode { get; set; } // get/set properties
   public int PlusFourExtension { get; set; }
}
```

```
// good design
public struct ZipCode {
    int fiveDigitCode;
    int plusFourExtension;

    public ZipCode(int fiveDigitCode, int plusFourExtension){...}
    public ZipCode(int fiveDigitCode):this(fiveDigitCode,0){}

    public int FiveDigitCode { get; } // get-only properties
    public int PlusFourExtension { get; }
}
```

✓ **DO** ensure that a state where all instance data is set to zero, false, or null (as appropriate) is valid.

This prevents accidental creation of invalid instances when an array of the structs is created. For example, the following struct is incorrectly designed. The parameterized constructor is meant to ensure a valid state, but the constructor is not executed when an array of the struct is created and so the instance field value gets initialized to 0, which is not a valid value for this type.

```
// bad design
public struct PositiveInteger {
    int value;

    public PositiveInteger(int value) {
        if (value <= 0) throw new ArgumentException(...);
        this.value = value;
    }

    public override string ToString() {
        return value.ToString();
    }
}
```

The problem can be fixed by ensuring that the default state (in this case, the value field equal to 0) is a valid logical state for the type.

```
// good design
public struct PositiveInteger {
    int value; // the logical value is value+1
```

```
    public PositiveInteger(int value) {
        if (value <= 0) throw new ArgumentException(...);
        this.value = value-1;
    }

    public override string ToString() {
        return (value+1).ToString();
    }
}
```

✓ **DO** implement `IEquatable<T>` on value types.

The `Object.Equals` method on value types causes boxing, and its default implementation is not very efficient, because it uses reflection. `IEquatable<T>.Equals` can have much better performance and can be implemented so that it will not cause boxing. See section 8.6 for guidelines on implementing `IEquatable<T>`.

✗ **DO NOT** explicitly extend `System.ValueType`. In fact, most languages prevent this.

In general, structs can be very useful but should only be used for small, single, immutable values that will not be boxed frequently.

The guidelines in the next section are for enum design, a more complex matter.

4.8 Enum Design

Enums are a special kind of value type. There are two kinds of enums: simple enums and flag enums.

Simple enums represent small closed sets of choices. A common example of the simple enum is a set of colors such as the following:

```
public enum Color {
    Red,
    Green,
    Blue,
    ...
}
```

Flag enums are designed to support bitwise operations on the enum values. A common example of the flags enum is a list of options like the following:

```
[Flags]
public enum AttributeTargets {
    Assembly   = 0x0001,
    Module     = 0x0002,
    Cass       = 0x0004,
    Struct     = 0x0008,
    ...
}
```

> ■ **BRAD ABRAMS**   We had some debates about what to call enums that are designed to be bitwise OR-ed together. We considered bitfields, bitflags, and even bitmasks but ultimately decided to use flag enums because the term is clear, simple, and approachable.

> ■ **STEVEN CLARKE**   I'm sure that less experienced developers will be able to understand bitwise operations on flags. The real question, though, is whether they would expect to have to do this. Most of the APIs that I have run through the labs don't require them to perform such operations, so I have a feeling that they would have the same experience that we observed during a recent study—it's just not something that they are used to doing, so they might not even think about it.
> Where it could get worse, I think, is that if less advanced developers don't realize they are working with a set of flags that can be combined with one another, they might just look at the list available and think that is all the functionality they can access. As we've seen in other studies, if an API makes it look to them as though a specific scenario or requirement isn't immediately possible, it's likely that they will change the requirement and do what does appear to be possible rather than being motivated to spend time investigating what they need to do to achieve the original goal.

Historically, many APIs (e.g., Win32 APIs) represented sets of values using integer constants. Enums make such sets more strongly typed and thus improve compile-time error checking, usability, and readability. For example, use of enums allows development tools to know the possible choices for a property or a parameter.

✓ **DO** use an enum to strongly type parameters, properties, and return values that represent sets of values.

✓ **DO** favor using an enum instead of static constants.

Intellisense provides support for specifying arguments to members with enum parameters. It does not have similar support for static constants.

```
// Avoid the following
public static class Color {
    public static int Red      = 0;
    public static int Green    = 1;
    public static int Blue     = 2;
    ...
}

// Favor the following
public enum Color {
    Red,
    Green,
    Blue,
    ...
}
```

JEFFREY RICHTER   An enum is a structure with a set of static constants. The reason to follow this guideline is because you will get some additional compiler and reflection support if you define an enum versus manually defining a structure with static constants.

✗ **DO NOT** use an enum for open sets (such as the operating system version, names of your friends, etc.).

✗ **DO NOT** provide reserved enum values that are intended for future use.

You can always simply add values to the existing enum at a later stage. See section 4.8.2 for more details on adding values to enums. Reserved values just pollute the set of real values and tend to lead to user errors.

```
public enum DeskType {
    Circular,
    Oblong,
    Rectangular,

    // the following two  values should not be here
    ReservedForFutureUse1,
    ReservedForFutureUse2,
}
```

✗ **AVOID** publicly exposing enums with only one value.

A common practice for ensuring future extensibility of C APIs is to add reserved parameters to method signatures. Such reserved parameters can be expressed as enums with a single default value. This should not be done in managed APIs. Method overloading allows adding parameters in future releases.

```
// Bad Design
public enum SomeOption {
  DefaultOption
  // we will add more options in the future
}

...

// The option parameter is not needed.
// It can always be added in the future
// to an overload of SomeMethod().
public void SomeMethod(SomeOption option) {
    ...
}
```

▪▪ **VANCE MORRISON**   While I agree that this example is not a good practice, I think it is OK to define enums with no values (or just one "sentinel" value). The key is whether the type safety (not being allowed to "accidentally" use an int) is valuable. If you pass out int as "handles" to your structure, passing them out as an enum rather than an int is a REALLY good thing because it prevents mistakes and makes the intent of the API clear (what can I do with this "handle" you returned to me?). When you do this, you may be defining enums with no values or maybe just one (a "Null" value).

JOE DUFFY   Although having enums with one value is a bad idea, enums with just two values are far more common. If you have a Boolean parameter and suspect that the choice may have a third possible value sometime in the future, it's usually a good idea to proactively add the parameter to a two-valued enum. This can help to avoid versioning problems down the road.

BRAD ABRAMS   Like Joe, I believe an enum with just two values is a fine and common practice. I much prefer this to a Boolean argument. The main reason is for code readability. For example, consider:

```
FileStream f = File.Open ("foo.txt", true, false);
```

This call gives you no context whatsoever for understanding the meaning behind true and false. Now consider if the call were:

```
FileStream f = File.Open ("foo.txt", CasingOptions.CaseSensitive,
FileMode.Open);
```

X **DO NOT** include sentinel values in enums.

Although they are sometimes helpful to framework developers, sentinel values are confusing to users of the framework. They are used to track the state of the enum rather than being one of the values from the set represented by the enum. The following example shows an enum with an additional sentinel value used to identify the last value of the enum, which is intended for use in range checks. This is bad practice in framework design.

```
public enum DeskType {
    Circular   = 1,
    Oblong     = 2,
    Rectangular = 3,

    LastValue  = 3 // this sentinel value should not be here
}
```

```
public void OrderDesk(DeskType desk){
    if((desk > DeskType.LastValue){
        throw new ArgumentOutOfRangeException(...);
    }
    ...
}
```

Rather than relying on sentinel values, framework developers should perform the check using one of the real enum values.

```
public void OrderDesk(DeskType desk){
    if(desk > DeskType.Rectangular || desk < DeskType.Circular){
        throw new ArgumentOutOfRangeException(...);
    }
    ...
}
```

■■ RICO MARIANI You can get yourself into a lot of trouble by trying to be too clever with enums. Sentinel values are a great example of this: People write code like the example shown, but they use the sentinel value LastValue instead of Rectangular, as recommended. When a new value comes along and LastValue is updated, their program "automatically" does the right thing and accepts the new input value without giving an ArgumentOutOfRangeException. That sounds grand except for all that we didn't show, the part that's doing the actual work and that might not yet expect or even handle the new value. By avoiding sentinel values you will be forced to revisit all the right places to ensure that the new value really is going to work. The few minutes you spend visiting those call sites will be more than repaid in time you save avoiding bugs.

✔ **DO** provide a value of zero on simple enums.

Consider calling the value something like "None." If such a value is not appropriate for this particular enum, the most common default value for the enum should be assigned the underlying value of zero.

```
public enum Compression {
    None = 0,
    GZip,
    Deflate,
}
```

```
public enum EventType {
    Error = 0,
    Warning,
    Information,
    ...
}
```

✓ **CONSIDER** using Int32 (the default in most programming languages) as the underlying type of an enum unless any of the following is true:

- The enum is a flags enum and you have more than 32 flags, or expect to have more in the future.

■ **BRAD ABRAMS** This might not be as uncommon a concern as you might first expect. We are only in version 2.0 of the .NET Framework and we are already running out of values in the CodeDom GeneratorSupport enum. In retrospect, we should have used a different mechanism for communicating the generator support options than an enum.

■ **RICO MARIANI** Did you know that the CLR supports enums with an underlying type of float or double even though most languages don't choose to expose it? This is very handy for strongly typed constants that happen to be floating point (e.g., a set of canonical conversion factors for different measuring systems). It's in the ECMA standard.

- The underlying type needs to be different than Int32 for easier interoperability with unmanaged code expecting different-size enums.
- A smaller underlying type would result in substantial savings in space. If you expect the enum to be used mainly as an argument for flow of control, the size makes little difference. The size savings might be significant if:
  - You expect the enum to be used as a field in a very frequently instantiated structure or class.
  - You expect users to create large arrays or collections of the enum instances.
  - You expect a large number of instances of the enum to be serialized.

For in-memory usage, be aware that managed objects are always DWORD-aligned, so you effectively need multiple enums or other small structures in an instance to pack a smaller enum with in order to make a difference, because the total instance size is always going to be rounded up to a DWORD.

> ▪▪ **BRAD ABRAMS**   Keep in mind that it is a binary breaking change to change the size of the enum type once you have shipped, so choose wisely—with an eye on the future. Our experience has been that `Int32` is usually the right choice and thus we made it the default.

✓ **DO** name flag enums with plural nouns or noun phrases and simple enums with singular nouns or noun phrases.

See section 3.5.3 for details.

✗ **DO NOT** extend `System.Enum` directly.

`System.Enum` is a special type used by the CLR to create user-defined enumerations. Most programming languages provide a programming element that gives you access to this functionality. For example, in C# the enum keyword is used to define an enumeration.

4.8.1 Designing Flag Enums

> ▪▪ **JEFFREY RICHTER**   I use flag enums quite frequently in my own programming. They store very efficiently in memory, and manipulation is very fast. In addition, they can be used with interlocked operations, making them ideal for solving thread synchronization problems. I'd love to see the `System.Enum` type offer a bunch of additional methods that could be easily inlined by the JIT compiler that would make source code easier to read and maintain. Here are some of the methods I'd like to see added to `System.Enum`: `IsExactlyOneBitSet`, `CountOnBits`, `AreAllBitsOn`, `AreAnyBitsOn`, and `TurnBitsOnOff`.

✓ **DO** apply the `System.FlagsAttribute` to flag enums. Do not apply this attribute to simple enums.

```
[Flags]
public enum AttributeTargets {
    ...
}
```

✓ **DO** use powers of two for the flag enum values so they can be freely combined using the bitwise OR operation.

```
[Flags]
public enum WatcherChangeTypes {
    Created = 0x0002,
    Deleted = 0x0004,
    Changed = 0x0008,
    Renamed = 0x0010,
}
```

✓ **CONSIDER** providing special enum values for commonly used combinations of flags.

Bitwise operations are an advanced concept and should not be required for simple tasks. `FileAccess.ReadWrite` is an example of such a special value.

```
[Flags]
public enum FileAccess {
    Read = 1,
    Write = 2,
    ReadWrite = Read | Write
}
```

✗ **AVOID** creating flag enums where certain combinations of values are invalid.

The `System.Reflection.BindingFlags` enum is an example of an incorrect design of this kind. The enum tries to represent many different concepts, such as visibility, staticness, member kind, and so on.

```
[Flags]
public enum BindingFlags {
    Instance,
    Static,

    NonPublic,
    Public,
```

```
        CreateInstance,
        GetField,
        SetField,
        GetProperty,
        SetProperty,
        InvokeMethod,
        ...
    }
```

Certain combinations of the values are not valid. For example, the `Type.`
`GetMembers` method accepts this enum as a parameter, but the documentation for the method warns users, "You must specify either
`BindingFlags.Instance` or `BindingFlags.Static` in order to get a
return." Similar warnings apply to several other values of the enum.

If you have an enum with this problem, you should separate the values
of the enum into two or more enums or other types. For example, the
Reflection APIs could have been designed as follows:

```
[Flags]
public enum Visibilities {
    Public,
    NonPublic
}

[Flags]
public enum MemberScopes {
    Instance,
    Static
}

[Flags]
public enum MemberKinds {
    Constructor,
    Field,
    PropertyGetter,
    PropertySetter,
    Method,
}

public class Type {
    public MemberInfo[] GetMembers(MemberKinds members,
                                   Visibilities visibility,
                                   MemberScopes scope);

}
```

✗ **AVOID** using flag enum values of zero unless the value represents "all flags are cleared" and is named appropriately, as prescribed by the next guideline.

The following example shows a common implementation of a check that programmers use to determine if a flag is set (see the if-statement in the example). The check works as expected for all flag enum values except the value of zero, where the Boolean expression always evaluates to true.

```
[Flags]
public enum SomeFlag {
    ValueA = 0,  // this might be confusing to users
    ValueB = 1,
    ValueC = 2,
    ValueBAndC = ValueB | ValueC,
}

SomeFlag flags = GetValue();
if ((flags & SomeFlag.ValueA) == SomeFlag.ValueA) {
    ...
}
```

■ **ANDERS HEJLSBERG** Note that in C# the literal constant 0 implicitly converts to any enum type, so you could just write:

```
if (Foo.SomeFlag == 0)...
```

We support this special conversion in order to provide programmers with a consistent way of writing the default value of an enum type, which by CLR decree is "all bits zero" for any value type.

✓ **DO** name the zero value of flag enums None. For a flag enum, the value must always mean "all flags are cleared."

```
[Flags]
public enum BorderStyle {
    Fixed3D       = 0x1,
    FixedSingle   = 0x2,
    None          = 0x0
}
if (foo.BorderStyle == BorderStyle.None)....
```

> **■ VANCE MORRISON**   Note that the zero value is special in that it is the default value that will be assigned if no other assignment is made. Thus, it has the potential to be the most common value. Your design should accommodate this. In particular, the zero value should be either of the following:
>
> - A very good default value (when there is such a default)
> - An error value that is checked by your APIs (when there is no good default value and you want to ensure that users set something)

4.8.2 Adding Values to Enums

It is very common to discover that you need to add values to an enum after you have already shipped it. There is a potential application compatibility problem when the newly added value is returned from an existing API, because poorly written applications might not handle the new value correctly. Documentation, samples, and FxCop rules encourage application developers to write robust code that can help applications deal with unexpected values. Therefore, it is generally acceptable to add values to enums, but as with most guidelines there might be exceptions to the rule based on the specifics of the framework.

✓ **CONSIDER** adding values to enums, despite a small compatibility risk.

If you have real data about application incompatibilities caused by additions to an enum, consider adding a new API that returns the new and old values, and deprecate the old API, which should continue returning just the old values. This will ensure that your existing applications remain compatible.

> **■ CLEMENS SZYPERSKI**   Adding a value to an enum presents a very real possibility of breaking a client. Before the addition of the new enum value, a client that was throwing unconditionally in the default case presumably never actually threw the exception, and the corresponding catch path is likely untested. Now that the new enum value can pop up, the client will throw and likely fold.

The biggest concern with adding values to enums is that you don't know whether clients perform an exhaustive switch over an enum or a progressive case analysis across wider-spread code. Even with these FxCop rules in place and even when it is assumed that client apps pass FxCop without warnings, we still would not know about code that performs things like `if (myEnum == someValue) ...` in various places.

Clients might instead perform point-wise case analyses across their code, resulting in fragility under enum versioning. It is important to provide specific guidelines to developers of enum client code detailing what they need to do to survive the addition of new elements to enums they use. Developing with the suspected future versioning of an enum in mind is the required attitude.

■ **ANTHONY MOORE** Enum values that have a usage pattern of method or property return values should usually not be changed (even by addition) after being shipped because of usage in `switch` or `enum` statements. `DateTimeKind` is an example of this.

Enums that are primarily used as input arguments are generally safe to add members to, because code that has followed the argument validation guidelines will at worst throw an `ArgumentException` if it encounters the new value. `FileAccess` on `FileStream` is an example of this.

In general, it is safe to add members to flags enums. Compared to regular enums, it is much harder to write code against them that would be broken by the presence of new values.

4.9 Nested Types

A nested type is a type defined within the scope of another type, which is called the enclosing type. A nested type has access to all members of its enclosing type. For example, it has access to private fields defined in the enclosing type and to protected fields defined in all ascendants of the enclosing type.

```
// enclosing type
public class OuterType {
    private string name;
```

```
    // nested type
    public class InnerType {
        public InnerType(OuterType outer){
            // the name field is private, but it works just fine
            Console.WriteLine(outer.name);
        }
    }
}
```

In general, nested types should be used sparingly. There are several reasons for this. Some developers are not fully familiar with the concept. These developers might, for example, have problems with the syntax of declaring variables of nested types. Nested types are also very tightly coupled with their enclosing types, and as such are not suited to be general-purpose types.

Nested types are best suited for modeling implementation details of their enclosing types. The end user should rarely have to declare variables of a nested type and almost never should have to explicitly instantiate nested types. For example, the enumerator of a collection can be a nested type of that collection. Enumerators are usually instantiated by their enclosing type, and because many languages support the foreach statement, enumerator variables rarely have to be declared by the end user.

✓ **DO** use nested types when the relationship between the nested type and its outer type is such that member-accessibility semantics are desirable.

For example, the nested type needs to have access to private members of the outer type.

```
public OrderCollection : IEnumerable<Order> {
    Order[] data = ...;

    public IEnumerator<Order> GetEnumerator(){
        return new OrderEnumerator(this);
    }

    // This nested type will have access to the data array
    // of its outer type.
    class OrderEnumerator : IEnumerator<Order> {
    }
}
```

✗ **DO NOT** use public nested types as a logical grouping construct; use namespaces for this.

✗ **AVOID** publicly exposed nested types. The only exception to this is if variables of the nested type need to be declared only in rare scenarios such as subclassing or other advanced customization scenarios.

> ■ **KRZYSZTOF CWALINA** The main motivation for this guideline is that many less skilled developers don't understand why some type names have dots in them and some don't. As long as they don't have to type in the type name, they don't care. But the moment you ask them to declare a variable of a nested type, they get lost. Therefore, in general, we avoid nested types and use them only in places where developers almost never have to declare variables of that type (e.g., collection enumerators).

✗ **DO NOT** use nested types if the type is likely to be referenced outside of the containing type.

For example, an enum passed to a method defined on a class should not be defined as a nested type in the class.

✗ **DO NOT** use nested types if they need to be instantiated by client code. If a type has a public constructor, it should probably not be nested.

If a type can be instantiated, that seems to indicate the type has a place in the framework on its own (you can create it, work with it, and destroy it without ever using the outer type), and thus should not be nested. Inner types should not be widely reused outside of the outer type without any relationship whatsoever to the outer type.

✗ **DO NOT** define a nested type as a member of an interface. Many languages do not support such a construct.

In general, nested types should be used sparingly, and exposure as public types should be avoided.

4.10 **Types and Assembly Metadata**

Types reside in assemblies, which in most cases are packaged in the form of DLLs or executables (EXEs). There are several important attributes that should be applied to assemblies that contain public types. This section describes guidelines related to these attributes.

✔ **DO** apply the `CLSCompliant(true)` attribute to assemblies with public types.

```
[assembly:CLSCompliant(true)]
```

The attribute is a declaration that the types contained in the assembly are CLS[3] compliant and so can be used by all .NET languages.[4] Some languages, such as C#, verify compliance[5] with the standard if the attribute is applied.

For example, unsigned integers are not in the CLS subset. Therefore, if you add an API that uses UIn32 (for example), C# is going to generate a compilation warning. To comply with the CLS standard, the assembly must provide a compliant alternative and explicitly declare the non-compliant API as `CLSCompliant(false)`.

```
public static class Console {

    [CLSCompliant(false)]
    public void Write(uint value); // not CLS compliant

    public void Write(long value); // CLS compliant alternative
}
```

---

3. The CLS standard is an interoperability agreement between framework developers and language developers as to what subset of the CLR type system can be used in framework APIs so that these APIs can be used by all CLS-compliant languages.

4. All that support the CLS standard and almost all of the CLR languages do.

5. C# verifies compliance with most of the CLS rules. Some rules are not automatically verifiable. For example, the standard does not say that an assembly cannot have noncompliant APIs. It only says that noncompliant APIs must be marked with `CLSCompliant(false)` and that a compliant alternative must exist. But, of course, the existence of an alternative to a noncompliant API cannot be verified automatically.

✓ **DO** apply `AssemblyVersionAttribute` to assemblies with public types.

```
[assembly:AssemblyVersion(...)]
```

✓ **CONSIDER** using the format <V>.<S>.<B>.<R> for the assembly version, where V is the major version number, S is the servicing number, B is the build number, and R is the build revision number.

For example, this is how the version attribute is applied in System.Core. dll, which shipped as part of .NET Framework 3.5:

```
[assembly:AssemblyVersion("3.5.21022.8")]
```

✓ **DO** apply the following informational attributes to assemblies. These attributes are used by tools, such as Visual Studio, to inform the user of the assembly about its contents.

```
[assembly:AssemblyTitle("System.Core.dll")]
[assembly:AssemblyCompany("Microsoft Corporation")]
[assembly:AssemblyProduct("Microsoft .NET Framework")]
[assembly:AssemblyDescription(...)]
```

✓ **CONSIDER** applying `ComVisible(false)` to your assembly. COM-callable APIs need to be designed explicitly. As a rule of thumb, .NET assemblies should not be visible to COM. If you do design the APIs to be COM-callable, you can apply `ComVisible(true)` either to the individual APIs or to the whole assembly.

✓ **CONSIDER** applying `AssemblyFileVersionAttribute` and `Assembly-CopyrightAttribute` in order to provide additional information about the assembly.

SUMMARY

This chapter presented guidelines that describe when and how to design classes, structs, and interfaces.

The next chapter goes to the next level in type design—the design of members.

5

Member Design

METHODS, PROPERTIES, EVENTS, constructors, and fields are collectively referred to as members. Members are ultimately the means by which framework functionality is exposed to the end users of a framework.

Members can be virtual or nonvirtual, concrete or abstract, static or instance, and can have several different scopes of accessibility. All this variety provides incredible expressiveness but at the same time requires care on the part of the framework designer.

This chapter offers basic guidelines that should be followed when designing members of any type. Chapter 6 spells out additional guidelines related to members that need to support extensibility.

5.1 General Member Design Guidelines

Most member design guidelines are specific to the kind of member being designed and are described later in this chapter. There are, however, some broad design conventions applicable to different kinds of members. This section discusses such conventions.

5.1.1 Member Overloading

Member overloading means creating two or more members on the same type that differ only in the number or type of parameters but have the same name. For example, in the following, the `WriteLine` method is overloaded:

```
public static class Console {
    public void WriteLine();
    public void WriteLine(string value);
    public void WriteLine(bool value);
    ...
}
```

Because only methods, constructors, and indexed properties can have parameters, only those members can be overloaded.

▪▪ **BRENT RECTOR** Technically, the CLR allows additional overloading. For example, multiple fields in the same scope can have the same name as long as the fields have differing types, and multiple methods in the same scope can have the same name, number, and type of parameters as long as the methods have differing return types. However, few languages above IL support such distinctions. If you created an API using such distinctions, the API wouldn't be usable from most programming languages. Therefore, it's a useful fiction to restrict discussion of overloading to methods, constructors, and indexed properties.

Overloading is one of the most important techniques for improving usability, productivity, and readability of reusable libraries. Overloading on the number of parameters makes it possible to provide simpler versions of constructors and methods. Overloading on the parameter type makes it possible to use the same member name for members performing identical operations on a selected set of different types.

For example, `System.DateTime` has several constructor overloads. The most powerful but at the same time the most complex one takes eight parameters. Thanks to constructor overloading, the type also supports a shortened constructor that takes only three simple parameters: hours, minutes, and seconds.

```
public struct DateTime {
    public DateTime(int year, int month, int day,
                    int hour, int minute, int second,
                    int millisecond, Calendar calendar) { ... }

    public DateTime(int hour, int minute, int second) { ... }
}
```

■ **RICO MARIANI** This is one case where a simpler API for the programmer also results in better code—most calls to the library do not need the complicated arguments, so the bulk of the call sites are abbreviated. Even though there might be internal forwarding to the more complicated API, that forwarding code is shared, so overall there is significantly less code. Less code means more cache hits, which means faster programs.

This section does not talk about the similarly named but quite different construct called operator overloading. Operator overloading is described in section 5.7.

✓ **DO** try to use descriptive parameter names to indicate the default used by shorter overloads.

In a family of members overloaded on the number of parameters, the longer overload should use parameter names that indicate the default value used by the corresponding shorter member. This is mostly applicable to Boolean parameters. For example, in the following code, the first short overload does a case-sensitive look-up. The second longer overload adds a Boolean parameter that can be used to control whether the look-up is case sensitive or not. The parameter is named `ignoreCase` rather than `caseSensitive` to indicate that the longer overload should be used to ignore case and that the shorter overload probably defaults to the opposite, a case-sensitive look-up.

```
public class Type {
    public MethodInfo GetMethod(string name); //ignoreCase = false
    public MethodInfo GetMethod(string name, Boolean ignoreCase);
}
```

■ **BRAD ABRAMS** Notice that this API would be even better if it used an enum rather than the Boolean parameter. As you see in section 5.8.1, an enum argument would make it easier to understand code calling this API.

✗ **AVOID** arbitrarily varying parameter names in overloads. If a parameter in one overload represents the same input as a parameter in another overload, the parameters should have the same name.

```
public class String {
    // correct
    public int IndexOf (string value) { ... }
    public int IndexOf (string value, int startIndex) { ... }

    // incorrect
    public int IndexOf (string value) { ... }
    public int IndexOf (string str, int startIndex) { ... }
}
```

✗ **AVOID** being inconsistent in the ordering of parameters in overloaded members. Parameters with the same name should appear in the same position in all overloads.

```
public class EventLog {
    public EventLog();
    public EventLog(string logName);
    public EventLog(string logName, string machineName);
    public EventLog(string logName, string machineName, string source);
}
```

There are specific cases where this otherwise very strict guideline can be broken. For example, a params array parameter has to be the last parameter in a parameter list. If a params array parameter appears in an overloaded member, the API designer might need to make a trade-off and either settle for inconsistent parameter ordering or not use the params modifier. For more information on the params array parameters, see section 5.8.4.

Another case where the guideline might need to be violated is when the parameter list contains out parameters. These parameters should in general appear at the end of the parameter list, which again means that the API designer might need to settle for a slightly inconsistent order of parameters in overloads with out parameters. See section 5.8 for more information about out parameters.

✓ **DO** make only the longest overload virtual (if extensibility is required).

Shorter overloads should simply call through to a longer overload.

```
public class String {
    public int IndexOf (string s){
        return IndexOf (s, 0);
    }
    public int IndexOf (string s, int startIndex){
        return IndexOf (s, startIndex, s.Length);
    }
    public virtual int IndexOf (string s, int startIndex, int count){
        //do real work here
    }
}
```

For more information on the design of virtual members, see Chapter 6.

■ **BRIAN PEPIN** Remember that you can apply this pattern to abstract classes, too. In your abstract class, you can perform all necessary argument checking in nonabstract, nonvirtual methods and then provide a single abstract method for the developer to implement.

■ **CHRIS SELLS** I love this guideline, not only because it makes the library code easier to reason about, but because it makes it easier for me to write. If I have to implement each overload from scratch instead of making the less complicated ones call the more complicated ones, then I have to test and maintain all that copied code, too, which I'm far too lazy to do properly.

Further, if I've got more than two overloads, I always make the less complicated ones call the next more complicated one and not the most complicated one, like the three overloads of IndexOf shown previously for String. That way, I'm not hard-coding defaults in more than one place—if I had to do that, I'd probably get it wrong.

✗ DO NOT use ref or out modifiers to overload members.

For example, you should not do the following:

```
public class SomeType {
    public void SomeMethod(string name){ ... }
    public void SomeMethod(out string name){ ... }
}
```

Some languages cannot resolve calls to overloads like this. In addition, such overloads usually have completely different semantics and probably should not be overloads but two separate methods instead.

✗ **DO NOT** have overloads with parameters at the same position and similar types yet with different semantics.

The following example is a bit extreme, but it does illustrate the point:

```
public class SomeType {
    public void Print(long value, string terminator){
        Console.Write("{0}{1}",value,terminator);
    }
    public void Print(int repetitions, string str){
        for(int i=0; i< repetitions; i++){
            Console.Write(str);
        }
    }
}
```

The methods just presented should not be overloads. They should have two different names.

It's difficult in some languages (in particular, dynamically typed languages) to resolve calls to overloads like these. In most cases, if two overloads called with a number and a string would do exactly the same thing, it would not matter which overload is called. For example, the following is fine, because these methods are semantically equivalent:

```
public static class Console {
    public void WriteLine(long value){ ... }
    public void WriteLine(int value){ ... }
}
```

✓ **DO** allow null to be passed for optional arguments.

If a method takes optional arguments that are reference types, allow null to be passed to indicate that the default value should be used. This avoids the problem of having to check for null before calling an API, as shown here:

```
if (geometry==null) DrawGeometry(brush, pen);
else DrawGeometry(brush, pen, geometry);
```

> ■ **BRAD ABRAMS**   Notice that this guideline is not intended to encourage developers to use null as a magic constant but to help them avoid explicit checking, as previously described. In fact, whenever you have to use literal null when calling an API, it indicates an error in your code or in the framework not providing the appropriate overload.

✓ **DO** use member overloading rather than defining members with default arguments.

Default arguments are not CLS compliant.

```vb
' Bad Design
Class Point
    Sub Move(x As Integer, Optional y As Integer = 0)
        Me.x = Me.x + x
        Me.y = Me.y + y
    End Sub
End Class

' Good Design
Class Point
    Sub Move(x As Integer)
        Move(x,0)
    End Sub
    Sub Move(x As Integer, y As Integer)
        Me.x = Me.x + x
        Me.y = Me.y + y
    End Sub
End Class
```

> ■ **RICO MARIANI**   Languages tend to implement default arguments by implementing only the full function and then padding out the provided arguments at each call site to the necessary full list using the defaults. This isn't necessarily the best thing to do at all, because now each call site has the code for the full argument list. It might be better if languages instead used default argument notation as "syntactic sugar" for creating the two overloads in the "good design." It looks like more code has to run, but the accrued benefits of code sharing can easily offset that extra cost and give you the net best performance with the good pattern. In addition, that pattern is CLS-compliant. Bottom line: The good pattern is likely to win on a performance basis as well as on a compliance basis.

> **JEFFREY RICHTER**   In addition to this not being CLS-compliant, there is also a versioning issue here, and the version issue is why C# and other languages don't even offer this feature. Imagine version 1 of a method that sets an optional parameter to 123. When compiling code that calls this method without specifying the optional parameter, the compiler will embed the default value (123) into the code at the call site. Now, if version 2 of the method changes the optional parameter to 863, then, if the calling code is not recompiled, it will call version 2 of the method passing in 123 (version 1's default, not version 2's default).

5.1.2 Implementing Interface Members Explicitly

Explicit interface member implementation allows an interface member to be implemented so that it is only callable when the instance is cast to the interface type. For example, consider the following definition:

```
public struct Int32 : IConvertible {
    int IConvertible.ToInt32 () {..}
    ...
}

// calling ToInt32 defined on Int32
int i = 0;
i.ToInt32(); // does not compile
((IConvertible)i).ToInt32(); // works just fine
```

In general, implementing interface members explicitly is straightforward and follows the same general guidelines as those for methods, properties, or events. However, there are some specific guidelines concerning implementing interface members explicitly and these are described next.

> **ANDERS HEJLSBERG**   Programmers working in other environments consistently complain about the need for internal methods to be public just so a class can implement some worker interface. Explicit member implementations are the correct solution to that problem. Yes, it is true that C# doesn't give you syntax to call the base implementation of such members, but I have seen very few actual requests for that feature.

✗ AVOID implementing interface members explicitly without having a strong reason to do so.

Explicitly implemented members can be confusing to developers because such members don't appear in the list of public members and can also cause unnecessary boxing of value types.

> ■ **KRZYSZTOF CWALINA**   You need to be especially careful when considering explicitly implementing members on value types. Casting a value type to an interface, which is the only way to call explicitly implemented members, causes boxing.

> ■ **RICO MARIANI**   Value types are often very simple types with very simple operations on them. You must be especially careful about incurring extra dispatching costs on any of these operations. If the main work at hand is something as simple as comparing one value to another or reinterpreting an integer in another format, then just the cost of the function calls might be more than the actual work you have to do. Keep this in mind or you might find that you have created a value type that is fundamentally unusable for its primary (cheap) purpose.

> ■ **JEFFREY RICHTER**   In general, the reason to explicitly implement an interface method is if your type also has another method with the same name and parameters but with a different return type, for example:
>
> ```
> class Collection : IEnumerable {
>   IEnumerator IEnumerable.GetEnumerator() { ... }
>   public MyEnumerator GetEnumerator() { ... }
> }
> ```
>
> The Collection class can't have two methods called GetEnumerator that differ only in return value unless the version that returns an IEnumerator is an explicitly implemented interface method (as shown earlier). Now, if someone calls GetEnumerator, they are calling the strongly typed version of the method that returns MyEnumerator. Aside from this example, there are few other reasons to implement an interface method explicitly.

> ▪▪ **STEVEN CLARKE**   One common observation we have made in the API usability studies is that many developers assume that the reason members have been implemented explicitly is that they are not supposed to be used in common scenarios. Thus, they sometimes have a tendency to avoid using these members and spend time looking for some other way to accomplish their task.

✓ **CONSIDER** implementing interface members explicitly if the members are intended to be called only through the interface.

This includes mainly members supporting framework infrastructure, such as data binding or serialization. For example, `ICollection<T>`. `IsReadOnly` is intended to be accessed mainly by the data-binding infrastructure through the `ICollection<T>` interface. It is almost never accessed directly when using types implementing the interface. Therefore, `List<T>` implements the member explicitly.

✓ **CONSIDER** implementing interface members explicitly to simulate variance (change parameters or return type in "overridden" members).

For example, `IList` implementations often change the type of the parameters and returned values to create strongly typed collections by explicitly implementing (hiding) the loosely typed member and adding the publicly implemented strongly typed member.

```
public class StringCollection : IList {
    public string this[int index]{ ... }
    object IList.this[int index] { ... }
    ...
}
```

✓ **CONSIDER** implementing interface members explicitly to hide a member and add an equivalent member with a better name.

You can say that this amounts to renaming a member. For example, `System.IO.FileStream` implements `IDisposable.Dispose` explicitly and renames it to `FileStream.Close`.

```
// this is not exactly how FileStream does it but this simplification
// best illustrates the concept
public class FileStream : IDisposable {
   void IDisposable.Dispose() { Close(); }
   public void Close() { ... }
}
```

Such member renaming should be done extremely sparingly. In most cases, the added confusion is a bigger problem than the suboptimal name of the interface member.

> ■ **RICO MARIANI**   Even this example is plagued with problems. Should `Close()` be calling `IDisposable.Dispose()` or should it call some shared helper function (that's `Dispose(true)` in this example)? And how does a client of your API know that it's really the same thing? Do they `Close()` and `Dispose()`? In what order? All of these questions will plague your clients, so the advice to do this extremely sparingly is well taken. I sometimes wish we had syntax to say `Close` = `Dispose` so that the equivalence of these methods would be discoverable by inspecting, and could even be enforced.

✘ **DO NOT** use explicit members as a security boundary.

Such members can be called by any code by simply casting an instance to the interface.

> ■ **RICO MARIANI**   Generally, objects that have security issues should expose the fewest possible interfaces and inherit as little as possible. Get your code reuse by encapsulation rather than inheritance and seal as much as you can. My biggest dissent with the guidelines is that they do not recommend sealing as often as I believe they should. Where there are security issues, be more careful and consider sealing more aggressively, inheriting less aggressively, and using explicit (sealed) implementations of those interfaces you need to offer.

✔ **DO** provide a protected virtual member that offers the same functionality as the explicitly implemented member if the functionality is meant to be specialized by derived classes.

Explicitly implemented members cannot be overridden. They can be redefined, but then it is impossible for subtypes to call the base method's implementation. It is recommended that you name the protected member by either using the same name or affixing `Core` to the interface member name.

```
[Serializable]
public class List<T> : ISerializable {
  ...
  void ISerializable.GetObjectData(
     SerializationInfo info, StreamingContext context) {
     GetObjectData(info,context);
  }

  protected virtual void GetObjectData(
     SerializationInfo info, StreamingContext context) {
     ...
  }
}
```

> ■ **RICO MARIANI**   Classes designed to be subclassed in normal use need extra care. The times when the `Core` functions are called is part of the contract, so document it well and try not to change it. Access to protected members might allow partially trusted code to do bad things to the internal state. You must code with the expectation that the subclass will be hostile.

5.1.3 Choosing Between Properties and Methods

When designing members of a type, one of the most common decisions a library designer must make is to choose whether a member should be a property or a method.

On a high level, there are two general styles of API design in terms of usage of properties and methods. In method-heavy APIs, methods have a large number of parameters, and the types have fewer properties.

```
public class PersonFinder {
  public string FindPersonsName (
     int height,
     int weight,
     string hairColor,
```

```
        string eyeColor,
        int shoeSize,
        Connection database
    );
}
```

In property-heavy APIs, methods have a small number of parameters and more properties to control the semantics of the methods.

```
public class PersonFinder {
    public int Height { get; set; }
    public int Weight { get; set; }
    public string HairColor { get;set; }
    public string EyeColor { get; set; }
    public int ShoeSize { get; set; }

    public string FindPersonsName (Connection database);
}
```

> **RICO MARIANI** Note the huge difference in semantics. With properties, you must (or can, if you see that as a benefit) set each field independently, and the `PersonFinder` can only be used for one call at one time because it captures the result of the find as well as the input. With the functional contract, multiple threads can use the very same finder and there is only one function call. This is not a small decision we are making here.

> **CHRIS ANDERSON** I have to firmly agree with the guideline encouraging the use of properties. Generally, methods with lots of arguments lend themselves to lots of overloads—you have 15 overloads of a method so you can get every combination of options. This produces APIs that are super hard to understand, and inconsistent. Look at `DrawRectangle` on `System.Drawing.Graphics` as a great example. There are a lot of overloads, and there is always one missing. When you add a new feature to the API, you have to add more overloads, making it less and less understandable over time. Properties provide a natural self-documentation aspect to the API, easy statement completion, progressive understanding, and simple versioning. You always have to balance performance, but in general properties really do add a huge amount of value.

All else being equal, the property-heavy design is generally preferable because methods with many parameters are less approachable to inexperienced developers. This is described in detail in Chapter 2.

Another reason to use properties when they are appropriate is that property values show up automatically in the debugger, and inspecting a value of a method is much more cumbersome.

> ■■ **CHRIS SELLS** I have yet to find any developer who prefers things to be harder than they need to be. If you make something more approachable for the "inexperienced developer," then it's more approachable for everyone.

However, it is worth noting that the method-heavy design has the advantage in terms of performance, and might result in better APIs for advanced users.

A rule of thumb is that methods should represent actions and properties should represent data. Properties are preferred over methods if everything else is equal.

> ■■ **RICO MARIANI** Properties probably result in more performance crimes than any other language feature. You must remember that the property looks like a simple field access to your customers and comes with an expectation that it is no more costly than a field access. You can expect your callers will write straightforward-looking code to access the properties, and they will be astonished if this is expensive. Similarly, they will be astonished if the behavior changes over time so that it becomes costly, or if it is costly with some subtypes and not with others.

> ■■ **JOE DUFFY** Properties should contain a tiny amount of code. If you avoid if-statements, try/catch blocks, calls to other methods, etc., and strive to make them nothing more than a simple field access, it is highly likely the CLR's JIT compiler will inline all accesses to them. Doing this helps to avoid the performance crimes that Rico mentions in his comment.

✓ **CONSIDER** using a property if the member represents a logical attribute of the type.

For example, Button.Color is a property because color is an attribute of a button.

> ■ **BRAD ABRAMS** Early in the implementation of the .NET Framework 1.0, when we first added a first-class construct of properties to the system, we went in and blanket-changed all the Get<Name> methods to <Name> properties. For example, Type.GetName() became Type.Name. This worked out well in many places, but not in the Guid class where we had a method called Guid.GetNext() that generated the next Guid in a sequence. When we changed it to a Guid.Next property, it became quite confusing because GUIDs do not naturally have a next-value attribute. Luckily, we fixed this back to a GetNext() method before we shipped.

✓ **DO** use a property, rather than a method, if the value of the property is stored in the process memory and the property would just provide access to the value.

For example, a member that retrieves the name of a Customer from a field stored in the object should be a property.

```
public Customer {
    public Customer(string name){
        this.name = name;
    }
    public string Name {
        get { return this.name; }
    }
    private string name;
}
```

✓ **DO** use a method, rather than a property, in the following situations:

- The operation is orders of magnitude slower than a field access would be. If you are even considering providing an asynchronous version of an operation to avoid blocking the thread, it is very likely that the operation is too expensive to be a property. In particular, operations that access the network or the file system (other than once for initialization) should likely be methods, not properties.

> **JEFFREY RICHTER**   If you follow the performance guideline to its logical extreme, types that are ultimately derived from `MarshalByRefObject` should never have any properties because the object could be on a remote machine somewhere and there is no telling how long accessing the property will take.

- The operation is a conversion, such as `Object.ToString` method.
- The operation returns a different result each time it is called, even if the parameters don't change. For example, the `Guid.NewGuid` method returns a different value each time it is called.

> **JEFFREY RICHTER**   The `DateTime.Now` property is an example of a place in the Framework where this property should have been a method because the operation returns a different result each time.

- The operation has a significant and observable side effect. Notice that populating an internal cache is not generally considered an observable side effect.

> **BRIAN PEPIN**   The `Handle` property on a Windows Forms control is an example of where too many side effects might occur. If the control has not had its handle created yet, accessing the `Handle` property will create it. I can't tell you how many times I've completely changed the result of a debugging session by setting up a watch on the `Handle` property. The debugger's watch will actually create the control's handle, often hiding your bug.

- The operation returns a copy of an internal state (this does not include copies of value type objects returned on the stack).
- The operation returns an array.

Properties that return arrays can be very misleading. Usually it is necessary to return a copy of an internal array so that the user cannot change the internal state. This could lead to inefficient code.

In the following example, the Employees property is accessed twice in every iteration of the loop. That would be 2n + 1 copies for the following short code sample:

```
Company microsoft = GetCompanyData("MSFT");
for (int i = 0; i < microsoft.Employees.Length; i++) {
    if (microsoft.Employees[i].Alias == "kcwalina"){
        ...
    }
}
```

This problem can be addressed in one of two ways:

- Change the property to a method, which communicates to callers that they are not just accessing an internal field and probably are creating an array every time they call the method. Given that, users are more likely to call the method once, cache the result, and work with the cached array.

```
Company microsoft = GetCompanyData("MSFT");
Employees[] employees = microsoft.GetEmployees();
for (int i = 0; i < employees.Length; i++) {
    if (employees[i].Alias == "kcwalina"){
        ...
    }
}
```

- Change the property to return a collection instead of an array. You can use ReadOnlyCollection<T> to provide public read-only access to a private array. Alternatively, you can use a subclass of Collection<T> to provide controlled read-write access, where you can be notified when the collection is modified by the user code. See section 8.3 for more details on using ReadOnlyCollection<T> and Collection<T>.

```
public ReadOnlyCollection<Employee> Employees {
    get { return roEmployees; }
}
private Employee[] employees;
private ReadOnlyCollection<Employee> roEmployees;
```

> ■ **BRAD ABRAMS**   Some of the guidelines in this book were debated and agreed on in the abstract; others were learned in the school of hard knocks. The guideline on properties that return arrays is in the school of hard knocks camp. When we were investigating some performance issues in version 1.0 of the .NET Framework, we noticed that thousands of arrays were being created and quickly trashed. It turns out that many places in the Framework itself ran into this pattern. Needless to say, we fixed those instances and the guidelines.

> ■ **RICO MARIANI**   I hope you've read this far—you really must understand that the preceding guideline is designed to avoid some pretty big problems. I'd encourage you to remember this shorthand: Use properties for simple access to simple data with a simple computation. Don't stray from that pattern.

5.2 Property Design

Although properties are technically very similar to methods, they are quite different in terms of their usage scenarios. They should be seen as smart fields. They have the calling syntax of fields, and the flexibility of methods.

✓ **DO** create get-only properties if the caller should not be able to change the value of the property.

Keep in mind that if the type of the property is a mutable reference type, the property value can be changed even if the property is get-only.

✗ **DO NOT** provide set-only properties or properties with the setter having broader accessibility than the getter.

For example, do not use properties with a public setter and a protected getter.

If the property getter cannot be provided, implement the functionality as a method instead. Consider starting the method name with `Set` and follow with what you would have named the property. For example, `AppDomain` has a method called `SetCachePath` instead of having a set-only property called `CachePath`.

✓ **DO** provide sensible default values for all properties, ensuring that the defaults do not result in a security hole or terribly inefficient code.

✓ **DO** allow properties to be set in any order even if this results in a temporary invalid state of the object.

It is common for two or more properties to be interrelated to a point where some values of one property might be invalid given the values of other properties on the same object. In such cases, exceptions resulting from the invalid state should be postponed until the interrelated properties are actually used together by the object.

■ **RICO MARIANI** This happens a lot in business objects used in a three-tier system. You cannot do much more than basic validation of the properties when they are set. You have to provide an explicit "commit" method of some kind so that you know the caller is completely done with the update. Avoid validation that you cannot do with local knowledge (i.e., don't go to the database, etc.). Remember that there is a strong expectation that setting a property is not much more expensive than setting a field.

■ **BRIAN PEPIN** While working on the code generator for the Windows Forms designer, I had a lot of people ask me for a way to tell the code generator how to order properties. I stubbornly refused every time, because it adds a huge amount of complexity for developers. It's easy to dictate an order for your properties, but how does your property ordering mix in with classes that derive from you? Also, if it is complicated to describe to a code generator how things need to be ordered, imagine how complicated it will be to explain this to developers.

✓ **DO** preserve the previous value if a property setter throws an exception.

✗ **AVOID** throwing exceptions from property getters.

Property getters should be simple operations and should not have any preconditions. If a getter can throw an exception, it should probably be redesigned to be a method. Notice that this rule does not apply to indexers, where we do expect exceptions as a result of validating the arguments.

PATRICK DUSSUD   Notice that this guideline only applies to property getters. It is OK to throw an exception in a property setter. It is very much like setting an array element, which can throw as well (and not just when checking the index bound but the possibility of type mismatch between the value and the array element type).

JASON CLARK   Patrick's guidance speaks to one of the key reasons that exceptions and object-oriented programming environments go hand in hand. Object-oriented environments impose many circumstances whereby the developer of a method has limited or no control of the methods signature. Properties, events, constructors, virtual overrides, and operator overloads are examples of this. What exceptions do is take the error response of a method call out of band of the signature or return type. This introduces the necessary flexibility to both reflect and react to failure in any method regardless of the syntax sugar that restricts signature decisions.

JOE DUFFY   Another pattern to avoid is blocking the thread inside of a property, because of either I/O or some synchronization operation. This is the extreme example of "doing too much work" inside of a property. In the worst case (deadlock), the property may never actually return to the caller. If the property accesses shared state, it may be necessary to acquire a lock in order to access it safely, but anything more complicated (like waiting on a `WaitHandle`) is an indication that a method is a better design choice.

5.2.1 Indexed Property Design

An indexed property is a special property that can have parameters and can be called with special syntax similar to array indexing.

```
public class String {
   public char this[int index] {
      get { ... }
   }
}
...

string city = "Seattle";
Console.WriteLine(city[0]); // this will print 'S'
```

Indexed properties are commonly referred to as indexers. Indexers should be used only in APIs that provide access to items in a logical collection. For example, a string is a collection of characters, and the indexer on System.String was added to access its characters.

RICO MARIANI Be extra careful with these—you can expect them to be called in a loop! Keep them very simple.

✓ **CONSIDER** using indexers to provide access to data stored in an internal array.

✓ **CONSIDER** providing indexers on types representing collections of items.

✗ **AVOID** using indexed properties with more than one parameter.

If the design requires multiple parameters, reconsider whether the property really represents an accessor to a logical collection. If it does not, use methods instead. Consider starting the method name with Get or Set.

✗ **AVOID** indexers with parameter types other than System.Int32, System.Int64, System.String, System.Object, or an enum.

If the design requires other types of parameters, strongly reevaluate whether the API really represents an accessor to a logical collection. If it does not, use a method. Consider starting the method name with Get or Set.

✓ **DO** use the name Item for indexed properties unless there is an obviously better name (e.g., see the Chars property on System.String).

In C#, indexers are by default named Item. The IndexerNameAttribute can be used to customize this name.

```
public sealed class String {
    [System.Runtime.CompilerServices.IndexerNameAttribute("Chars")]
    public char this[int index] {
        get { ... }
    }
    ...
}
```

✗ **DO NOT** provide both an indexer and methods that are semantically equivalent.

In the following example, the indexer should be changed to a method.

```
// Bad design
public class Type {
    [System.Runtime.CompilerServices.IndexerNameAttribute("Members")]
    public MemberInfo this[string memberName]{ ... }
    public MemberInfo GetMember(string memberName, Boolean ignoreCase){ ... }
}
```

✗ **DO NOT** provide more than one family of overloaded indexers in one type.

This is enforced by the C# compiler.

✗ **DO NOT** use nondefault indexed properties.

This is enforced by the C# compiler.

5.2.2 Property Change Notification Events

Sometimes it is useful to provide an event notifying the user of changes in a property value. For example, System.Windows.Forms.Control raises a TextChanged event after the value of its Text property has changed.

```
public class Control : Component{
    string text = String.Empty;

    public event EventHandler<EventArgs> TextChanged;

    public string Text{
        get{ return text; }
```

```
        set{
            if (text!=value) {
                text = value;
                OnTextChanged();
            }
        }
    }

    protected virtual void OnTextChanged(){
        EventHandler<EventArgs> handler = TextChanged;
        if(handler!=null){
            handler(this,EventArgs.Empty);
        }
    }
}
```

The guidelines that follow describe when property change events are appropriate and their recommended design for these APIs.

> ■ **RICO MARIANI** Recall some of the previous rules about properties: They should look and act like fields as much as possible, because library users will think of them and use them as though they were fields. Here we're practically guaranteeing that the property setter will have a side effect because we're allowing arbitrary user code to run. We're also causing multiple function calls to be made for each set. All of that cross-wiring of objects and handlers often causes "object spaghetti." If the notifications are not at a high enough level, they will be much too frequent and the connections too complex, rendering the system both unusable and indescribable.

> ■ **CHRIS SELLS** For data binding to work properly in WPF or Windows Forms, objects with properties must raise property change events, preferably via `INotifyPropertyChanged`.

✓ **CONSIDER** raising change notification events when property values in high-level APIs (usually designer components) are modified.

If there is a good scenario for a user to know when a property of an object is changing, the object should raise a change notification event for the property.

However, it is unlikely to be worth the overhead to raise such events for low-level APIs such as base types or collections. For example, List<T> would not raise such events when a new item is added to the list and the Count property changes.

■■ **CHRIS SELLS** Because List<T> doesn't implement any of the notification APIs for data binding, and because I like data binding, I find myself using ObservableCollection<T> instead, which implements INotify-CollectionChanged.

✓ **CONSIDER** raising change notification events when the value of a property changes via external forces.

If a property value changes via some external force (in a way other than by calling methods on the object), raise events indicate to the developer that the value is changing and has changed. A good example is the Text property of a text box control. When the user types text in a TextBox, the property value automatically changes.

The next section provides guidelines for constructor design.

5.3 Constructor Design

There are two kinds of constructors: type constructors and instance constructors.

```
public class Customer {
    public Customer() { ... } // instance constructor
    static Customer() { ... } // type constructor
}
```

Type constructors are static and are run by the CLR before the type is used. Instance constructors run when an instance of a type is created.

Type constructors cannot take any parameters. Instance constructors can. Instance constructors that don't take any parameters are often called default constructors.

Constructors are the most natural way to create instances of a type. Most developers will search and try to use a constructor before they consider alternative ways of creating instances (such as factory methods).

✓ **CONSIDER** providing simple, ideally default, constructors.

A simple constructor has a very small number of parameters, and all parameters are primitives or enums. Such simple constructors increase usability of the framework.

■ **PHIL HAACK**   If you have a type that has a required dependency on another type, that is, an instance of your type won't work if it doesn't have a proper instance of this type, then you should allow passing that type in via a constructor parameter.

I see the constructor parameter list as defining the set of required dependencies for your type. Following this approach makes your type more amenable to dependency injection.

At the same time, I think it's a good practice to have default constructors that provide reasonable defaults for these required dependencies.

✓ **CONSIDER** using a static factory method instead of a constructor if the semantics of the desired operation do not map directly to the construction of a new instance, or if following the constructor design guidelines feels unnatural.

See section 9.5 for more details on factory method design.

✓ **DO** use constructor parameters as shortcuts for setting main properties.

There should be no difference in semantics between using the empty constructor followed by some property sets and using a constructor with multiple arguments. The following three code examples are equivalent:

```
//1
var applicationLog = new EventLog();
applicationLog.MachineName = "BillingServer";
applicationLog.Log = "Application";
```

```
//2
var applicationLog = new EventLog("Application");
applicationLog.MachineName = "BillingServer";

//3
var applicationLog = new EventLog("Application", "BillingServer");
```

✓ **DO** use the same name for constructor parameters and a property if the constructor parameters are used to simply set the property.

The only difference between such parameters and the properties should be casing.

```
public class EventLog {
    public EventLog(string logName){
        this.LogName = logName;
    }
    public string LogName {
        get { ... }
        set { ... }
    }
}
```

✓ **DO** minimal work in the constructor.

Constructors should not do much work other than capture the constructor parameters. The cost of any other processing should be delayed until required.

✓ **DO** throw exceptions from instance constructors, if appropriate.

> ■ **CHRISTOPHER BRUMME**   When an exception propagates out of a constructor, the object is already created despite the fact that the new operator does not return the object reference. If the type defines a `Finalize` method, the method will run when the object becomes eligible for garbage collection. This means that you should make sure the `Finalize` method can run on partially constructed objects.

■ JEFFREY RICHTER Alternatively, you could call GC.Suppress-Finalize from within the constructor itself to avoid having the Finalize method called and to improve performance.

```
// finalizable type constructor that can throw
public FinalizableType(){
    try{
        SomeOperationThatCanThrow();
        handle = ... // allocate resource that needs to be finalized
    }
    catch(Exception){
        GC.SuppressFinalize(this);
        throw;
    }
}
```

■ BRIAN GRUNKEMEYER Note that if your constructor throws an exception, the finalizer for your type will still run! So the finalizer and the Dispose(false) code path in your type must be prepared to handle an uninitialized state. Worse yet, if your app must deal with asynchronous exceptions such as ThreadAbortException or OutOfMemoryException, your finalizer may have to deal with partially initialized state if your constructor threw an exception halfway through! This surprising fact is usually pretty easy to deal with, but it may take you several years to realize it.

■ JOE DUFFY A related constructor anti-pattern can lead to the same problem that Chris describes. If a constructor prematurely shares the *this* reference, the object may be accessible even if it has thrown an exception before it was fully constructed. This could happen by setting a field on an object passed in as an argument, or via a static variable, for example. Avoid doing this at all costs.

✓ **DO** explicitly declare the public default constructor in classes, if such a constructor is required.

If you don't explicitly declare any constructors on a type, many languages (such as C#) will automatically add a public default constructor.

(Abstract classes get a protected constructor.) For example, the following two declarations are equivalent in C#:

```
public class Customer {
}

public class Customer {
    public Customer(){}
}
```

Adding a parameterized constructor to a class prevents the compiler from adding the default constructor. This often causes accidental breaking changes. Consider a class defined as shown in the following example:

```
public class Customer {
}
```

Users of the class can call the default constructor, which the compiler automatically added in this case, to create an instance of the class.

```
var customer = new Customer();
```

It is quite common to add a parameterized constructor to an existing type with a default constructor. If the addition is not done carefully, the default constructor might not be emitted anymore. For example, the following addition to the type just declared will "remove" the default constructor:

```
public class Customer {
    public Customer(string name) { ... }
}
```

This will break code relying on the default constructor and is unlikely to be caught in a code review. Therefore, the best practice is to always specify the public default constructor explicitly.

Note that this does not apply to structs. Structs implicitly get default constructors even if they have a parameterized constructor defined.

✗ **AVOID** explicitly defining default constructors on structs.

This makes array creation faster, because if the default constructor is not defined, it does not have to be run on every slot in the array.[1] Note that many compilers, including C#, don't allow structs to have parameterless constructors for this reason.

Consider List<T>, which has a private array field. It would be very unfortunate if constructors would have to run on every slot when the array is created, because the collection items are added to the array after its creation.

Even if a struct does not have a default constructor, instances of the struct can be created using the default constructor syntax.

```
public struct Token {
    public Token(Guid id) { this.id = id; }
    internal Guid id;
}
...
var token = new Token(); // this compiles and executes just fine.
```

The runtime will initialize all of the fields of the struct to their default values (0/null).

✗ **AVOID** calling virtual members on an object inside its constructor.

Calling a virtual member will cause the most derived override to be called, even if the constructor of the most derived type has not been fully run yet.

Consider the following example, which prints out "What is wrong?" when a new instance of Derived is created. The implementer of the derived class assumes that the value will be set before anyone can call the Method. However, that is not true, because the Base constructor is called before the Derived constructor finishes, so any calls it makes to Method might operate on data that is not yet initialized.

---

1. A struct without an explicitly defined constructor still gets one that is provided by the CLR implicitly, but because the implicit constructor is empty (does not do anything), the runtime does not have to run it on value types in a newly created array.

```
public abstract class Base {
   public Base() {
      Method();
   }
   public abstract void Method();
}

public class Derived: Base {
   private int value;
   public Derived() {
      value = 1;
   }

   public override void Method() {
      if (value == 1){
         Console.WriteLine("All is good");
      }
      else {
         Console.WriteLine("What is wrong?");
      }
   }
}
```

Occasionally, the benefits associated with calling virtual members from a constructor might outweigh the risks. An example of this case is a helper constructor that initializes virtual properties using parameters passed to the constructor. It's acceptable to call virtual members from constructors, given that all the risks are carefully analyzed and you document the virtual members that you call for the users overriding the virtual members.

■ CHRISTOPHER BRUMME In unmanaged C++, the vtable is updated during the construction so that a call to a virtual function during construction only calls to the level of the object hierarchy that has been constructed.

It's been my experience that many programmers are as confused by the C++ behavior as they are about the managed behavior. The fact is that most programmers don't think about the semantics of virtual calls during construction and destruction until they have just finished debugging a failure related to this.

Either behavior is appropriate for some programs and inappropriate for others. Both behaviors can be logically defended. For the CLR, the decision is ultimately based on our desire to support extremely fast object creation.

5.3.1 **Type Constructor Guidelines**

A type constructor, also called a static constructor, is used to initialize a type. The runtime calls the static constructor before the first instance of the type is created or any static members of the type are accessed.

✓ **DO** make static constructors private.

A static constructor, also called a class constructor, is used to initialize a type. The CLR calls the static constructor before the first instance of the type is created or any static members on that type are called. The user has no control over when the static constructor is called. If a static constructor is not private, it can be called by code other than the CLR. Depending on the operations performed in the constructor, this can cause unexpected behavior. The C# compiler forces static constructors to be private.

✗ **DO NOT** throw exceptions from static constructors.

If an exception is thrown from a type constructor, the type is not usable in the current application domain.

CHRISTOPHER BRUMME The only time it's OK to throw from a static constructor is if the type must never again be used in this application domain. You are basically making the type off-limits in the application domain where you throw, so you'd better have a good reason, such as if some important invariant is broken and you would not be secure if usage were to be permitted.

VANCE MORRISON To be clear on this rule, it does not apply to just explicitly throwing, but any exception, which implies that if the body of the class constructor has the potential to make method calls (and this is very likely the case) you need a "try-catch" around the body of your class constructor.

✓ **CONSIDER** initializing static fields inline rather than explicitly using static constructors, because the runtime is able to optimize the performance of types that don't have an explicitly defined static constructor.

```
// unoptimized code
public class Foo {
    public static readonly int Value;
    static Foo() {
        Value = 63;
    }
    public static void PrintValue() {
        Console.WriteLine(Value);
    }
}

// optimized code
public class Foo {
    public static readonly int Value = 63;
    public static void PrintValue() {
        Console.WriteLine(Value);
    }
}
```

■ **CHRISTOPHER BRUMME**   Be aware that initializing static fields inline has very loose guarantees about when the fields will be initialized. The guarantee is that the fields will be initialized before the first time they are accessed, but it could potentially be much earlier. The CLR reserves the right to do the initialization before the program even starts running (e.g., using NGEN techniques). Explicit static constructors make a very precise guarantee. They are run before the first static member (code or data) is accessed, but no earlier.

■ **VANCE MORRISON**   Generally, doing nontrivial work in a class constructor is bad because if it fails, you make the class unavailable, and you have made some nontrivial semantic effect happen at a potentially surprising time (do all your users know the rules for precise class construction?). Thus you should seriously reconsider any design that does nontrivial work in class constructors. Initializing statics is really the reason class constructors exist, and for that you *don't* need the static class {} syntax (use static initialization functions instead). It has less guarantees, but you should not need stronger guarantees, and the flexibility you give the runtime allows class construction to be more efficient.

5.4 Event Design

Events are the most commonly used form of callbacks (constructs that allow the framework to call into user code). Other callback mechanisms include members taking delegates, virtual members, and interface-based plug-ins. Data from usability studies indicate that the majority of developers are more comfortable using events than they are using the other callback mechanisms. Events are nicely integrated with Visual Studio and many languages.

Under the covers, events are not much more than fields that have a type that is a delegate, plus two methods to manipulate the field. Delegates used by events have special signatures (by convention) and are referred to as event handlers.

When users subscribe to an event, they provide an instance of the event handler bound to a method that will be called when the event is raised. The method provided by the user is referred to as an event handling method.

The event handler determines the event handling method's signature. By convention, the return type of the method is void and takes two parameters. The first parameter represents the object that raised the event. The second parameter represents event-related data that the object raising the event wants to pass to the event handling method. The data are often referred to as event arguments.

```
var timer = new Timer(1000);
timer.Elapsed += new ElapsedEventHandler(TimerElapsedHandlingMethod);
...

// event handling method for Timer.Elapsed
void TimerElapsedHandlingMethod(object sender, ElapsedEventArgs e){
    ...
}
```

It is important to note that there are two groups of events: events raised before a state of the system changes, called pre-events, and events raised after a state changes, called post-events. An example of a pre-event would be Form.Closing, which is raised before a form is closed. An example of a post-event would be Form.Closed, which is raised after a form is closed.

The following sample shows an `AlarmClock` class defining an `AlarmRaised` post-event.

```
public class AlarmClock {
    public AlarmClock() {
        timer.Elapsed += new ElapsedEventHandler(TimerElapsed);
    }

    public event EventHandler<AlarmRaisedEventArgs> AlarmRaised;

    public DateTimeOffset AlarmTime {
        get { return alarmTime; }
        set {
            if (alarmTime != value) {
                timer.Enabled = false;
                alarmTime = value;
                TimeSpan delay = alarmTime - DateTimeOffset.Now;
                timer.Interval = delay.TotalMilliseconds;
                timer.Enabled = true;
            }
        }
    }

    protected virtual void OnAlarmRaised(AlarmRaisedEventArgs e){
        EventHandler<AlarmRaisedEventArgs> handler = AlarmRaised;
        if (handler != null) {
            handler(this, e);
        }
    }

    private void TimerElapsed(object sender, ElapsedEventArgs e){
        OnAlarmRaised(AlarmRaisedEventArgs.Empty);
    }
    private Timer timer = new Timer();
    private DateTimeOffset alarmTime;
}
public class AlarmRaisedEventArgs : EventArgs {
    new internal static readonly
        AlarmRaisedEventArgs Empty = new AlarmRaisedEventArgs();
}
```

✓ **DO** use the term "raise" for events rather than "fire" or "trigger."

When referring to events in documentation, use the phrase "an event was raised" instead of "an event was fired" or "an event was triggered."

> **BRAD ABRAMS** Why did we decide to use "raised" rather than "fired?" Well, we certainly have some prior art on our side on this one, but we also felt like fire was too negative a term. After all, you fire a gun or you fire an employee. Raise sounds more peaceful.

✓ **DO** use `System.EventHandler<T>` instead of manually creating new delegates to be used as event handlers.

```
public class NotifyingContactCollection : Collection<Contact> {
    public event EventHandler<ContactAddedEventArgs> ContactAdded;
    ...
}
```

If you're adding new events to an existing feature area that uses traditional event handlers, then keep using those in order to remain consistent within the feature area. For example, `System.Windows.Forms` might want to continue using manually created handlers.

Also, this guideline does not apply to frameworks that need to run on one of the early versions of the CLR that does not support Generics.

> **BRIAN PEPIN** You wouldn't believe how long we debated this. On one hand, `EventHandler<T>` doesn't really buy you that much over the one-line declaration of your own event handler. In fact, the syntax is quite a bit more confusing. On the other hand, reducing the number of classes that need to be loaded by your code improves performance. I've never been a big fan of choosing performance over ease of use (performance gets better over time; ease of use doesn't). The current round of compilers allows you to leave out the new `EventHandler<ContactAddedEventArgs>()` business, however, so this doesn't really impact ease of use that much. We also finally solved the last hurdle—getting the Visual Studio designers to understand generic events—so I'll be glad to finally put this debate to bed.

✓ **CONSIDER** using a subclass of `EventArgs` as the event argument, unless you are absolutely sure the event will never need to carry any data to the event handling method, in which case you can use the `EventArgs` type directly.

```
public class AlarmRaisedEventArgs : EventArgs {
}
```

If you ship an API using `EventArgs` directly, you will never be able to add any data to be carried with the event without breaking compatibility. If you use a subclass, even if initially completely empty, you will be able to add properties to the subclass when needed.

```
public class AlarmRaisedEventArgs : EventArgs {
    public DateTimeOffset AlarmTime { get; }
}
```

✓ **DO** use a protected virtual method to raise each event. This is only applicable to nonstatic events on unsealed classes, not to structs, sealed classes, or static events.

For each event, include a corresponding protected virtual method that raises the event. The purpose of the method is to provide a way for a derived class to handle the event using an override. Overriding is a more flexible, faster, and more natural way to handle base class events in derived classes. By convention, the name of the method should start with "On" and be followed with the name of the event.

▪▪ **RICO MARIANI** Note that using an event handler mechanism gives you maximum flexibility in terms of code that can receive the event—in principle, any object could be notified. Sometimes all that's necessary is for the object to notify itself or more generally the subtype. If that's the case, an event might be overkill and all you need is a virtual protected `OnWhatever()` method. This is both cheaper and simpler than an event.

```
public class AlarmClock {
    public event EventHandler<AlarmRaisedEventArgs> AlarmRaised;

    protected virtual void OnAlarmRaised(AlarmRaisedEventArgs e){
        EventHandler<AlarmRaisedEventArgs> handler = AlarmRaised;
```

```
        if (handler != null) {
            handler(this, e);
        }
    }
}
```

The derived class can choose not to call the base implementation of the method in its override. Be prepared for this by not including any processing in the method that is required for the base class to work correctly.

ERIC GUNNERSON If you have an event in a class, you need to add a null test before you call the delegate. Typically, you would write:

```
if (Click != null) Click(this, e);
```

There is actually a possible race condition here: The event can be cleared between the first and second line. You would actually want to write:

```
ClickHandler handler = Click;
if (handler != null) handler(this, e);
```

You might want to do some other sort of synchronization in other scenarios. So back to the main question: Why is the null test required? We can't change the existing behavior of calling through a delegate, because some apps might depend on it, so it would have to be an addition to the language. We have talked about adding an Invoke keyword to the language to make this easier, but after a fair bit of discussion, we decided that we couldn't do the right thing all the time, so we elected not to change the way the C# compiler behaved.

JOE DUFFY An example of other kinds of synchronization you might need, as Eric alludes to, is event handlers. This is because the code generated for adding and removing event handlers is *not* threadsafe. If you need to support multiple threads subscribing or removing handlers simultaneously, you'll need to write custom event add and remove methods that use locking internally. The AppDomain class does this, for example, so that threads subscribing to its events (such as ProcessExit) don't race with one another, which leads to missed subscriptions.

✓ **DO** take one parameter to the protected method that raises an event. The parameter should be named e and should be typed as the event argument class.

```
protected virtual void OnAlarmRaised(AlarmRaisedEventArgs e){
    EventHandler<AlarmRaisedEventArgs> handler = AlarmRaised;
        if (handler != null) {
            handler(this, e);
        }
    }
}
```

✗ **DO NOT** pass null as the sender when raising a nonstatic event.

✓ **DO** pass null as the sender when raising a static event.

```
EventHandler<EventArgs> handler = ...;
if (handler!=null) handler(null,...);
```

✗ **DO NOT** pass null as the event data parameter when raising an event.

You should pass EventArgs.Empty if you don't want to pass any data to the event handling method. Developers expect this parameter not to be null.

✓ **CONSIDER** raising events that the end user can cancel. This only applies to pre-events.

Use System.ComponentModel.CancelEventArgs or its subclass as the event argument to allow the end user to cancel events. For example, System.Windows.Forms.Form raises a Closing event before a form closes. The user can cancel the close operation, as shown in the following example:

```
void ClosingHandler(object sender, CancelEventArgs e) {
    e.Cancel = true;
}
```

The next section describes custom event handler design.

5.4.1 **Custom Event Handler Design**

There are cases in which EventHandler<T> cannot be used, such as when the framework needs to work with earlier versions of the CLR, which did not support Generics. In such cases, you might need to design and develop a custom event handler delegate.

✓ **DO** use a return type of void for event handlers.

An event handler can invoke multiple event handling methods, possibly on multiple objects. If event handling methods were allowed to return a value, there would be multiple return values for each event invocation.

✓ **DO** use object as the type of the first parameter of the event handler, and call it sender.

✓ **DO** use System.EventArgs or its subclass as the type of the second parameter of the event handler, and call it e.

✗ **DO NOT** have more than two parameters on event handlers.

The following event handler follows all of the preceding guidelines.

```
public delegate void ClickedEventHandler(object sender, ClickedEventArgs e);
```

CHRIS ANDERSON Why? People always ask this. In the end, this is just about a pattern. By having event arguments packaged in a class you get better versioning semantics. By having a common pattern (sender, e) it is easily learned as the signature for all events. I think back to how bad it was with Win32—when data was in WPARAM versus LPARAM, and so on. The pattern becomes noise and developers just assume that event handlers have scope to the sender and arguments of the event.

5.5 **Field Design**

The principle of encapsulation is one of the most important notions in object-oriented design. This principle states that data stored inside an object should be accessible only to that object.

A useful way to interpret the principle is to say that a type should be designed so that changes to fields of that type (name or type changes) can be made without breaking code other than for members of the type. This interpretation immediately implies that all fields must be private.

We exclude constant and static read-only fields from this strict restriction, because such fields, almost by definition, are never required to change.

✗ DO NOT provide instance fields that are public or protected.

You should provide properties for accessing fields instead of making them public or protected.

Very trivial property accessors, as shown here, can be inlined by the Just-in-Time (JIT) compiler and provide performance on a par with that of accessing a field.

```
public struct Point{
    private int x;
    private int y;

    public Point(int x, int y){
        this.x = x;
        this.y = y;
    }

    public int X {
        get{ return x; }
    }

    public int Y{
        get{ return y; }
    }
}
```

By not exposing fields directly to the developer, the type can be versioned more easily, and for the following reasons:

- A field cannot be changed to a property while maintaining binary compatibility.
- The presence of executable code in get and set property accessors allows later improvements, such as demand-creation of an object on usage of the property, or a property change notification.

> **CHRIS ANDERSON**   Fields are the bane of my existence. Because reflection treats fields and properties as different constructs, any system that walks an object graph must special-case both of them. Data binding always looks only at properties; runtime serialization looks only at fields. The fact that we didn't unify these two (treating properties as smart fields) is definitely a regret of mine. However, as Rico Mariani would say, properties have additional overhead. And as I would say, fields don't version. You can never promote a field to be a property when you want to add validation, change notification, put it in an interface, and so on. Fields are private data; they are the stores behind your public contract, which should be implemented with properties, methods, and events.

> **JEFFREY RICHTER**   Personally, I always make my fields private. I don't even expose fields as internal, because doing so would give me no protection from code in my own assembly.

✓ **DO** use constant fields for constants that will never change.

The compiler burns the values of const fields directly into calling code. Therefore, const values can never be changed without the risk of breaking compatibility.

```
public struct Int32 {
   public const int MaxValue = 0x7fffffff;
   public const int MinValue = unchecked((int)0x80000000);
}
```

✓ **DO** use public static readonly fields for predefined object instances.

If there are predefined instances of the type, declare them as public readonly static fields of the type itself.

```
public struct Color{
   public static readonly Color Red = new Color(0x0000FF);
   public static readonly Color Green = new Color(0x00FF00);
   public static readonly Color Blue = new Color(0xFF0000);
   ...
}
```

✗ **DO NOT** assign instances of mutable types to `readonly` fields.

A mutable type is a type with instances that can be modified after they are instantiated. For example, arrays, most collections, and streams are mutable types, but `System.Int32`, `System.Uri`, and `System.String` are all immutable. The read-only modifier on a reference type field prevents the instance stored in the field from being replaced, but it does not prevent the field's instance data from being modified by calling members changing the instance. The following example shows how it is possible to change the value of an object referred to by a `readonly` field.

```
public class SomeType {
    public static readonly int[] Numbers = new int[10];
}
...

SomeType.Numbers[5] = 10; // changes a value in the array
```

> ▪▪ **JOE DUFFY**   The real distinction here is *deep* versus *shallow* immutability. A deeply immutable type is one whose fields are all `readonly`, and each field is of a type that itself is also deeply immutable. This ensures that a whole object graph is transitively immutable. While this is certainly the most useful kind, shallow immutability can also be useful. What this guideline is trying to protect you from is believing you've exposed a deeply immutable object graph when in fact it is shallow, and then writing code that assumes the whole graph is immutable.

The next section offers guidelines for operator overload design.

5.6 Extension Methods

Extension methods are a language feature that allows static methods to be called using instance method call syntax. These methods must take at least one parameter, which represents the instance the method is to operate on. For example, in C#, this is done by using the *this* modifier on such a parameter when defining the method.

```
public static class StringExtensions {
    public static bool IsPalindrome(this string s){
        ...
    }
}
```

This extension method can be called as follows:

```
if("hello world".IsPalindrome()){
    ...
}
```

The class that defines such extension methods is referred to as the "sponsor" class, and it must be declared as static. To use extension methods, one must import the namespace defining the sponsor class.

✗ **AVOID** frivolously defining extension methods, especially on types you don't own.

If you do own source code of a type, consider using regular instance methods instead. If you don't own, and you want to add a method, be very careful. Liberal use of extension methods has the potential of cluttering APIs of types that were not designed to have these methods.

Another thing to consider is that extension methods are a compile-time facility, and not all languages provide support for them. These languages will have to use the regular static method call syntax to call extension methods.

There are, of course, scenarios in which extension methods should be employed. These are outlined in the guidelines that follow.

✓ **CONSIDER** using extension methods in any of the following scenarios:

- To provide helper functionality relevant to every implementation of an interface, if said functionality can be written in terms of the core interface. This is because concrete implementations cannot otherwise be assigned to interfaces. For example, the LINQ to Objects operators are implemented as extension methods for all IEnumerable<T> types. Thus, any IEnumerable<> implementation is automatically LINQ-enabled.

- When an instance method would introduce a dependency on some type, but such a dependency would break dependency management rules. For example, a dependency from `String` to `System.Uri` is probably not desirable, and so `String.ToUri()` instance method returning `System.Uri` would be the wrong design from a dependency management perspective. A static extension method `Uri.ToUri(this string str)` returning `System.Uri` would be a much better design.

> **■ RICO MARIANI** The value of this cannot be overstated. Extension methods provide you with a way to give interfaces not just one default implementation but as many as you need, and you can choose between them simply by bringing the right namespace(s) into your lexical scope with `using`. However, this could be easily abused in the same way that complex `#include` combinations in C++ can make the final code hard to read.
>
> Another interesting feature of this manner of adding functionality to a class is that you could potentially partition (extension) methods of the same class into different assemblies for performance reasons. Again, this should not be done lightly, because you could cause great confusion.
>
> This is one of the many times I like to quote from Spiderman—"With great power comes great responsibility."

> **■ PHIL HAACK** Section 2.2.4.1 covers the topic of layering in namespaces, which I think applies well to extension methods.
>
> One scenario I've seen is to put functionality that is more advanced or esoteric in a separate namespace. That way, for core scenarios, these extra methods do not "pollute" the API. But for those who know about the namespace, or need these alternate scenarios, they can add the namespace and gain access to these extra methods.
>
> The drawback, of course, is that this results in a "hidden" API that is not very discoverable.

> **■ JOE DUFFY** Extension methods can also be used to provide actual concrete method implementations for interfaces. For example, if you ship an `IFoo` interface, you can also have a static `Foo` class with a method `public static void Bar(this IFoo f)` that makes all instances of `IFoo` effectively have an extra `Bar` method.

✗ **AVOID** defining extension methods on System.Object.

VB users will not be able to call such methods on object references using the extension method syntax. VB does not support calling such methods because, in VB, declaring a reference as Object forces all method invocations on it to be late bound (actual member called is determined at runtime), while bindings to extension methods are determined at compile-time (early bound). For example:

```
// C# declaration of the extension method
public static class SomeExtensions{
    static void SomeMethod(this object o){...}
}


' VB will fail to compile as VB.NET does not support calling extension
' methods on references types as Object
Dim o As Object = ...
o.SomeMethod();
```

VB users will have to call the method using the regular static method call syntax.

```
SomeExtensions.SomeMethod(o)
```

Note that the guideline applies to other languages where the same binding behavior is present, or where extension methods are not supported.

✗ **DO NOT** put extension methods in the same namespace as the extended type unless it is for adding methods to interfaces or for dependency management.

Of course, in the latter case, the type would be in a different assembly.

✗ **AVOID** defining two or more extension methods with the same signature, even if they reside in different namespaces.

For example, if two different namespaces defined the same extension method on the same type, it would be impossible to import both namespaces in the same file—the compiler would report an ambiguity if one of the methods is called.

```
namespace A{
  public static class AExtensions{
          public static void ExtensionMethod(this Foo foo){...}
  }
}
namespace B{
  public static class BExtensions{
          public static void ExtensionMethod(this Foo foo){...}
  }
}
```

■■ **RICO MARIANI**   There can be reasons to violate this guideline; for example, there might be a framework that allowed developers to choose:

```
using SomeType.Routing.SpeedOptimized;
```

or

```
using SomeType.Routing.SpaceOptimized;
```

In this case, both namespaces could offer the same services, and developers simply choose which flavor to use.

The key here is that a natural mutual exclusion exists for a given consumer of the extension so that it avoids the ambiguity. If you tried to use both, you would want to see the error so that you would realize you have a conflict.

■■ **MIRCEA TROFIN**   Such a situation may occur when using a mix of third-party libraries. To resolve it, import in a file only one namespace defining extension methods on a type, and use fully qualified static method calls for extension methods defined on the same type in a different namespace.

```
using A;
...
T someObj = ...
someObj.ExtentionMethod(); //this calls AExtensions.ExtensionMethod
// to avoid compilation errors,
// we call explicitly the extension method defined in namespace B
B.BExtensions.ExtensionMethod(someObj);
```

✓ **CONSIDER** defining extension methods in the same namespace as the extended type if the type is an interface and if the extension methods are meant to be used in most or all cases.

✗ **DO NOT** define extension methods implementing a feature in namespaces normally associated with other features. Instead, define them in the namespace associated with the feature they belong to.

For example, do not define `Uri.ToUri(this string string):Uri` in the `System` namespace (the namespace containing `String`). Such an extension method should probably be defined in the `System.Net` namespace.

✗ **AVOID** generic naming of namespaces dedicated to extension methods (e.g., "Extensions"). Use a descriptive name (e.g., "Routing") instead.

> ■ **ANTHONY MOORE**   Many developers love the power and expressivity of extension methods and are tempted to use them in ways that clearly violate these guidelines. In many ways, this seems a lot like operator overloading in the early days of C++, where there was initially vigorous and "creative" use of operators for nonintuitive cases, including the runtime libraries of the language.
>
> Over time the painful lesson was learned, and operator overloading was one of the features that many companies using C++ all but banned. It provides a one-off saving of some typing at the expense of future transparency of the code, and code is read a lot more times than it is written. Using extension methods for reasons other than the scenarios for interfaces or layering is very similar to this situation.
>
> As an example, I've had some frustrating experiences with using APIs that enthusiastically use extensions. On a multilanguage project I found that a pleasant and intuitive object model in one language was awkward in a language without the support for extension methods. I've also had cases where I was misled about the type of an instance because some local code was injecting extensions into it.
>
> Please use extension methods with caution.

> ■ **BRIAN PEPIN** When working on the implementation of the WPF
> designer for Visual Studio, we made careful use of extension methods. In
> many places in our code we needed to identify properties based on the
> values of certain attributes defined for XAML. For example, the content
> property of a control can be identified by looking for a `ContentProperty-`
> `Attribute` on the type, and then using the value of that attribute to look
> for a property on the type. Having this code everywhere was cumber-
> some, so we wrote a set of internal extension methods to Type to do the
> work for us:
>
> ```
> internal static class XamlTypeExtensions {
>     internal static PropertyInfo GetContentProperty(this Type source) {
>         var attrs = source.GetCustomAttributes(typeof
>                                         (ContentPropertyAttribute), true);
>         if (attrs.Length > 0) {
>             return source.GetProperty(((ContentPropertyAttribute)
>                                         attrs[0]).Name);
>         }
>         return null;
>     }
> }
> ```
>
> Centralizing these types of operations in a set of internal extension meth-
> ods allowed our code to be much cleaner and allowed us to optimize imple-
> mentations in one place.

5.7 Operator Overloads

Operator overloads allow framework types to appear as if they were built-
in language primitives. The following snippet shows some of the most
important operator overloads defined by `System.Decimal`.

```
public struct Decimal {
    public static Decimal operator+(Decimal d);
    public static Decimal operator-(Decimal d);
    public static Decimal operator++(Decimal d);
    public static Decimal operator--(Decimal d);
    public static Decimal operator+(Decimal d1, Decimal d2);
    public static Decimal operator-(Decimal d1, Decimal d2);
    public static Decimal operator*(Decimal d1, Decimal d2);
    public static Decimal operator/(Decimal d1, Decimal d2);
    public static Decimal operator%(Decimal d1, Decimal d2);
```

```
public static bool operator==(Decimal d1, Decimal d2);
public static bool operator!=(Decimal d1, Decimal d2);
public static bool operator<(Decimal d1, Decimal d2);
public static bool operator<=(Decimal d1, Decimal d2) ;
public static bool operator>(Decimal d1, Decimal d2) ;
public static bool operator>=(Decimal d1, Decimal d2);


public static implicit operator Decimal(int value);
public static implicit operator Decimal(long value);
public static explicit operator Decimal(float value);
public static explicit operator Decimal(double value);
...


public static explicit operator int(Decimal value);
public static explicit operator long(Decimal value);
public static explicit operator float(Decimal value);
public static explicit operator double(Decimal value);
...
}
```

Although allowed and useful in some situations, operator overloads should be used cautiously. There are many cases in which operator overloading has been abused, such as when framework designers started to use operators for operations that should be simple methods. The following guidelines should help you decide when and how to use operator overloading.

■ **CHRIS SELLS**   Operator overloads don't show up in Intellisense, so for most developers, they don't exist. Keep that in mind before you go through the complicated exercise of making sure your operators work and act like the same operators on the built-in types.

■ **KRZYSZTOF CWALINA**   Normally, overloading is understood as having more than one member with the same name but different parameters defined by one type. In the case of operators, they are said to be overloaded despite the fact that there might be only one such operator member on a type. This terminology can be quite confusing, but there is a reason for the seemingly confusing name.

Overloading happens when an addition of a member means the compiler will have to use the argument list, in addition to the member name, to resolve which member should be called. So, for example, the moment you add an `operator+` to a custom type, the compiler has to know the types of arguments (operands) of the following call to know which operator needs to be called.

```
public struct BigInteger {
    public static BigInteger operator+(BigInt left, BigInt right);
}
...
// if x and y are BigInteger instances the operator above will be used
object result = x + y;
```

✗ **AVOID** defining operator overloads, except in types that should feel like primitive (built-in) types.

✓ **CONSIDER** defining operator overloads in a type that should feel like a primitive type.

For example, `System.String` has `operator==` and `operator!=` defined.

✓ **DO** define operator overloads in structs that represent numbers (such as `System.Decimal`).

✗ **DO NOT** be cute when defining operator overloads.

Operator overloading is useful in cases in which it is immediately obvious what the result of the operation will be. For example, it makes sense to be able to subtract one `DateTime` from another `DateTime` and get a `TimeSpan`. However, it is not appropriate to use the logical union operator to union two database queries, or to use the shift operator to write to a stream.

✗ **DO NOT** provide operator overloads unless at least one of the operands is of the type defining the overload.

In other words, operators should operate on types that define them. The C# compiler enforces this guideline.

```
public struct RangedInt32 {
    public static RangedInt32 operator-(RangedInt32 left, RangedInt32 right);
    public static RangedInt32 operator-(RangedInt32 left, int right);
    public static RangedInt32 operator-(int left, RangedInt32 right);

    // the following would violate the guideline and in fact does not
    // compile in C#.
    // public static RangedInt32 operator-(int left, int right);
}
```

✔ **DO** overload operators in a symmetric fashion.

For example, if you overload the operator==, you should also overload the operator!=. Similarly, if you overload the operator<, you should also overload the operator>, and so on.

> **■ RICO MARIANI** More generally, if you haven't defined a whole family of overloads (because maybe they don't all make sense), there's a good chance that operator overloading isn't really the best way to express your class. Remember that there are no bonus points for using fewer characters in your method calls.

✔ **CONSIDER** providing methods with friendly names that correspond to each overloaded operator.

Many languages do not support operator overloading. For this reason, it is recommended that types that overload operators include a secondary method with an appropriate domain-specific name that provides equivalent functionality. The following example illustrates this point.

```
public struct DateTimeOffset {
    public static TimeSpan operator-(DateTimeOffset left, DateTimeOffset
right) { ... }
    public TimeSpan Subtract(DateTimeOffset value) { ... }
}
```

Table 5-1 contains a list of operators and the corresponding friendly method names.

T<small>ABLE</small> 5-1: Operators and Corresponding Method Names

C# Operator Symbol	Metadata Name	Friendly Name
N/A	op_Implicit	To<TypeName>/From<TypeName>
N/A	op_Explicit	To<TypeName>/From<TypeName>
+ (binary)	op_Addition	Add
- (binary)	op_Subtraction	Subtract
* (binary)	op_Multiply	Multiply
/	op_Division	Divide
%	op_Modulus	Mod or Remainder
^	op_ExclusiveOr	Xor
& (binary)	op_BitwiseAnd	BitwiseAnd
|	op_BitwiseOr	BitwiseOr
&&	op_LogicalAnd	And
||	op_LogicalOr	Or
=	op_Assign	Assign
<<	op_LeftShift	LeftShift
>>	op_RightShift	RightShift
N/A	op_SignedRightShift	SignedRightShift
N/A	op_UnsignedRightShift	UnsignedRightShift
==	op_Equality	Equals
!=	op_Inequality	Equals
>	op_GreaterThan	CompareTo
<	op_LessThan	CompareTo
>=	op_GreaterThanOrEqual	CompareTo

C# Operator Symbol	Metadata Name	Friendly Name
<=	op_LessThanOrEqual	CompareTo
*=	op_MultiplicationAssignment	Multiply
-=	op_SubtractionAssignment	Subtract
^=	op_ExclusiveOrAssignment	Xor
<<=	op_LeftShiftAssignment	LeftShift
%=	op_ModulusAssignment	Mod
+=	op_AdditionAssignment	Add
&=	op_BitwiseAndAssignment	BitwiseAnd
|=	op_BitwiseOrAssignment	BitwiseOr
,	op_Comma	Comma
/=	op_DivisionAssignment	Divide
--	op_Decrement	Decrement
++	op_Increment	Increment
- (unary)	op_UnaryNegation	Negate
+ (unary)	op_UnaryPlus	Plus
~	op_OnesComplement	OnesComplement

5.7.1 **Overloading** Operator ==

Overloading operator == is quite complicated. The semantics of the operator need to be compatible with several other members, such as Object.Equals. For information on this subject, see section 8.9.1.

5.7.2 **Conversion Operators**

Conversion operators are unary operators that allow conversion from one type to another. The operators must be defined as static members on either the operand or the return type. There are two types of conversion operators: implicit and explicit.

```
public struct RangedInt32 {
    public static implicit operator int(RangedInt32 value){ ... }
    public static explicit operator RangedInt32(int value) { ... }
    ...
}
```

✗ **DO NOT** provide a conversion operator if such conversion is not clearly expected by the end users.

Ideally, you should have some customer research data showing that the conversion is expected, or some prior art examples where a similar type needed such conversion.

✗ **DO NOT** define conversion operators outside of a type's domain.

For example, Int32, Double, and Decimal are all numeric types, whereas DateTime is not. Therefore, there should be no conversion operator to convert a Double(long) to a DateTime. A constructor is preferred in such a case.

```
public struct DateTime {
    public DateTime(long ticks){ ... }
}
```

✗ **DO NOT** provide an implicit conversion operator if the conversion is potentially lossy.

For example, there should not be an implicit conversion from Double to Int32 because Double has a wider range than Int32. An explicit conversion operator can be provided even if the conversion is potentially lossy.

✗ **DO NOT** throw exceptions from implicit casts.

It is very difficult for end users to understand what is happening, because they might not be aware that a conversion is taking place.

✓ **DO** throw `System.InvalidCastException` if a call to a cast operator results in a lossy conversion and the contract of the operator does not allow lossy conversions.

```
public static explicit operator RangedInt32(long value) {
    if (value < Int32.MinValue || value > Int32.MaxValue) {
        throw new InvalidCastException();
    }
    return new RangedInt32((int)value, Int32.MinValue, Int32.MaxValue);
}
```

For information on overloading `operator==`, see section 8.13. The next section presents guidelines on parameter design.

5.8 Parameter Design

This section provides broad guidelines on parameter design, including sections with guidelines for checking arguments. In addition, you should refer to the parameter naming guidelines described in Chapter 3.

✓ **DO** use the least derived parameter type that provides the functionality required by the member.

For example, suppose you want to design a method that enumerates a collection and prints each item to the console. Such a method should take `IEnumerable` as the parameter, not `ArrayList` or `IList`, for example.

```
public void WriteItemsToConsole(IEnumerable collection){
    foreach(object item in collection){
        Console.WriteLine(item.ToString());
    }
}
```

None of the specific `IList` members needs to be used inside the method. Typing the parameter as `IEnumerable` allows the end user to pass collections that implement only `IEnumerable` and not `IList`.

> ■■ RICO MARIANI   Interface isn't everything. If your algorithm needs a more specialized type to get decent performance, there's no point in pretending that you only need a base type. Best to make your needs clear—ask for the type that is required to get the designed behavior. Likewise, if your method requires certain thread-safety or security features provided by subtypes, insist on those features in the contract. There's no point in allowing users to make calls that won't work.

✗ **DO NOT** use reserved parameters.

If more input to a member is needed in some future version, a new overload can be added. For example, it would be bad to reserve a parameter as follows:

```
public void Method(SomeOption option, object reserved);
```

It is better to simply add a parameter in a future version, as shown in the following example:

```
public void Method(SomeOption option);

// added in a future version
public void Method(SomeOption option, string path);
```

✗ **DO NOT** have publicly exposed methods that take pointers, arrays of pointers, or multidimensional arrays as parameters.

Pointers and multidimensional arrays are relatively difficult to use properly. In almost all cases, APIs can be redesigned to avoid taking these types as parameters.

> ■■ RICO MARIANI   Sometimes people try these sorts of things to squeeze out more performance. But remember that you aren't helping anyone if it's fast but also virtually impossible to use correctly.

✓ **DO** place all out parameters following all of the by-value and ref parameters (excluding parameter arrays), even if it results in an inconsistency in parameter ordering between overloads (see section 5.1.1).

The out parameters can be seen as extra return values, and grouping them together makes the method signature easier to understand. For example:

```
public struct DateTimeOffset {
    public static bool TryParse(string input, out DateTimeOffset result);
    public static bool TryParse(string input, IFormatProvider
formatProvider, DateTimeStyles styles, out DateTimeOffset result);
}
```

✓ **DO** be consistent in naming parameters when overriding members or implementing interface members.

This better communicates the relationship between the methods.

```
public interface IComparable<T> {
    int CompareTo(T other);
}

public class Nullable<T> : IComparable<Nullable<T>> {
    // correct
    public int CompareTo(Nullable<T> other) { ... }

    // incorrect
    public int CompareTo(Nullable<T> nullable) { ... }
}

public class Object {
    public virtual bool Equals(object obj) { ... }
}

public class String {
    // correct, the parameter to the base method is called 'obj'
    public override bool Equals(object obj) { ... }

    // incorrect, the parameter should be called 'obj'
    public override bool Equals(object value) { ... }
}
```

5.8.1 Choosing Between Enum and Boolean Parameters

A framework designer often must decide when to use enums and when to use Booleans for parameters. In general, you should favor using enums where it improves the readability of the client code, especially in commonly used APIs. If using enums would add unneeded complexity and actually hurt readability, or if the API is very rarely used, Booleans should be preferred.

✓ **DO** use enums if a member would otherwise have two or more Boolean parameters.

Enums are much more readable when it comes to books, documentation, source code reviews, and so on. For example, look at the following method call:

```
Stream stream = File.Open ("foo.txt", true, false);
```

This call gives the reader no context within which to understand the meaning behind true and false. The call would be much more usable if it were to use enums, as follows:

```
Stream stream = File.Open("foo.txt", CasingOptions.CaseSensitive,
FileMode.Open);
```

ANTHONY MOORE Some have asked why we don't have a similar guideline for integers, doubles, and so on. Should we find a way to "name" them as well? There is a big difference between numeric types and Booleans. You almost always use constants and variables to pass numeric values around, because it is good programming practice and you don't want to have "magic numbers." However, if you take a look at real-life source code, this is almost never true of Booleans. Eighty percent of the time a Boolean argument is passed in as a literal constant, and its intention is to turn a piece of behavior on or off. We could alternatively try to establish a coding guideline that you should never pass a literal value to a method or constructor, but I don't think it would be practical. I certainly don't want to define a constant for each Boolean parameter I'm passing in.

JON PINCUS Methods with two Boolean parameters, like the one in the preceding example, allow developers to inadvertently switch the arguments, and the compiler and static analysis tools can't help you. Even with just one parameter, I tend to believe it's still somewhat easier to make a mistake with Booleans ... let's see, does true mean case insensitive or case sensitive?

■ **STEVEN CLARKE**   The worst example of an unreadable Boolean param-eter that I had to deal with was the `CWnd::UpdateData` method in MFC. It takes a Boolean that indicates whether a dialog is being initialized or data is being retrieved. I always had to look up whether to pass true or false to this method each time I called it. Likewise, each time I read code that called the method, I had to look it up to see what it meant.

✗ DO NOT use Booleans unless you are absolutely sure there will never be a need for more than two values.

Enums give you some room for future addition of values, but you should be aware of all the implications of adding values to enums, which are described in section 4.8.2.

■ **BRAD ABRAMS**   We have seen a couple of places in the Framework where we added a Boolean in one version and in the next one we were forced to add another Boolean option to account for what could have been a foreseeable change. Don't let this happen to you: If there is even a slight possibility of needing more options in the future, use an enum now.

✓ CONSIDER using Booleans for constructor parameters that are truly two-state values and are simply used to initialize Boolean properties.

■ **ANTHONY MOORE**   An interesting clarification of this guideline for constructor parameters that map onto properties is that if the value is typi-cally set in the constructor, an enum value is better. If the value is usually set using the property setter, a Boolean value is better. This thinking helped us clarify a recent `CodeDom` work item to add `IsGlobal` on `CodeTypeReference`. In this case, it should be an enum because it is typically set in the construc-tor, but the `IsPartial` property on `CodeTypeDeclaration` should be a Boolean.

5.8.2 Validating Arguments

Rigorous checks on arguments passed to members are a crucial element of modern reusable libraries. Although argument checks might have a slight impact on performance, end users are in general willing to pay the price for the benefit of better error reporting, which becomes possible if arguments are validated as high on the call stack as possible.

> **■ RICO MARIANI**   The key words for me here are "high on the call stack." When you get low in the call stack, the amount of work that the functions are doing is so small that the argument validation becomes a significant, even dominant, factor in performance. At that point it's a lousy deal. Where do I tend to just let the runtime throw exceptions rather than prevalidate? Typically, in comparison and hashing functions; you can expect those to be called often and with tight requirements. Regular measurements will help you spot any validations that are too low in the stack.

✓ **DO** validate arguments passed to public, protected, or explicitly implemented members. Throw `System.ArgumentException`, or one of its subclasses, if the validation fails.

```
public class StringCollection : IList {
    int IList.Add(object item){
        string str = item as string;
        if(str==null) throw new ArgumentNullException(...);
        return Add(str);
    }
}
```

Note that the actual validation does not necessarily have to happen in the public or protected member itself. It could happen at a lower level in some private or internal routine. The main point is that the entire surface area that is exposed to the end users checks the arguments.

✓ **DO** throw `ArgumentNullException` if a null argument is passed and the member does not support null arguments.

✓ **DO** validate enum parameters.

Do not assume enum arguments will be in the range defined by the enum. The CLR allows casting any integer value into an enum value even if the value is not defined in the enum.

```
public void PickColor(Color color) {
   if(color > Color.Black || color < Color.White){
      throw new ArgumentOutOfRangeException(...);
   }
   ...
}
```

■ VANCE MORRISON   I am not a believer in always validating [Flags] enums. Typically, all you can usefully do for them is to confirm that "unused" flags are not used, but this also makes your code unnecessarily fragile (now adding a new flag is a breaking change!). Your code "naturally" would simply ignore unused flags, and I think that is a reasonable semantics. Note, however, that if certain combinations of flags are illegal, that should certainly be checked and an appropriate error thrown.

✗ DO NOT use Enum.IsDefined for enum range checks.

■ BRAD ABRAMS   There are really two problems with Enum.IsDefined. First, it loads reflection and a bunch of cold type metadata, making it a surprisingly expensive call. Second, there is a versioning issue here. Consider an alternate way to validate enum values.

```
public void PickColor(Color color) {
   // the following check is incorrect!
   if (!Enum.IsDefined (typeof(Color), color) {
      throw new InvalidEnumArgumentException(...);
   }
   // issue: never pass a negative color value
   NativeMethods.SetImageColor (color, byte[] image);
}
 // callsite
Foo.PickColor ((Color) -1); //throws InvalidEnumArgumentException
```

This looks pretty good, even if you know this (mythical) native API has a buffer overrun if you pass a color value that is negative. You know this because you know the enum only defined positive values and you are sure that any value passed was one of the ones defined in the enum, right? Well, only half right. You don't know what values are defined in the enum. Checking at the moment you write this code is not good enough because IsDefined takes the value of the enum at runtime. So if someone later added a new value (say `Ultraviolet = -1`) to the enum, `IsDefined` will start allowing the value `-1` through. This is true whether the enum is defined in the same assembly as the method or in another assembly.

```
public enum Color {
    Red = 1,
    Green = 2,
    Blue = 3,
    Ultraviolet = -1, //new value added this version
}
```

Now, that same call site no longer throws.

```
//causes a buffer overrun in NativeMethods.SetImageColor() Foo.PickColor
((Color) -1);
```

The moral of the story is twofold. First, be very careful when you use `Enum.IsDefined` in your code. Second, when you design an API to simplify a situation, be sure the fix isn't worse than the current problem.

BRENT RECTOR `Enum.IsDefined` is surprisingly expensive. However, I think using `Enum.IsDefined` is appropriate *when you want to determine whether a value equals a definition in an enumerated type*—but that's not what the prior example is trying to do.

In the preceding example, the issue is that there is a condition required before calling the native `SetImageColor` method: The `Color` argument cannot have a negative value. As Brad mentions, the values defined in an enumerated type may change from compilation to compilation. In other words, the constraint applicable to the argument value (which must not be negative) doesn't necessarily hold over time for the values defined in the enumerated type. Therefore, validating that the `Color` argument is not negative by testing whether its value matches a definition in an enumerated type simply isn't proper validation.

The example is great, though, in that it demonstrates how easily you can unintentionally misuse `Enum.IsDefined`, so use it thoughtfully.

✓ **DO** be aware that mutable arguments might have changed after they were validated.

If the member is security sensitive, you are encouraged to make a copy and then validate and process the argument.

> ■ **RICO MARIANI** This is one of the many places where you can cash in on the fact that CLR strings are immutable; there is no need to copy them in security-sensitive operations.

5.8.3 Parameter Passing

From the perspective of a framework designer, there are three main groups of parameters: by-value parameters, `ref` parameters, and `out` parameters.

When an argument is passed through a by-value parameter, the member receives a copy of the actual argument passed in. If the argument is a value type, a copy of the argument is put on the stack. If the argument is a reference type, a copy of the reference is put on the stack. Most popular CLR languages, such as C#, VB.NET, and C++, default to passing parameters by value.

```
public void Add (object value) {...}
```

> ■ **PAUL VICK** When moving to .NET, VB changed the default for parameters from by-reference to by-value. We did this because the vast majority of parameters are by-value and so having a default of by-reference meant that parameters could unintentionally side effect quite easily. Thus, defaulting to by-value was a safer default and meant that choosing by-reference semantics was a conscious, rather than accidental, decision.

When an argument is passed through a `ref` parameter, the member receives a reference to the actual argument passed in. If the argument is a value type, a reference to the argument is put on the stack. If the argument is a reference type, a reference to the reference is put on the stack. `Ref` parameters can be used to allow the member to modify arguments passed by the caller.

```
public static void Swap(ref object obj1, ref object obj2){
    object temp = obj1;
    obj1 = obj2;
    obj2 = temp;
}
```

Out parameters are similar to `ref` parameters, with some small differences. The parameter is initially considered unassigned and cannot be read in the member body before it is assigned some value. Also, the parameter has to be assigned some value before the member returns. For example, the following sample will not compile and generates compiler error "Use of unassigned out parameter 'uri.'"

```
public class Uri {
    public bool TryParse(string uriString, out Uri uri){
        Trace.WriteLine(uri);
        ...
    }
}
```

■ **RICO MARIANI**   Out is the same as the `ref` in mechanism, but there are different (stronger) verification rules because the intent has been made clear to the compiler and the runtime.

✗ **AVOID** using out or ref parameters.

Using out or ref parameters requires experience with pointers, understanding how value types and reference types differ, and handling methods with multiple return values. Also, the difference between out and ref parameters is not widely understood. Framework architects designing for a general audience should not expect users to master working with out or ref parameters.

ANDERS HEJLSBERG   As a rule, I am not too crazy about `ref` and `out` parameters in APIs. Such APIs compose very poorly, forcing you to declare temporary variables. I much prefer functional designs that convey the entire result in the return value.

BRIAN PEPIN   If you need to return several pieces of data from a call, wrap that data up into a class or struct. For example, the .NET Framework has an API to perform hit testing of controls that returns a `HitTestResult` object.

JASON CLARK   Generics and `ref/out` parameters interact very nicely. Normally, the variable used to make a `ref` call must be an exact type match, which can be inconvenient. However, if the method is defined with a generic argument that is merely constrained to the required base type, then variables of derived types can be used to make the call. Meanwhile, inference by the compiler makes it unlikely that the caller is impacted by the generic syntax for the method. Very nice!

✗ **DO NOT** pass reference types by reference.

There are some limited exceptions to the rule, such as a method that can be used to swap references.

```
public static class Reference {
    public void Swap<T>(ref T obj1, ref T obj2){
        T temp = obj1;
        obj1 = obj2;
        obj2 = temp;
    }
}
```

CHRIS SELLS   Swap always comes up in these discussions, but I have not written code that actually needed a swap function since college. Unless you've got a very good reason, avoid `out` and `ref` altogether.

5.8.4 **Members with Variable Number of Parameters**

Members that can take a variable number of arguments are expressed by providing an array parameter. For example, String provides the following method:

```
public class String {
    public static string Format(string format, object[] parameters);
}
```

A user can then call the String.Format method, as follows:

```
String.Format("File {0} not found in {1}",new object[]{filename,directory});
```

Adding the C# params keyword to an array parameter changes the parameter to a so-called params array parameter and provides a shortcut to creating a temporary array.

```
public class String {
    public static string Format(string format, params object[] parameters);
}
```

Doing this allows the user to call the method by passing the array elements directly in the argument list.

```
String.Format("File {0} not found in {1}",filename,directory);
```

Note that the params keyword can be added only to the last parameter in the parameter list.

> ■_ **RICO MARIANI** Creating a temporary object array just to make a function call might sound like a scary thing to do from a performance perspective—and it can be—but keep in mind that allocations on the GC heap are quite zippy. The amortized cost of temporary objects is only about double (or so) what it would cost to do an alloca() in unmanaged code; that is, it is about double the cost of raw stack use. If the function that you are calling has a good bit of work to do (e.g., WriteLine()), then the argument cost won't be a big percentage. On the other hand, an otherwise very cheap function will suffer measurably if called with a params array.

✓ **CONSIDER** adding the params keyword to array parameters if you expect the end users to pass arrays with a small number of elements.

If it's expected that lots of elements will be passed in common scenarios, users will probably not pass these elements inline anyway, and so the params keyword is not necessary.

BRIAN PEPIN There are several places in the Framework where we didn't do this, and it still grates on me whenever I have to write code that creates a bunch of temporary arrays. In many cases, we were able to add params in a later version, but in other cases adding params made the method ambiguous and was a source-code breaking change.

✗ **AVOID** using params arrays if the caller would almost always have the input already in an array.

For example, members with byte array parameters would almost never be called by passing individual bytes. For this reason, byte array parameters in the .NET Framework do not use the params keyword.

✗ **DO NOT** use params arrays if the array is modified by the member taking the params array parameter.

Because of the fact that many compilers turn the arguments to the member into a temporary array at the call site, the array might be a temporary object, and therefore any modifications to the array will be lost.

✓ **CONSIDER** using the params keyword in a simple overload, even if a more complex overload could not use it.

Ask yourself if users would value having the params array in one overload even if it wasn't in all overloads. Consider the following overloaded method:

```
public class Graphics {
    FillPolygon(Brush brush, params Point[] points) { ... }
    FillPolygon(Brush brush, Point[] points, FillMode fillMode) {
        ...
    }
}
```

The array parameter of the second overload is not the last parameter in the parameter list. Therefore, it cannot use the params keyword. This does not mean that the keyword should not be used in the first over-load, where it is the last parameter. If the first overload is used often, users will appreciate the addition.

✓ **DO** try to order parameters to make it possible to use the params keyword.

Consider the following overloads on `PropertyDescriptorCollection`:

```
Sort()
Sort(IComparer comparer)
Sort(string[] names, IComparer comparer)
Sort(params string[] names)
```

Because of the order of parameters on the third overload, the opportunity to use the params keyword has been lost. The parameters could be reordered to allow for the params keyword in both overloads.

```
Sort()
Sort(IComparer comparer)
Sort(IComparer comparer, params string[] names)
Sort(params string[] names)
```

✓ **CONSIDER** providing special overloads and code paths for calls with a small number of arguments in extremely performance-sensitive APIs.

This makes it possible to avoid creating array objects when the API is called with a small number of arguments. Form the names of the parameters by taking a singular form of the array parameter and adding a numeric suffix.

```
void Format (string formatString, object arg1)
    void Format (string formatString, object arg1, object arg2)
...
    void Format (string formatString, params object[] args)
```

You should only do this if you are going to special-case the entire code path, not just create an array and call the more general method.

> ▪ **RICO MARIANI** You might also do this if you want to specialize the code path at some point, even if you can't do it in your first release. That way, you can change your internal implementation without having your clients recompile, and you can do the most important specializations first.

✔ **DO** be aware that null could be passed as a params array argument.

You should validate that the array is not null before processing.

```
static void Main() {
   Sum(1, 2, 3, 4, 5); //result == 15
   Sum(null);
}
static int Sum(params int[] values) {
   if(values==null) throw ArgumentNullException(...);
   int sum = 0;
   foreach (int value in values) {
      sum += value;
   }
   return sum;
}
```

> ▪ **RICO MARIANI** Very low-level functions (those doing only a tiny amount of work) will find the cost of temporary array creation and array validation a significant burden. All of this argues in favor of using the params construct higher up in your stack—in bigger functions that are doing more work.

✗ **DO NOT** use the varargs methods, otherwise known as the ellipsis.

Some CLR languages, such as C++, support an alternative convention for passing variable parameter lists called varargs methods. The convention should not be used in frameworks, because it is not CLS compliant.

> ▪ **RICO MARIANI** Of course "never" in this context means not in the framework APIs—varargs wasn't added lightly to C++. If varargs help you in your internal implementation, by all means use them. Just remember it isn't CLS-compliant, so it's bad form to use it in public APIs.

5.8.5 **Pointer Parameters**

In general, pointers should not appear in the public surface area of a well-designed managed code framework. Most of the time, pointers should be encapsulated. However, in some cases pointers are required for interoperability reasons, and using pointers in such cases is appropriate.

✓ **DO** provide an alternative for any member that takes a pointer argument, because pointers are not CLS-compliant.

```
[CLSCompliant(false)]
public unsafe int GetBytes(char* chars, int charCount,
byte* bytes, int byteCount);

public int GetBytes(char[] chars, int charIndex, int charCount,
byte[] bytes, int byteIndex, int byteCount)
```

✗ **AVOID** doing expensive argument checking of pointer arguments.

In general, argument checking is well worth the cost, but for APIs that are performance-critical enough to require using pointers, the overhead is often not worth it.

> ▪▪ **RICO MARIANI**   This is right in line with my general advice. Put the argument checking at the right level of your abstraction stack. That will get you the best diagnostics at the best price. After you get this close to the metal, those extra tests can be a significant fraction of the job at hand.

✓ **DO** follow common pointer-related conventions when designing members with pointers.

For example, there is no need to pass the start index, because simple pointer arithmetic can be used to accomplish the same result.

```
//Bad practice
public unsafe int GetBytes(char* chars, int charIndex, int charCount,
byte* bytes, int byteIndex, int byteCount)

//Better practice
public unsafe int GetBytes(char* chars, int charCount,
byte* bytes, int byteCount)
```

```
//example callsite
GetBytes(chars + charIndex, charCount, bytes + byteIndex, byteCount);
```

BRAD ABRAMS   For developers working with pointer-based APIs, it is more natural to think of the world with a pointer-oriented mindset. Although it is common in "safe" managed code, in pointer-based code, passing an index is uncommon; it is more natural to use pointer arithmetic.

SUMMARY

This chapter offers comprehensive guidelines for general member design. As you could see from several of the annotations, member design is one of the most complex parts of designing a framework. This is a natural consequence of the richness of concepts related to member design.

The next chapter covers design issues relating to extensibility.

6
Designing for Extensibility

O NE IMPORTANT ASPECT of designing a framework is making sure the extensibility of the framework has been carefully considered. This requires that you understand the costs and benefits associated with various extensibility mechanisms. This chapter helps you decide which of the extensibility mechanisms—subclassing, events, virtual members, callbacks, and so on—can best meet the requirements of your framework. This chapter does not talk about the design details of these mechanisms. Such details are discussed in other parts of the book, and this chapter simply provides cross-references to sections that describe those details.

A good understanding of OOP is a necessary prerequisite to designing an effective framework and, in particular, to understanding the concepts discussed in this chapter. However, we do not cover the basics of object-orientation in this book, because there are already excellent books entirely devoted to the topic. A list of some of them is provided in the Suggested Reading List at the end of the book.

6.1 Extensibility Mechanisms

There are many ways to allow extensibility in frameworks. They range from less powerful but less costly to very powerful but expensive. For any given extensibility requirement, you should choose the least costly extensibility mechanism that meets the requirements. Keep in mind that it's usually possible to add more extensibility later, but you can never take it away without introducing breaking changes.

This section discusses some of the framework extensibility mechanisms in detail.

6.1.1 Unsealed Classes

Sealed classes cannot be inherited from, and they prevent extensibility. In contrast, classes that can be inherited from are called unsealed classes.

```
// string cannot be inherited from
public sealed class String { ... }

// TraceSource can be inherited from
public class TraceSource { ... }
```

Subclasses can add new members, apply attributes, and implement additional interfaces. Although subclasses can access protected members and override virtual members, these extensibility mechanisms result in significantly different costs and benefits. Subclasses are described in sections 6.1.2 and 6.1.4. Adding protected and virtual members to a class can have expensive ramifications if not done with care, so if you are looking for simple, inexpensive extensibility, an unsealed class that does not declare any virtual or protected members is a good way to do it.

✓ **CONSIDER** using unsealed classes with no added virtual or protected members as a great way to provide inexpensive yet much appreciated extensibility to a framework.

Developers often want to inherit from unsealed classes so as to add convenience members such as custom constructors, new methods, or method overloads.[1] For example, System.Messaging.MessageQueue is unsealed and thus allows users to create custom queues that default to a particular queue path or to add custom methods that simplify the API

---

1. Some convenience methods can be added to sealed types as extension methods.

for specific scenarios (in the following example, the scenario is for a method sending Order objects to the queue).

```
public class OrdersQueue : MessageQueue {
    public OrdersQueue() : base(OrdersQueue.Path){
        this.Formatter = new BinaryMessageFormatter();
    }
    public void SendOrder(Order order){
        Send(order,order.Id);
    }
}
```

■ **PHIL HAACK** Because Test-Driven Development has caught fire in the .NET developer community, many developers want to inherit from unsealed classes (often dynamically using a mock framework) in order to substitute a test double in the place of the real implementation.

At the very least, if you've gone to the trouble of making your class unsealed, consider making key members virtual, perhaps via the Template Method Pattern, in order to provide more control.

Classes are unsealed by default in most programming languages, and this is also the recommended default for most classes in frameworks. The extensibility afforded by unsealed types is much appreciated by framework users and quite inexpensive to provide because of relatively low test costs associated with unsealed types.

■ **VANCE MORRISON** The key word in this advice is "CONSIDER." Keep in mind that you always have the option of unsealing a class in the future (it is not a breaking change), but once unsealed, a class must remain unsealed. Also, unsealing does inhibit some optimizations (e.g., converting virtual calls to more efficient nonvirtual calls (and then inlining)). Finally, unsealing only helps your users if they control the creation of the class (sometimes true, sometimes not). In short, designs are only rarely usefully extensible "by accident." Being unsealed is part of the contract of a class and its users, and like everything about the contract deserves to be a conscious, deliberate choice on the part of the designer.

6.1.2 **Protected Members**

Protected members by themselves do not provide any extensibility, but they can make extensibility through subclassing more powerful. They can be used to expose advanced customization options without unnecessarily complicating the main public interface. For example, the `SourceSwitch.Value` property is protected because it is intended for use only in advanced customization scenarios.

```
public class FlowSwitch : SourceSwitch {
    protected override void  OnValueChanged() {
        switch (this.Value) {
            case "None"    : Level = FlowSwitchSetting.None;       break;
            case "Both"    : Level = FlowSwitchSetting.Both;       break;
            case "Entering": Level = FlowSwitchSetting.Entering; break;
            case "Exiting" : Level = FlowSwitchSetting.Exiting;  break;
        }
    }
}
```

Framework designers need to be careful with protected members because the name "protected" can give a false sense of security. Anyone is able to subclass an unsealed class and access protected members, and so all the same defensive coding practices used for public members apply to protected members.

✓ **CONSIDER** using protected members for advanced customization.

Protected members are a great way to provide advanced customization without complicating the public interface.

✓ **DO** treat protected members in unsealed classes as public for the purpose of security, documentation, and compatibility analysis.

Anyone can inherit from a class and access the protected members.

■ **BRAD ABRAMS** Protected members are just as much a part of your publicly callable interface as public members. In designing the Framework, we considered protected and public to be roughly equivalent. We generally did the same level of review and error checking in protected APIs as we did in public APIs because they can be called from any code that just happens to subclass.

6.1.3 Events and Callbacks

Callbacks are extensibility points that allow a framework to call back into user code through a delegate. These delegates are usually passed to the framework through a parameter of a method.

```
List<string> cityNames = ...
cityNames.RemoveAll(delegate(string name) {
    return name.StartsWith("Seattle");
});
```

Events are a special case of callbacks that supports convenient and consistent syntax for supplying the delegate (an event handler). In addition, Visual Studio's statement completion and designers provide help in using event-based APIs.

```
var timer = new Timer(1000);
timer.Elapsed += delegate {
    Console.WriteLine("Time is up!");
};
timerStart();
```

General event design is discussed in section 5.4.

Callbacks and events can be used to provide quite powerful extensibility, comparable to virtual members. At the same time, callbacks, and even more so, events, are more approachable to a broader range of developers because they don't require a thorough understanding of object-oriented design. Also, callbacks can provide extensibility at runtime, while virtual members can only be customized at compile-time.

The main disadvantage of callbacks is that they are more heavyweight than virtual members. The performance of calling through a delegate is worse than it is for calling a virtual member. In addition, delegates are objects and thus affect memory consumption.

You should also be aware that by accepting and calling a delegate, you are executing arbitrary code in the context of your framework. Therefore, a careful analysis of all such callback extensibility points from the security, correctness, and compatibility points of view is required.

✓ **CONSIDER** using callbacks to allow users to provide custom code to be executed by the framework.

✓ **CONSIDER** using events to allow users to customize the behavior of a framework without the need for understanding object-oriented design.

✓ **DO** prefer events over plain callbacks, because they are more familiar to a broader range of developers and are integrated with Visual Studio statement completion.

✗ **AVOID** using callbacks in performance-sensitive APIs.

> ■ **KRZYSZTOF CWALINA**   Delegate calls were made much faster in the CLR 2.0, but they are still about two times slower than direct calls to virtual members. In addition, delegate-based APIs are generally less efficient in terms of memory usage. Having said that, the differences are relatively small and should only matter if the API is called very frequently.

✓ **DO** use the new Func<...>, Action<...>, or Expression<...> types instead of custom delegates, when defining APIs with callbacks.

Func<...> and Action<...> represent generic delegates. The following is how .NET Framework defines them:

```
public delegate void Action()
public delegate void Action<T1, T2>(T1 arg1, T2 arg2)
public delegate void Action<T1, T2, T3>(T1 arg1, T2 arg2, T3 arg3)
public delegate void Action<T1, T2, T3, T4>(T1 arg1, T2 arg2, T3 arg3, T4
arg4)
public delegate TResult Func<TResult>()
public delegate TResult Func<T, TResult>(T arg)
public delegate TResult Func<T1, T2, TResult>(T1 arg1, T2 arg2)
public delegate TResult Func<T1, T2, T3, TResult>(T1 arg1, T2 arg2, T3
arg3)
public delegate TResult Func<T1, T2, T3, T4, TResult>(T1 arg1, T2 arg2, T3
arg3, T4 arg4)
```

They can be used as follows:

```
Func<int,int,double> divide = (x,y)=>(double)x/(double)y;
Action<double> write = (d)=>Console.WriteLine(d);
write(divide(2,3));
```

Expression<...> represents function definitions that can be compiled and subsequently invoked at runtime but can also be serialized and passed to remote processes. Continuing with our example:

```
Expression<Func<int,int,double>> expression =(x,y)=>(double)x/(double)y;
Func<int,int,double> divide = expression.Compile();
write(divide2(2,3));
```

Notice how the syntax for constructing an Expression<> object is very similar to the one used to construct a Func<> object; in fact, the only difference is the static type declaration of the variable (Expression<> instead of Func<...>).

> ■ **RICO MARIANI** Most times you're going to want Func or Action if all that needs to happen is to run some code. You need Expression when the code needs to be analyzed, serialized, or optimized before it is run. Expression is for thinking about code, Func/Action is for running it.

✔ **DO** measure and understand performance implications of using Expression<...>, instead of using Func<...> and Action<...> delegates.

Expression<...> types are in most cases logically equivalent to Func<...> and Action<...> delegates. The main difference between them is that the delegates are intended to be used in local process scenarios; expressions are intended for cases where it's beneficial and possible to evaluate the expression in a remote process or machine.

> ■ **RICO MARIANI** The remoteness of the evaluation is sort of incidental. The main thing about Expressions is that you use them when you are going to need to reason over the code to be executed, often over a composition of expressions such as in a LINQ query, and then, having considered the whole and the execution options, you create some kind of optimized plan for doing the work. This is how LINQ to SQL is able to create a single SQL fragment from a composition of loose-looking expressions.
>
> This plan could easily go wrong. You could do too much analysis of expressions or too little. You could use up too much space holding expression trees or you could avoid all the trees but then find you have bad performance because you have so many small anonymous delegates.

If you look at the patterns that were used in the LINQ implementations in the .NET Framework, you'll see several good ways to make use of these constructs:

- Use expressions only if you need to "think" about the code and not just run it.
- Don't blindly compose and run code that could be meaningfully optimized if you "thought" about it before running it.
- Don't create systems that optimize the code so much before running it that it would have been faster to just run it directly without optimizing.
- Optimization isn't the only use for expression trees, but it is an important one.

✓ **DO** understand that by calling a delegate, you are executing arbitrary code and that could have security, correctness, and compatibility repercussions.

▪▪ **BRIAN PEPIN**   The Windows Forms team bumped up against this issue when writing some of the low-level code in `SystemEvents`. `SystemEvents` defines a static API and therefore needs to be threadsafe. Internally, it uses locks to ensure thread safety. Early code in `SystemEvents` would grab a lock and then raise an event. Here's an example:

```
lock(someInternalLock) {
    if(eventHandler!=null) eventHandler(sender, EventArgs.Empty);
}
```

This is bad because you have no idea what the user code in the event handler is going to do. If the user code signals a thread and waits on its own lock, you might have just introduced a deadlock. This would be better code:

```
EventHandler localHandler = eventHandler;
if(localHandler != null) localHandler(sender, EventArgs.Empty);
```

This way, the user's code will never deadlock due to your own internal implementation. Note that because assignments in managed code are atomic, I didn't need a lock at all in this case. That won't always be true. For example, if your code needed to check more than one variable, you'd still need a lock:

```
EventHandler localHandler = null;
lock(someInternalLock) {
    if (eventHandler != null && shouldRaiseEvents) {
        localHandler = eventHandler;
    }
}
if(localHandler!=null) localHandler(sender,EventArgs.Empty);
```

▪ **JOE DUFFY**   In addition to deadlock, invoking a callback under a lock like this can cause reentrancy. Locks on the CLR support recursive acquires, so if the callback somehow manages to call back into the same object that initiated the callback, the results are often not good. Locks are typically used to isolate invariants that are temporarily broken, and yet this practice can expose them at the reentrant boundary. Needless to say, this is apt to cause weird exceptions and unexpected behavior.

   That said, sometimes this practice is necessary. If the callback is being used to make a decision—as would be the case with a predicate—and that decision needs to be made under a lock, you will have no choice. When unavoidable, be sure to carefully document the restrictions (no inter-thread communication, no reentrancy). And you must ensure that, should a developer violate these restrictions, the result will not lead to security vulnerabilities. The risk here is usually greater than the reward.

6.1.4 Virtual Members

Virtual members can be overridden, thus changing the behavior of the subclass. They are quite similar to callbacks in terms of the extensibility they provide, but they are better in terms of execution performance and memory consumption. Also, virtual members feel more natural in scenarios that require creating a special kind of an existing type (specialization).

   The main disadvantage of virtual members is that the behavior of a virtual member can only be modified at the time of compilation. The behavior of a callback can be modified at runtime.

   Virtual members, like callbacks (and maybe more than callbacks), are costly to design, test, and maintain because any call to a virtual member can be overridden in unpredictable ways and can execute arbitrary code. Also, much more effort is usually required to clearly define the contract of virtual members, so the cost of designing and documenting them is higher.

KRZYSZTOF CWALINA   A common question I get is whether documentation for virtual members should say that the overrides must call the base implementation. The answer is that overrides should preserve the contract of the base class. They can do it by calling the base implementation or by some other means. It is rare that a member can claim that the only way to preserve its contract (in the override) is to call it. In a lot of cases, calling the base might be the easiest way to preserve the contract (and docs should point that out), but it's rarely absolutely required.

Because of the risks and costs, limiting extensibility of virtual members should be considered. Extensibility through virtual members today should be limited to those areas that have a clear scenario requiring extensibility. This section presents guidelines for when to allow it and when and how to limit it.

✗ DO NOT make members virtual unless you have a good reason to do so and you are aware of all the costs related to designing, testing, and maintaining virtual members.

Virtual members are less forgiving in terms of changes that can be made to them without breaking compatibility. Also, they are slower than nonvirtual members, mostly because calls to virtual members are not inlined.

RICO MARIANI   Be sure you understand your extensibility requirements completely before you make decisions in the name of extensibility. A common mistake is sprinkling classes with virtual methods and properties only to find that the needed extensibility still can't be realized and everything is now (and forever) slower.

JAN GRAY   The peril: If you ship types with virtual members, you are promising to forever abide by subtle and complex observable behaviors and subclass interactions. I think framework designers underestimate their peril. For example, we found that `ArrayList` item enumeration calls several virtual methods for each `MoveNext` and `Current`. Fixing those performance problems could (but probably doesn't) break user-defined implementations of virtual members on the `ArrayList` class that are dependent on virtual method call order and frequency.

✓ **CONSIDER** limiting extensibility to only what is absolutely necessary through the use of the Template Method Pattern, described in section 9.9.

✓ **DO** prefer protected accessibility over public accessibility for virtual members. Public members should provide extensibility (if required) by calling into a protected virtual member.

The public members of a class should provide the right set of functionality for direct consumers of that class. Virtual members are designed to be overridden in subclasses, and protected accessibility is a great way to scope all virtual extensibility points to where they can be used.

```
public Control{
   public void SetBounds(...){
   ...
      SetBoundsCore (...);
   }

   protected virtual void SetBoundsCore(...){
      // Do the real work here.
   }
}
```

You can see more on this subject in section 9.9.

▪ **JEFFREY RICHTER**   It is common for a type to define multiple overloaded methods for caller convenience. These methods typically allow the caller to pass fewer arguments to the method and then, internally, the method calls a more complex method, passing additional arguments with good default values. If your type offers convenience methods, these methods should not be virtual, but internally they should call the one virtual method that contains the actual implementation of the method (which can be overridden).

6.1.5 Abstractions (Abstract Types and Interfaces)

An abstraction is a type that describes a contract but does not provide a full implementation of the contract. Abstractions are usually implemented as abstract classes or interfaces, and they come with a well-defined set of reference documentation describing the required semantics of the types implementing the contract. Some of the most important abstractions in the .NET Framework include `Stream`, `IEnumerable<T>`, and `Object`. Section 4.3 discusses how to choose between an interface and a class when designing an abstraction.

You can extend frameworks by implementing a concrete type that supports the contract of an abstraction and using this concrete type with framework APIs consuming (operating on) the abstraction.

A meaningful and useful abstraction that is able to withstand the test of time is very difficult to design. The main difficulty is getting the right set of members, no more and no fewer. If an abstraction has too many members, it becomes difficult or even impossible to implement. If it has too few members for the promised functionality, it becomes useless in many interesting scenarios. Also, abstractions without first-class documentation that clearly spells out all the pre- and post-conditions often end up being failures in the long term. Because of this, abstractions have a very high design cost.

> ■ JEFFREY RICHTER   The `ICloneable` interface is an example of very simple abstraction with a contract that was never explicitly documented. Some types that implement this interface's `Clone` method implement it so that it performs a shallow copy of the object, whereas some implementations perform a deep-copy. Because what this interface's `Clone` method should do was never fully documented, when using an object with a type that implements `ICloneable`, you never know what you're going to get. This makes the interface useless.

Too many abstractions in a framework also negatively affect usability of the framework. It is often quite difficult to understand an abstraction without understanding how it fits into the larger picture of the concrete implementations and the APIs operating on the abstraction. Also, names of abstractions and their members are necessarily abstract, which often makes them cryptic and unapproachable without first understanding the broader context of their usage.

However, abstractions provide extremely powerful extensibility that the other extensibility mechanisms cannot often match. They are at the core of many architectural patterns, such as plug-ins, inversion of control (IoC), pipelines, and so on. They are also extremely important for testability of frameworks. Good abstractions make it possible to stub out heavy dependencies for the purpose of unit testing. In summary, abstractions are responsible for the sought-after richness of the modern object-oriented frameworks.

✗ **DO NOT** provide abstractions unless they are tested by developing several concrete implementations and APIs consuming the abstractions.

> ■ **KRZYSZTOF CWALINA** The PowerCollections project is a framework extending the `System.Collections.Generic` namespace. It has been a great source of feedback and validation for the abstractions contained in the namespace. Based on the feedback, we fixed several design issues that would otherwise probably not have been discovered until after the release, at which point it's usually too late to fix abstractions, because the fixes require breaking changes.

✓ **DO** choose carefully between an abstract class and an interface when designing an abstraction. See section 4.3 for more details on this subject.

✓ **CONSIDER** providing reference tests for concrete implementations of abstractions. Such tests should allow users to test whether their implementations correctly implement the contract.

> ■ **JEFFREY RICHTER** I like what the Windows Forms team did: They defined an interface called `System.ComponentModel.IComponent`. Of course, any type can implement this interface. But the Windows Forms team also provided a `System.ComponentModel.Component` class that implements the `IComponent` interface. So a type could choose to derive from `Component` and get the implementation for free, or the type could derive from a different base class and then manually implement the `IComponent` interface. By having available an interface and a base class, developers get to choose whichever works best for them.

6.2 Base Classes

Strictly speaking, a class becomes a base class when another class is derived from it. For the purpose of this section, however, a base class is a class designed mainly to provide a common abstraction or for other classes to reuse some default implementation though inheritance. Base classes usually sit in the middle of inheritance hierarchies, between an abstraction at the root of a hierarchy and several custom implementations at the bottom.

They serve as implementation helpers for implementing abstractions. For example, one of the Framework's abstractions for ordered collections of items is the `IList<T>` interface. Implementing `IList<T>` is not trivial, and therefore the Framework provides several base classes, such as `Collection<T>` and `KeyedCollection<TKey,TItem>`, which serve as helpers for implementing custom collections.

```
public class OrderCollection : Collection<Order> {
    protected override void SetItem(int index, Order item) {
        if(item==null) throw new ArgumentNullException(...);
        base.SetItem(index,item);
    }
}
```

Base classes are usually not suited to serve as abstractions by themselves, because they tend to contain too much implementation. For example, the `Collection<T>` base class contains lots of implementation related to the fact that it implements the nongeneric `IList` interface (to integrate better with nongeneric collections) and to the fact that it is a collection of items stored in memory in one of its fields.

> ■■ **KRZYSZTOF CWALINA**   `Collection<T>` can also be used directly, without the need to create subclasses, but its main purpose is to provide an easy way to implement custom collections.

As previously discussed, base classes can provide invaluable help for users who need to implement abstractions, but at the same time they can be a significant liability. They add surface area and increase the depth of inheritance hierarchies and so conceptually complicate the framework. Therefore, base classes should be used only if they provide significant value to the users of the framework. They should be avoided if they provide value only to the implementers of the framework, in which case delegation to an internal implementation instead of inheritance from a base class should be strongly considered.

✓ **CONSIDER** making base classes abstract even if they don't contain any abstract members. This clearly communicates to the users that the class is designed solely to be inherited from.

✓ **CONSIDER** placing base classes in a separate namespace from the mainline scenario types. By definition, base classes are intended for advanced extensibility scenarios and therefore are not interesting to the majority of users. See section 2.2.4 for details.

✗ **AVOID** naming base classes with a "Base" suffix if the class is intended for use in public APIs.

For example, despite the fact that `Collection<T>` is designed to be inherited from, in many cases frameworks expose APIs typed as the base class, not as its subclasses, mainly because of the cost associated with a new public type.

```
public Directory {
    public Collection<string> GetFilenames(){
        return new FilenameCollection(this);
    }

    private class FilenameCollection : Collection<string> {
        ...
    }
}
```

The fact that `Collection<T>` is a base class is irrelevant for the user of the `GetFilename` method, so the "Base" suffix would only create an unnecessary distraction for the user of the method.

6.3 Sealing

One of the features of object-oriented frameworks is that developers can extend and customize them in ways unanticipated by the framework designers. This is both the power and danger of extensible design. When you design your framework, it is, therefore, very important to carefully design for extensibility when it is desired, and to limit extensibility when it is dangerous.

> ◾ **KRZYSZTOF CWALINA** Sometimes framework designers want to limit the extensibility of a type hierarchy to a fixed set of classes. For example, let's say you want to create a hierarchy of living organisms that is split into two and only two subgroups: animals and plants. One way to do it is to make the constructor of LivingOrganism internal and then provide two subclasses (Plant and Animal) in the same assembly and give them protected constructors. Because the constructor of LivingOrganism is internal, third parties can only extend Animal and Plant, but not LivingOrganism.
>
> ```
> public class LivingOrganism {
>     internal LivingOrganism(){}
>     ...
> }
> public class Animal : LivingOrganism {
>     protected Animal() {}
>     ...
> }
> public class Plant : LivingOrganism {
>     protected Plant() {}
>     ...
> }
> ```

A powerful mechanism that prevents extensibility is sealing. You can seal either the class or individual members. Sealing a class prevents users from inheriting from the class. Sealing a member prevents users from overriding a particular member.

```
public class NonNullCollection<T> : Collection<T> {
    protected sealed override void SetItem(int index, T item) {
        if(item==null) throw new ArgumentNullException();
        base.SetItem(index,item);
    }
}
```

Because one of the key differentiating points of frameworks is that they offer some degree of extensibility, sealing classes and members will likely feel very abrasive to developers using your framework. Therefore, you should seal only when there are good reasons to do so.

✗ **DO NOT** seal classes without having a good reason to do so.

Sealing a class because you cannot think of an extensibility scenario is not a good reason. Framework users like to inherit from classes for various nonobvious reasons, like adding convenience members. See section 6.1.1 for examples of nonobvious reasons users want to inherit from a type.

Good reasons for sealing a class include the following:

- The class is a static class. For more information on static classes, see section 4.5.
- The class stores security-sensitive secrets in inherited protected members.
- The class inherits many virtual members and the cost of sealing them individually would outweigh the benefits of leaving the class unsealed.
- The class is an attribute that requires very fast runtime look-up. Sealed attributes have slightly higher performance levels than unsealed ones. For more information on attribute design, see section 8.2.

▪ **BRAD ABRAMS**   Having classes that are open to some level of customization is one of the core differences between a framework and a library. With an API library (such as the Win32 API), you basically get what you get. It is very difficult to extend the data structures and APIs. With a framework such as MFC or AWT, clients can extend and customize the classes. The productivity boost from this is obvious.

▪ **KRZYSZTOF CWALINA**   People often ask what the cost of sealing individual members is. The cost is relatively small, but it is nonzero and should be taken into account. There is development cost (typing in the overrides), testing cost (have you called the base class from the override?), assembly size cost (new overrides), and working set cost (if both the overrides and the base implementation are ever called).

✗ **DO NOT** declare protected or virtual members on sealed types.

By definition, sealed types cannot be inherited from. This means that protected members on sealed types cannot be called, and virtual methods on sealed types cannot be overridden.

✓ **CONSIDER** sealing members that you override.

```
public class FlowSwitch : SourceSwitch {
    protected sealed override void  OnValueChanged() {
       ...
    }
}
```

Problems that can result from introducing virtual members (discussed in section 6.1.4) apply to overrides as well, although to a slightly lesser degree. Sealing an override shields you from these problems starting from that point in the inheritance hierarchy.

In short, part of designing for extensibility is knowing when to limit it, and sealed types are one of the mechanisms by which to do that.

SUMMARY

Designing for extensibility is a critical aspect of designing frameworks. Understanding the costs and benefits provided by various extensibility mechanisms permits the design of frameworks that are flexible without many of the pitfalls that lead to trouble later.

7

Exceptions

EXCEPTION HANDLING HAS many advantages over return-value-based error reporting. Good framework design helps the application developer realize the benefits of exceptions. This section discusses the benefits of exceptions and presents guidelines for using them effectively.

Exception handling offers the following benefits:

- Exceptions integrate well with object-oriented languages. Object-oriented languages tend to impose constraints on member signatures that are not imposed by functions in non-OO languages. For example, in the case of constructors, operator overloads, and properties, the developer has no choice in the return value. For this reason, it is not possible to standardize on return-value-based error reporting for object-oriented frameworks. An error reporting method, such as exceptions, which is out of band of the method signature is the only option.

JEFFREY RICHTER From my perspective, this is the most important reason why exceptions must be used to report problems. In an OO system (like .NET), return codes could not be used for certain constructs, and an out-of-band mechanism must be used. Now the question becomes whether to use exceptions for everything or to use them for the special constructs and use return codes for methods. Obviously, having two different error reporting mechanisms is worse than having one, so it should be obvious that exceptions should be used to report all errors for all code constructs.

■ **CHRIS SELLS**   Jeff is right: Always use exceptions for communicating errors and never use them for anything else.

- Exceptions promote API consistency. This is because they are designed to be used for failure reporting and nothing else. In contrast, return values have many uses, of which failure reporting is only a subset. For this reason, it is likely that APIs that report failure through return values will find a number of patterns, whereas exceptions can be constrained to specific patterns. The Win32 API is a clear example of this inconsistency through usage of BOOLs, HRESULTS, and GetLastError, among others.
- With return-value-based error reporting, error handling code is always very near to the code that could fail. However, with exception handling the application developer has a choice. Code can be written to catch exceptions near the failure point, or the handling code can be centralized by locating it further up in the call stack.
- Error handling code is more easily localized. Very robust code that reports failure through return values tends to have an if-statement for nearly every functional line of code. The job of these if-statements is to handle the failure case. With exception-based error reporting, robust code can often be written so that a number of methods and operations can be performed with the error handling logic grouped just after the try block or even higher in the call stack.

■ **STEVEN CLARKE**   In one API usability study we performed, developers had to call an `Insert` method to insert one or more records into a database. If the method did not throw an exception, the implication was that the records had been inserted successfully. However, this wasn't clear to participants in the study. They expected the method to return the number of records that were successfully inserted. Although return codes should not be used to indicate failure, you can still consider returning status information in the case of a successful operation.

- Error codes can be easily ignored, and often are. Exceptions, on the other hand, take an active role in the flow of your code. This makes failures reported as exceptions impossible to ignore and improves the robustness of code.

■ **JEFFREY RICHTER**   It should be pointed out that this means that more bugs are caught during the testing of your code and that the code that ships will be more robust. Also, because the shipping code is more robust, there will probably be very few exceptions that get thrown when the shipping code is running out in the wild.

For example, the Win32 API `CloseHandle` fails very rarely, so it is common (and appropriate) for many applications to ignore the return value of the API. However, if any application has a bug that causes `CloseHandle` to be called twice on the same handle, it would not be obvious unless the code was written to test the return value. A managed equivalent to this API would throw an exception in this case, and the unhandled exception handler would log the failure and the bug would be found.

■ **BRAD ABRAMS**   With the return-code error handling model, if the API you are calling fails, the program will muddle on with incorrect results, causing your program to crash or corrupt data at some point in the future. With the exception handling model, when an error occurs the thread is suspended and the calling code is given a chance to handle the exception. When that method doesn't handle the exception, the method that calls it is given a chance to handle it. When no method up the stack handles the exception, your application is terminated. It is better to terminate the application than to let it muddle on—at least the error is eventually fixed.

JEFFREY RICHTER   I completely agree with Brad here. There are also potential security issues that could come up when you let a program continue to run after something fails. I know there are a lot of programmers who do not want their application to crash out in the field, and they are willing to do almost anything to stop that from happening—like swallow exceptions and let the program continue to run. But this is absolutely the wrong thing to do; it is much better for a program to crash than to continue running with unpredictable behavior and potential security vulnerabilities. Many other examples exist. For examples, Windows blue screens occur due to an unhandled exception in kernel-mode code. If a kernel-mode operation fails unexpectedly (an unhandled exception), then Windows doesn't want to just keep running, so it blue screens, all applications are stopped, and all data in memory is lost. In fact, all Microsoft applications, such as Office and Visual Studio, display dialog boxes when they experience an unhandled exception, and they terminate the application. The operating system and these applications are doing the right thing: Do not let your application keep running in the case of an unexpected failure.

BRENT RECTOR   A corollary to the preceding is that your application should handle only those exceptions that it understands. It is generally impossible to restore the possibly corrupted state of an application to a normal state after "something" has gone wrong. Handle only those exceptions for which your application can respond reasonably. Let all others go unhandled and let the operating system terminate your application.

- Exceptions can carry very rich information describing the cause of the failure.

- Exceptions allow for unhandled exception handlers. Ideally, every application is written to intelligently handle all forms of failure. However, this is unrealistic, because all forms of failure can't be known. With error codes, unexpected failures can be easily ignored by calling code, and the application continues to run with undefined results. With well-written exception-based code, unexpected failures eventually cause an unhandled exception handler to be called. This handler can be designed to log the failure and can also make the choice to shut down the application. This is by far preferable to running with indeterminate results and also provides for logging that makes it possible to add more significant error handling for the previously unexpected case. For example, Microsoft Office uses an unhandled exception handler to gracefully recover and relaunch the application, as well as to send error information to Microsoft to improve the product.

> **■ CHRISTOPHER BRUMME** You should have a custom unhandled exception handler only if you have application-specific work to do in the handler. If you just want error reporting to occur, the runtime will handle that automatically for you, and you do not need to (and should not) use an unhandled exception filter (UEF). An application should only register a UEF if it can provide functionality above and beyond the standard error reporting that comes with the system and runtime.

> **■ JEFFREY RICHTER** In addition to what Chris says, only applications should even think about using a UEF. Components should not be using one of these at all. UEFs are always application-model-specific. In other words, a Windows Form application will probably pop up a window, a Windows NT service will probably log to the event log, and a Web service will probably send a SOAP fault. The component doesn't know in which application model it is being used, and therefore components should leave this up to the application developer who is using their component.

- Exceptions promote instrumentation. Exceptions are a well-defined method-failure model. Because of this, it is possible for tools such as debuggers, profilers, performance counters, and others to be intimately aware of exceptions. For example, the Performance Monitor keeps track of exception statistics, and debuggers can be instructed to break when an exception is thrown. Methods that return failure do not share in the benefits of instrumentation.

> **■ BRAD ABRAMS** It is worthwhile to note that the exception handling feature can easily be defeated by poorly designed frameworks. If the framework designer chooses to use return codes for error handling, none of the benefits apply.

7.1 Exception Throwing

Exception-throwing guidelines described in this section require a good definition of the meaning of execution failure. Execution failure occurs whenever a member cannot do what it was designed to do (what the member name implies). For example, if the `OpenFile` method cannot return an opened file handle to the caller, it would be considered an execution failure.

> **KRZYSZTOF CWALINA**   One of the biggest misconceptions about exceptions is that they are for "exceptional conditions." The reality is that they are for communicating error conditions. From a framework design perspective, there is no such thing as an "exceptional condition." Whether a condition is exceptional or not depends on the context of usage, but reusable libraries rarely know how they will be used. For example, `OutOfMemoryException` might be exceptional for a simple data entry application; it's not so exceptional for applications doing their own memory management (e.g., SQL Server). In other words, one man's exceptional condition is another man's chronic condition.

Most developers have become comfortable with using exceptions for usage errors such as division by zero or null references. In the Framework, exceptions are used for all error conditions, including execution errors. At first, it can be difficult to embrace exception handling as the means of reporting all failures. However, it is important to design all public methods of a framework to report method failures by throwing an exception.

There are a variety of excuses for not using exceptions, but most boil down to the two perceptions that exception handling syntax is undesirable, so returning an error code is somehow preferable, or that a thrown exception does not perform as well as returning an error code. The performance concerns are addressed in sections 7.5.1 and 7.5.2. The concern over syntax is largely a matter of familiarity. We recognize that developers who are new to exceptions find the syntax awkward, but this becomes much less of a problem over time as developers get used to exception handling.

▪▪ **JEFFREY RICHTER**   In addition, different programming languages will offer different syntax for developers to express exception handling. Even for existing languages, like C#, new syntax could be provided in the future. Or code editors could spit out the code, making the coding a little less tedious. Certainly, I agree that syntax should not be a factor in determining exception usage.

✗ **DO NOT** return error codes.

Exceptions are the primary means of reporting errors in frameworks. The beginning section of the chapter describes the benefits of exceptions in detail.

▪▪ **KRZYSZTOF CWALINA**   It's OK for exceptions to have a property returning some kind of error code, but I would be very careful about this. Each exception can carry two main pieces of information: the exception message explaining to the developer what went wrong and how to fix it, and the exception type that should be used by handlers to decide what programmatic action to take. If you think you need to have a property on your exception that would return additional error code, ask yourself who this code is for. Is it for the developer or for the exception handler? If for the developer, add additional information to the message. If for the handlers, add a new exception type.

▪▪ **CHRISTOPHE NASARRE**   The error code property in a System. Exception is useful when you need to bind the issue to external documentation that details how to fix the problem. This is particularly important with different layers of a framework where the upper layer does not always (and should not) know how the lower layer is implemented. For example, a Web service call could get an exception because the associated database on the server is not started. In that case, you don't expect the client code to explain how to restart the database when the exception is caught. Instead, you provide a pointer to the documentation and the right section where the whole restarting process is explained.

✓ **DO** report execution failures by throwing exceptions.

If a member cannot successfully do what it is designed to do, it should be considered an execution failure, and an exception should be thrown.

> ■■ **JASON CLARK**   A good rule of thumb is that if a method does not do what its name suggests, it should be considered a method-level failure, resulting in an exception. For example, a method called `ReadByte` should throw if there are no more bytes left in a stream to be read. Meanwhile, a method named `ReadChar` should not throw when it reaches end of stream, because EOF is a valid char (in most character sets) that can be returned in this case while still achieving what the method's name suggests. So a char can be "read" successfully at the end of a stream, whereas a byte cannot.

✓ **CONSIDER** terminating the process by calling `System.Environment.FailFast` (.NET Framework 2.0 feature) instead of throwing an exception if your code encounters a situation where it is unsafe for further execution.

> ■■ **CHRISTOPHER BRUMME**   An example of the operating system performing a fail fast occurs when the stack is so corrupt that the operating system cannot propagate exceptions through it. In this case, the invariant expectations of the application (i.e., that exceptions propagate) can no longer be satisfied, so the application must terminate.
>
> An example of the CLR performing a fail fast occurs when the GC heap is so corrupt that we can no longer track managed objects. In this case, a process-wide resource is required for further processing, but it is now corrupt and cannot be returned to a functional state.
>
> Similar legitimate reasons for fail fast can occur in managed code. For example, if the application cannot revert a security impersonation on a thread (i.e., exceptions are thrown from `WindowsImpersonationContext.Dispose`), that thread must be doomed. But if there is no good way for the application to ensure that no more code runs on this thread, perhaps because it is the Finalizer thread or a ThreadPool thread, then the process must be destroyed. `Environment.FailFast` can be used for this purpose.

✗ **DO NOT** use exceptions for the normal flow of control, if possible.

Except for system failures and operations with potential race conditions, framework designers should design APIs so users can write code that does not throw exceptions. For example, you can provide a way to check preconditions before calling a member so users can write code that does not throw exceptions.

```
ICollection<int> collection = ...
if(!collection.IsReadOnly){
   collection.Add(additionalNumber);
}
```

The member used to check preconditions of another member is often referred to as a tester, and the member that actually does the work is called a doer. See section 7.5.1 for more information on the Tester-Doer Pattern.

There are cases when the Tester-Doer Pattern can have an unacceptable performance overhead. In such cases, the so-called Try-Parse Pattern should be considered (see section 7.5.2 for more information).

JEFFREY RICHTER This pattern should be used with caution. The potential problem occurs when you have multiple threads accessing the object at the same time. For example, one thread could execute the tester method, which reports that all is OK, and before the doer method executes, another thread could change the object, causing the doer to fail. Although this pattern might improve performance, it introduces race conditions and must be used with extreme caution.

✓ **CONSIDER** the performance implications of throwing exceptions. Throw rates above 100 per second are likely to noticeably impact the performance of most applications. See section 7.5 for details.

✓ **DO** document all exceptions thrown by publicly callable members because of a violation of the member contract (rather than a system failure) and treat them as part of your contract.

Exceptions that are a part of the contract should not change from one version to the next (i.e., exception type should not change, and new exceptions should not be added).

✗ **DO NOT** have public members that can either throw or not based on some option.

```
// bad design
public Type GetType(string name, bool throwOnError)
```

> ■ **BRAD ABRAMS**   An API such as this one usually reflects the inability of the framework designer to make a decision. A method either completes successfully or it does not, in which case it should throw an exception. Failure to decide forces the decision on the caller of the API, who likely does not have enough context on implementation details of the API to make an informed decision.

✗ **DO NOT** have public members that return exceptions as the return value or an out parameter.

Returning exceptions from public APIs instead of throwing them defeats many of the benefits of exception-based error reporting.

```
// bad design
public Exception DoSomething() { ... }
```

✓ **CONSIDER** using exception builder methods.

It is common to throw the same exception from different places. To avoid code bloat, use helper methods that create exceptions and initialize their properties.

Also, members that throw exceptions are not getting inlined. Moving the throw statement inside the builder might allow the member to be inlined. For example:

```
class File{
   string fileName;

   public byte[] Read(int bytes){
      if (!ReadFile(handle, bytes)) ThrowNewFileIOException(...);
   }
```

```
void ThrowNewFileIOException(...){
   string description = // build localized string
   throw new FileIOException(description);
}
}
```

✗ **DO NOT** throw exceptions from exception filter blocks.

When an exception filter raises an exception, the exception is caught by the CLR, and the filter returns false. This behavior is indistinguishable from the filter executing and returning false explicitly and is therefore very difficult to debug.

```
' VB sample
' This is bad design. The exception filter (When clause)
' may throw an exception when the InnerException property
' returns null
Try
   ...
Catch e As ArgumentException _
When e.InnerException.Message.StartsWith("File")
   ...
End Try
```

▪ **KRZYSZTOF CWALINA** Not all CLR languages support exception filters. For example, Visual Basic .NET and C++ support exception filters, but C# does not.

✗ **AVOID** explicitly throwing exceptions from finally blocks. Implicitly thrown exceptions resulting from calling methods that throw are acceptable.

This section covered the general issues on throwing exceptions. The next section deals with how to decide which type of exception to throw.

7.2 Choosing the Right Type of Exception to Throw

After you have decided when you need to throw exceptions, the next step is to pick the right type of exception to throw. This section provides those guidelines.

You should first decide whether the error condition represents a usage error or an execution error.

A usage error represents an incorrectly written program and is something that can be avoided by changing the code that calls your API. There is no reason to programmatically handle usage errors; instead the calling code should be changed. For example, if a routine gets into an error state when a null is passed as one of its arguments (an error condition usually represented by an `ArgumentNullException`), the calling code can be modified to ensure that null is never passed. In other words, usage errors can be fixed at compile-time, and the developer can ensure that they never occur at runtime.

An execution error is something that cannot be completely avoided by writing "better" code. For example, `File.Open` throws `FileNotFoundException` when it tries to open a file that does not exist. Even if the caller of the API checks whether the file exists before calling `File.Open`, the file can get deleted or corrupted between the call to `File.Exists` and the call to `File.Open`.

Execution errors need to be further divided into two groups: program errors and system failures.

A program error is an execution error that can be handled programmatically. For example, if `File.Open` throws `FileNotFoundException`, the calling code can catch the exception and handle it by creating a new file. This is in contrast to the usage error example described earlier where you would never write code that first passes an argument to a method, catches the `NullArgumentException`, and in the handler calls the method with a non-null argument.

A system failure is an execution error that cannot be handled programmatically. For example, you really cannot handle an out-of-memory exception resulting from the Just-in-Time (JIT) compiler running out of memory.[1]

✗ **DO NOT** create new exception types to communicate usage errors. Throw one of the existing Framework exceptions instead. See section 7.3 for detailed usage guidelines for the most common standard exception types.

Usage errors need to be communicated to the developer calling the API and should not be handled directly in code. The exception type is

---

1. And so by default the CLR shuts down the process in such case instead of throwing an exception.

generally less important to developers trying to fix their code than the message string. Therefore, for exceptions that are thrown as a result of usage errors, you should concentrate on designing a really good (i.e., explanatory) exception message and using one of the existing .NET Framework exception types: `ArgumentNullException`, `Argument-Exception`, `InvalidOperationException`, `NotSupportedException`, and so on.

> ■ **JASON CLARK**   This guideline should be followed with great caution. The exception's type is an "identity" for a type of failure. If code in the application catches the exception, its mitigation is going to be custom-made for failures of a particular nature. If you reuse an exception type simply because it has a relevant-sounding name, then you will probably have trouble down the road. Some exceptions have extremely clear meanings and are meant to be rethrown by all managed code; `ArgumentException` and its inheritors are good examples of this. Some virtual methods specify specific exceptions that you should throw to indicate certain expected failures to the caller. But most often you should be throwing your own exception types if you expect callers to handle the exception in a unique way.

✓ **CONSIDER** creating and throwing custom exceptions if you have a program error condition that can be programmatically handled in a different way than any other existing exception. Otherwise, throw one of the existing exceptions. See section 7.4 for details on creating custom exceptions.

Program errors are errors that can be, and often are, handled in code. The way to handle such errors is to catch the exception and execute some "compensating" logic. Whether the catch statement executes is determined by the type of the exception the catch block claims it can handle. This means that a program error is an error condition (actually the only error condition) where the exception type matters, and so you should consider creating a new exception type.

If you think you are dealing with a program error, validate this belief by actually writing code or describing very precisely what the catch handler would do when it catches the exception to allow the program to continue its execution. If you cannot describe it, or if the error can be avoided by changing the calling code, you are probably dealing with a usage error or a system failure.

✗ DO NOT create a new exception type if the exception would not be handled differently than an existing Framework exception. Throw the existing Framework exception in such case. See section 7.3 for detailed usage guidelines for the most common standard exception types.

Of course, the existing exception type must make sense for your error condition. For example, you don't want to throw `FileNotFound-Exception` from an API unrelated to accessing files.

Also, make sure that reusing the exception will not make an error condition ambiguous. That is, make sure that the code that wants to handle the specific error will always be able to tell whether the exception was thrown because of the error or because of some other error that happens to use the same exception. For example, you don't want to throw (reuse) `FileNotFoundException` from a routine that calls Framework's file I/O APIs, and so can throw the same exception, unless it does not matter to the calling code whether your code or the Framework threw the exception.

✓ DO create a new exception type to communicate a unique program error that cannot be communicated using an existing Framework exception. See section 7.4 for details on creating custom exceptions.

> **■■ KRZYSZTOF CWALINA** Keep in mind that it's not a breaking change to change an exception your code throws to a subtype of that exception. For example, if the first version of your framework throws `FooException`, in any future version of your library, you can start throwing a subtype for `FooException` without breaking code that was compiled against the previous version of your library. This means, when in doubt, I would consider not creating new exception types until you are sure you need them. At that point, you can create a new exception type by inheriting from the currently thrown type. Sometimes it might result in slightly strange exception hierarchy (for example, a custom exception inheriting from `InvalidOperation-Exception`), but it's not a big deal in comparison to the cost of having unnecessary exception types in your library, which makes the library more complex, adds development cost, increases working set, and so on.

✗ **AVOID** creating APIs that when called can result in a system failure. If such a failure can occur, call `Environment.FailFast` instead of throwing an exception when the system failure occurs.

System failures are errors that cannot be handled by the developer or the program. The good thing is that system failures are extremely rare in reusable libraries. They are mostly caused by the execution engine. The best way to shut down a process in such cases is to call `Environment.FailFast`, which logs the state of the system, something that is very useful in diagnosing the problem.

✗ **DO NOT** create and throw new exceptions just to have your team's exception.

✓ **DO** throw the most specific (the most derived) exception that makes sense.

For example, throw `ArgumentNullException` and not its base type, `ArgumentException`, if a null argument is passed.

> ■ **JEFFREY RICHTER**   Throwing `System.Exception`, the base class of all CLS-compliant exceptions, is always the wrong thing to do.

> ■ **BRENT RECTOR**   As described in more detail later, catching `System.Exception` is nearly always the wrong thing to do as well.

Now that you have chosen the correct exception type, you can focus on ensuring that the error message your exception delivers says what you need it to say.

7.2.1 **Error Message Design**

The guidelines in this section define best practices for creating the exception message text.

✓ **DO** provide a rich and meaningful message text targeted at the developer when throwing an exception.

The message should explain the cause of the exception and clearly describe what needs to be done to avoid the exception.

> ■■ **BRAD ABRAMS** This guideline applies to frameworks. It is likely quite appropriate in application code for the exception message to be targeted at an admin or even an end user. The high-level advice is that the message text should be targeted at whoever will have to make sense out of it.

✓ **DO** ensure that exception messages are grammatically correct.

Top-level exception handlers can show the exception message to application end users.

✓ **DO** ensure that each sentence of the message text ends with a period.

This way, code that displays exception messages to the user does not have to handle the case in which a developer forgot the final period, which is relatively cumbersome and expensive.

✗ **AVOID** question marks and exclamation points in exception messages.

✗ **DO NOT** disclose security-sensitive information in exception messages without demanding appropriate permissions.

✓ **CONSIDER** localizing the exception messages thrown by your components if you expect your components to be used by developers speaking different languages.

> ■■ **JEFFREY RICHTER** Exception messages are not relevant when an exception is handled; they only come into play when an exception is unhandled. An unhandled exception indicates a real bug in the application because the application will be terminated. The only way to fix the application now is to have the failure reported, the source code modified, recompiled, and to update the deployments in the field. So the error messages should be geared toward helping developers fix bugs in their code. End users should not see these messages. When a Microsoft Office application gets an unhandled exception, all the dialog box says is something like this: "Microsoft Word has encountered a problem and needs to close. We are sorry for the inconvenience." There is a bit more to the message, but there is nothing computerese in the message. The user does have the option of clicking a button that will show them what's in the error report that gets sent back to Microsoft, and this error report is very geeky.

7.2.2 Exception Handling

Having decided when to throw exceptions, their type, and the message design, the next thing to focus on is how to handle exceptions. First, let's define some terminology. You handle an exception when you have a catch block for a specific exception type and you fully understand the implications of continuing execution of the application after executing the catch block; for example, if you try to open a configuration file, catch `FileNotFoundException` if the file is not present, and fall back to the default configuration. You swallow an exception when you catch a very generic type of exception (usually) and without fully understanding or responding to the failure continue with the execution of the application.

✗ **DO NOT** swallow errors by catching nonspecific exceptions, such as `System.Exception`, `System.SystemException`, and so on, in framework code.

```
try{
    File.Open(...);
}
catch(Exception e){ } // swallow "all" exceptions - don't do this!
```

A legitimate reason for catching a nonspecific exception is so that you can transfer that exception to another thread. This can happen, for example, when a GUI application transfers an operation to the UI thread, when doing asynchronous programming, using thread pool operations, and so on. Obviously, if you are transferring an exception to another thread, you aren't actually swallowing it.

> ■ **JOE DUFFY**   When transferring exceptions across threads, it is imperative that you have put safeguards in place that prevent the exception from getting missed. For example, if you catch the exception and stuff it into a list that no other thread in the system ever gets around to checking, you have essentially swallowed it. And the effects can be as disastrous as ignoring an error code in Win32.

✗ **AVOID** swallowing errors by catching nonspecific exceptions, such as `System.Exception`, `System.SystemException`, and so on, in application code.

There are cases when swallowing errors in applications is acceptable, but such cases are rare.

If you decide to swallow exceptions, you must realize that you don't know exactly what went wrong, so you generally cannot predict what state might now be inconsistent. By swallowing exceptions, you are making a trade-off that the value of continuing to execute code in this application domain or process exceeds the risk of executing in the face of inconsistencies. Because a security attack might be able to exploit those inconsistencies, your decision here has deep consequences.

■ **VANCE MORRISON** There is surprisingly little you can do when catching an exception unless you know the following:

- Exactly what component threw it, and what the contract was (what state the object was left in).
- The WHOLE call stack between the thrower and the catcher, and you have determined that every method in that stack properly cleaned up any global state changes before returning.

If you don't know these two items, then you don't know that some global state has been left in a "half done" state, which will cause strange errors if the program continues. This is *especially* true for exceptions like `OutOfMemoryException`, `StackOverflowException`, or `ThreadAbortException`, which can happen in a great many places.

In practice, you don't know the whole call stack unless the caller and the thrower are right next to each other. This means that if you are trying to catch "any" exception, you should not continue execution. You should only be doing things like error logging and persisting critical information as a prelude to shutting down (and possibly relaunching the process). These latter operations are best done in a finally block.

✗ **DO NOT** exclude any special exceptions when catching for the purpose of transferring exceptions.

```
catch (Exception e) {
    // bad code
    // do not do this!
```

```
    if (e is StackOverflowException ||
        e is OutOfMemoryException ||
        e is ThreadAbortException
    ) throw;
    ...
}
```

> ■ **BRAD ABRAMS** There are some sets of exceptions that quite frankly can't be legitimately handled. Exceptions such as `StackOverflowException`, for example, are thrown by the runtime for fatal conditions. However, it is not recommended that you put special case code in every catch clause as just shown because such code is hard to maintain and prone to errors.

✓ **CONSIDER** catching a specific exception when you understand why it was thrown in a given context and can respond to the failure programmatically.

> ■ **JEFFREY RICHTER** You should only catch an exception when you know you can gracefully recover from it. When performing some operation, you might know why an exception was thrown, but if you don't know how you'd recover from it, do not catch it.

✗ **DO NOT** overcatch. Exceptions should often be allowed to propagate up the call stack.

> ■ **JEFFREY RICHTER** This can't be stressed enough. Far too many times I've seen developers catch an exception, which basically hides a bug that is in their program. Do not catch; flush out the bugs during testing and ship a better, more robust product.

> ■ **ERIC GUNNERSON** Exception handling is robust by default—every exception that is thrown will propagate up, looking for a handler. Every place you write an exception handler is a chance for you to remove robustness from the system, and if you make a mistake it will often be hard to track down. So be minimal about it.

✓ **DO** use try-finally and avoid using try-catch for cleanup code. In well-written exception code, try-finally is far more common than try-catch.

It might seem counterintuitive at first, but catch blocks are not needed in a surprising number of cases. On the other hand, you should always consider whether try-finally could be of use for cleanup to ensure a consistent state of the system when an exception is thrown. Usually, the cleanup logic rolls back resource allocations.

```
FileStream stream = null;
try{
    stream = new FileStream(...);
    ...
}finally{
    if(stream != null) stream.Close();
}
```

C# and VB.NET[2] provide the using statement, which can be used instead of plain try-finally to clean up objects implementing the IDisposable interface.

```
using(var stream = new FileStream(...)){
    ...
}
```

■ **CHRISTOPHER BRUMME** If you use catch clauses for cleanup, you should know that any code that comes after the end of the catch might not be executed. In CLR 2.0, the finally and catch blocks get special protection from thread aborts. Code after a catch does not.

■ **BRENT RECTOR** Don't use catch blocks for cleanup code. Use catch blocks for error recovery code and finally blocks for cleanup code. A catch block only runs when an exception of a particular type occurs within the try block. A finally block always runs. If you always need to clean up (the typical case), you need to perform that logic in a finally block.

---

2. The using statement was added to VB.NET in the Visual Studio 2005 release.

▪▪ **JEFFREY RICHTER** I completely agree with this guideline. I recommend that almost all cleanup code go inside finally blocks, and it is quite convenient that C# and VB.NET offer many language constructs that emit try-finally blocks automatically for you. Examples are C#/VB's using statement, C#'s lock statement, VB's SyncLock statement, C#'s foreach statement, and VB's For Each statement. In addition, when you define a finalizer in C#, the compiler makes sure that the base class's `Finalize` is called by placing the call within a finally block. In fact, I have designed many of my own types to have methods that return an `IDisposable` object so that they can be easily used with C#/VB's using statement.

✓ **DO** prefer using an empty throw when catching and rethrowing an exception. This is the best way to preserve the exception call stack.

```
public void DoSomething(FileStream file){
    long position = file.Position;
    try{
        ... // do some reading with the file
    }catch{
        file.Position = position; // unwind on failure
        throw; // rethrow
    }
}
```

▪▪ **CHRISTOPHER BRUMME** Every time you catch and throw and rethrow, you impact the debuggability of the system. Debugging of exceptions is based on the notion that we detect exceptions going unhandled during the first pass, when no state changes have occurred. By attaching a debugger at that time, we see the state at the time when the exception was thrown. If there is a series of catch and throw and rethrow segments up the stack, then debugging might be limited to inspecting the very last segment. This is an arbitrary distance from the original fault. The same state changes will reduce the effectiveness of Watson dumps.

▪▪ **JEFFREY RICHTER** In addition, when you throw a new exception (versus rethrowing the original exception), you are reporting a different failure than the failure that actually occurred. This also hurts your ability to debug the application. Therefore, always prefer a rethrow to a throw and try to avoid catching and (re)throwing altogether.

✗ **DO NOT** handle non-CLS-compliant exceptions (exceptions that don't derive from System.Exception) using a parameterless catch block.

Languages that support non-Exception-derived exceptions are free to handle these exceptions.

```
try{ ... }
catch{ ... }
```

The CLR 2.0 has been modified and is delivering noncompliant exceptions to compliant catch blocks wrapped up in RuntimeWrapped-Exception.

7.2.3 Wrapping Exceptions

Sometimes exceptions raised in a lower layer would be meaningless if they were allowed to propagate from a higher layer. In such cases, it is sometimes beneficial to wrap the lower-layer exception in an exception that is meaningful to the users of the higher layer. For example, a FileNotFoundException would be completely meaningless if allowed to propagate from transaction management APIs. The user of the transaction APIs might not even be aware that transactions can be stored on the file system. In other cases, the actual exception type is less important than the fact that it was raised in some particular code path. For example, even if an otherwise benign exception is thrown from a static constructor, the type will be unusable in the current application domain. In such a case, it is much more important to communicate to the user that an exception occurred in the constructor than what caused the exception. Therefore, the CLR wraps all exceptions propagating out of the static constructors into TypeInitializationException.

> ■ **STEVEN CLARKE** Make sure that the terminology used in the error message will make sense in the context in which it is being consumed. In an API usability study we ran, the lower-level details of the API had been factored out so that developers were only exposed to the high-level details. Unfortunately, exceptions were thrown from the lower level and caught at the higher level. The error message described concepts that would have made sense only to someone working at the lower level of the API and thus was no good at communicating the reason for the problem.

✓ **CONSIDER** wrapping specific exceptions thrown from a lower layer in a more appropriate exception if the lower-layer exception does not make sense in the context of the higher-layer operation.

Such wrapping should be quite rare in a typical framework. It will likely have a negative impact on the ability to debug.

```
try {
    // read the transaction file
}
catch(FileNotFoundException e) {
    throw new TransactionFileMissingException(...,e);
}
```

> ■ **RICO MARIANI**   Chris Brumme's previous annotation on rethrowing also applies to this context. The example given illustrates the point nicely: For rethrowing to help, the original exception context has to be nearly meaningless and certainly uninteresting to debug. That the original call stack was uninteresting is the controlling factor, in my opinion. In this case, nobody thinks that there is anything wrong with the file opening services—you might as well rethrow something more meaningful to indicate where we had trouble opening files and what file we were trying to open.

> ■ **ERIC GUNNERSON**   Another way of stating this is: "Don't wrap if your users will ever want to look at the inner exception." By far the worst position to be in is to have to look at an inner exception and base your behavior on the type of the inner exception.

✗ **AVOID** catching and wrapping nonspecific exceptions.

The catch and wrap practice is often undesired and is just another form of swallowing errors. There are exceptions to this rule. They include cases in which the wrapper exception communicates a severe condition that is much more interesting to the caller than the actual type of the original exception. For example, the `TypeInitializationException` wraps all exceptions propagating from static constructors.

✓ **DO** specify the inner exception when wrapping exceptions.

```
throw new ConfigurationFileMissingException(...,e);
```

> ■ **JEFFREY RICHTER** It cannot be stressed enough how carefully this needs to be thought through. When in doubt, do not wrap an exception with another. An example in the CLR where wrapping is known to cause all kinds of trouble is with reflection. When you invoke a method using reflection, if that method throws an exception, the CLR catches it and throws a new `TargetInvocationException`. This is incredibly annoying because it hides the actual method and location in the method that had the problem. I have wasted much time trying to debug my code because of this exception wrapping.

7.3 Using Standard Exception Types

This section describes the standard exceptions provided by the Framework and the details of their usage. The list is by no means exhaustive. Please refer to the .NET Framework reference documentation for usage of other Framework exception types.

7.3.1 Exception and SystemException

✗ **DO NOT** throw `System.Exception` or `System.SystemException`.

✗ **DO NOT** catch `System.Exception` or `System.SystemException` in framework code, unless you intend to rethrow.

✗ **AVOID** catching `System.Exception` or `System.SystemException`, except in top-level exception handlers.

7.3.2 ApplicationException

✗ **DO NOT** throw or derive from `System.ApplicationException`.

■ **JEFFREY RICHTER**   `System.ApplicationException` is a class that should not be part of the .NET Framework. The original idea was that classes derived from `SystemException` would indicate exceptions thrown from the CLR (or system) itself, whereas non-CLR exceptions would be derived from `ApplicationException`. However, a lot of exception classes didn't follow this pattern. For example, `TargetInvocationException` (which is thrown by the CLR) is derived from `ApplicationException`. So the `ApplicationException` class lost all meaning. The reason to derive from this base class is to allow some code higher up the call stack to catch the base class. It was no longer possible to catch all application exceptions.

7.3.3 InvalidOperationException

✓ **DO** throw an `InvalidOperationException` if the object is in an inappropriate state.

The `System.InvalidOperationException` exception should be thrown if a property set or a method call is not appropriate given the object's current state. An example of this is writing to a `FileStream` that's been opened for reading.

■ **KRZYSZTOF CWALINA**   The difference between `InvalidOperation-Exception` and `ArgumentException` is that `ArgumentException` does not rely on the state of any other object besides the argument itself to determine whether it needs to be thrown. For example, if client code tries to access a nonexistent resource, `InvalidOperationException` should be thrown. On the other hand, if client code tries to access a resource using a malformed identifier, `ArgumentException` should be thrown.

7.3.4 ArgumentException, ArgumentNullException, and ArgumentOutOfRangeException

✓ **DO** throw `ArgumentException` or one of its subtypes if bad arguments are passed to a member. Prefer the most derived exception type, if applicable.

✓ **DO** set the `ParamName` property when throwing one of the subclasses of `ArgumentExceptions`.

This property represents the name of the parameter that caused the exception to be thrown. Note that the property can be set using one of the constructor overloads.

```
public static FileAttributes GetAttributes(string path){
    if(path==null){
        throw new ArgumentNullException("path",...);
    }
}
```

✓ **DO** use `value` for the name of the implicit value parameter of property setters.

```
public FileAttributes Attributes {
    set {
        if(value==null){
            throw new ArgumentNullException("value",...);
        }
    }
}
```

■ **JEFFREY RICHTER**   It is very unusual to find code that catches any of these argument exceptions. When one of these exceptions is thrown, you almost always want the application to die. Then look at the exception stack trace, fix your source code so that you are passing the right argument, recompile the code, and retest.

■ **JASON CLARK**   Jeffrey is absolutely correct here. And it is the infrequency with which these exception types are caught that makes them safe to broadly reuse for throwing in your code.

7.3.5 NullReferenceException, IndexOutOfRangeException, and AccessViolationException

✗ **DO NOT** allow publicly callable APIs to explicitly or implicitly throw NullReferenceException, AccessViolationException, or IndexOutOfRangeException. These exceptions are reserved and thrown by the execution engine and in most cases indicate a bug.

Do argument checking to avoid throwing these exceptions. Throwing these exceptions exposes implementation details of your method that might change over time.

> ▪▪ **CHRISTOPHER BRUMME**   Prior to CLR 2.0, there was no distinction between NullReferenceException and AccessViolationException. In CLR 2.0, if you are running on an NT-based operating system rather than Win9x, the CLR will distinguish all the potentially corrupting access violations as AccessViolationException rather than NullReference-Exception.
>
> My advice is to treat NullReferenceException just like any other application exception. Generally, it is neither dangerous nor exotic. However, if you have a place where you know an AccessViolationException could occur, you have a bug that you must not ship. Based on all the cases I have seen, AccessViolationException should only be seen during development, where it indicates corruption.

7.3.6 StackOverflowException

✗ **DO NOT** explicitly throw StackOverflowException. The exception should be explicitly thrown only by the CLR.

✗ **DO NOT** catch StackOverflowException.

It is almost impossible to write managed code that remains consistent in the presence of arbitrary stack overflows. The unmanaged parts of the CLR remain consistent by using probes to move stack overflows to well-defined places rather than by backing out from arbitrary stack overflows.

> **CHRISTOPHER BRUMME** Generally you should never special-case `StackOverflowException`. Default policy in CLR 2.0 will result in a fast shutdown of the process when a stack overflows. There are strong security and reliability reasons for this decision. In a normal process, a stack overflow won't even result in a managed exception.

7.3.7 `OutOfMemoryException`

✗ **DO NOT** explicitly throw `OutOfMemoryException`. This exception is to be thrown only by the CLR infrastructure.

> **CHRISTOPHER BRUMME** At one end of the spectrum, an `OutOfMemoryException` could be the result of a failure to obtain 12 bytes for implicitly autoboxing, or a failure to JIT some code that is required for critical backout. These cases are catastrophic failures and ideally would result in termination of the process. At the other end of the spectrum, an `OutOfMemoryException` could be the result of a thread asking for a 1 GB byte array. The fact that we failed this allocation attempt has no impact on the consistency and viability of the rest of the process.
>
> The sad fact is that CLR 2.0 cannot distinguish among any points on this spectrum. In most managed processes, all `OutOfMemoryExceptions` are considered equivalent and they all result in a managed exception being propagated up the thread. However, you cannot depend on your backout code being executed, because we might fail to JIT some of your backout methods, or we might fail to execute static constructors required for backout.
>
> Also, keep in mind that all other exceptions can get folded into an `OutOfMemoryException` if there isn't enough memory to instantiate those other exception objects. Also, we will give you a unique `OutOfMemoryException` with its own stack trace if we can. But if we are tight enough on memory, you will share an uninteresting global instance with everyone else in the process.
>
> My best recommendation is that you treat `OutOfMemoryException` like any other application exception. You make your best attempts to handle it and remain consistent. In the future, I hope the CLR can do a better job of distinguishing catastrophic OOM from the 1 GB byte array case. If so, we might provoke termination of the process for the catastrophic cases, leaving the application to deal with the less risky ones. By treating all OOM cases as the less risky ones, you are preparing for that day.

7.3.8 ComException, SEHException, **and** ExecutionEngineException

✗ **DO NOT** explicitly throw ComException, ExecutionEngineException, and SEHException. These exceptions are to be thrown only by the CLR infrastructure.

> ▪ **CHRISTOPHER BRUMME** If you see an ExecutionEngineException thrown, treat it like any other Framework exception. It was thrown from a place where the CLR is not actually in an invalid state. For instance, there are some invalid operations in the security code that throw this exception, and backward compatibility requirements prevent us from changing the exception type.

7.4 **Designing Custom Exceptions**

In some cases, it will not be possible to use existing exceptions (section 7.2 describes in detail how to make such determination). In those cases, you'll need to define custom exceptions. The guidelines in this section provide help on doing that.

✓ **DO** derive exceptions from System.Exception or one of the other common base exceptions.

✗ **AVOID** deep exception hierarchies.

There are limited cases where it's good to create a more elaborate hierarchy of exceptions, but it's extremely rare. The reason is that code that handles exceptions almost never cares about the hierarchy, because it almost never wants to handle more than one error at a time. If two or more errors can be handled the same way, they should not be expressed using different exception types. Of course, there are exceptions to the rule and in some cases, it may be better to create a deeper hierarchy.

✓ **DO** end exception class names with the "Exception" suffix.

✓ **DO** make exceptions runtime serializable. An exception must be serializable to work correctly across application domain and remoting boundaries.

✓ **DO** provide (at least) these common constructors on all exceptions. Make sure the names and types of the parameters are exactly as shown in the following example.

```
public class SomeException: Exception, ISerializable {
    public SomeException();
    public SomeException(string message);
    public SomeException(string message, Exception inner);

    // this constructor is needed for serialization.
    protected SomeException(SerializationInfo info, StreamingContext
context);
}
```

✓ **DO** report security-sensitive information through an override of ToString only after demanding an appropriate permission.

If the permission demand fails, return a string excluding the security-sensitive information.

> ■■ **RICO MARIANI** Do not store the results of ToString in any generally accessible data structure unless that data structure suitably secures the string from untrusted code. This advice applies to all strings, but because exception strings frequently contain sensitive information (such as file paths), I reiterate the advice here.

✓ **DO** store useful security-sensitive information in a private exception state. Ensure only trusted code can get the information.

✓ **CONSIDER** providing exception properties for programmatic access to extra information (besides the message string) relevant to the exception.

7.5 **Exceptions and Performance**

One common concern related to exceptions is that if exceptions are used for code that routinely fails, the performance of the implementation will be unacceptable. This is a valid concern. When a member throws an exception, its performance can be orders of magnitude slower. However, it is

possible to achieve good performance while strictly adhering to the exception guidelines that disallow using error codes. Two patterns described in
this section suggest ways to do this.

✗ **DO NOT** use error codes because of concerns that exceptions might affect
performance negatively.

To improve performance, it is possible to use either the Tester-Doer
Pattern or the Try-Parse Pattern, described in the next two sections.

7.5.1 **Tester-Doer Pattern**

Sometimes performance of an exception-throwing member can be
improved by breaking the member into two. Let's look at the Add method
of the ICollection<T> interface.

```
ICollection<int> numbers = ...
numbers.Add(1);
```

The method Add throws if the collection is read-only. This can be a performance problem in scenarios where the method call is expected to fail
often. One of the ways to mitigate the problem is to test whether the collection is writable before trying to add a value.

```
ICollection<int> numbers = ...
...
if(!numbers.IsReadOnly){
    numbers.Add(1);
}
```

The member used to test a condition, which in our example is the property IsReadOnly, is referred to as the tester. The member used to perform a
potentially throwing operation, the Add method in our example, is referred
to as the doer.

✓ **CONSIDER** the Tester-Doer Pattern for members that might throw
exceptions in common scenarios to avoid performance problems related
to exceptions.

> ■ **RICO MARIANI** Consider this when the "test" is much cheaper than
> the "do."

> ■■ **JEFFREY RICHTER**   This pattern needs to be used carefully. The potential problem occurs when you have multiple threads accessing the object at the same time. For example, one thread could execute the tester method, which reports that all is OK, and before the doer method executes, another thread could change the object, causing the doer to fail. Although this pattern might improve performance, it might introduce race conditions and must be used with extreme caution.

> ■■ **VANCE MORRISON**   Jeff's comment about races is true, but it only rarely should impact your design. The reason is that unless you specifically designed your class to be threadsafe (operate properly while multiple threads simultaneously use it), it almost certainly is not. Of the thousands of classes in the .NET Framework, only a handful are designed to be threadsafe (and this is specifically noted in the documentation). If your class is not threadsafe (the default), any user must use locks to ensure that only one thread uses it at a time. As long as both the "test" and "do" are done under the same lock (this will typically happen naturally), there is not a problem.
> Thus, Jeff's concern only applies to the design of threadsafe classes.

7.5.2 Try-Parse Pattern

For extremely performance-sensitive APIs, an even faster pattern than the Tester-Doer Pattern described in the previous section should be used. The pattern calls for adjusting the member name to make a well-defined test case a part of the member semantics. For example, `DateTime` defines a `Parse` method that throws an exception if parsing of a string fails. It also defines a corresponding `TryParse` method that attempts to parse, but returns false if parsing is unsuccessful and returns the result of a successful parsing using an out parameter.

```
public struct DateTime {
    public static DateTime Parse(string dateTime){
        ...
    }
    public static bool TryParse(string dateTime, out DateTime result){
        ...
    }
}
```

When using this pattern, it is important to define the try functionality in strict terms. If the member fails for any reason other than the well-defined try, the member must still throw a corresponding exception.

✓ **CONSIDER** the Try-Parse Pattern for members that might throw exceptions in common scenarios to avoid performance problems related to exceptions.

> ■ **JEFFREY RICHTER** I like this guideline a lot. It solves the race-condition problem and the performance problem. Besides the `DateTime.TryParse`, the `Dictionary` class has a `TryGetValue` method.

✓ **DO** use the prefix "Try" and Boolean return type for methods implementing this pattern.

✓ **DO** provide an exception-throwing member for each member using the Try-Parse Pattern.

```
public struct DateTime {
    public static DateTime Parse(string dateTime){ ... }
    public static bool TryParse(string dateTime, out DateTime result){ ... }
}
```

> ■ **RICO MARIANI** But don't provide members that nobody could reasonably use. There's no reason to set your clients up for failure by giving them an API that's almost guaranteed to be too slow to use. The most obvious way to use your system should also be the best way.

SUMMARY

In designing frameworks, it is important to use exceptions as your error handling mechanism, for all of the reasons detailed in this chapter. In the end, it will make your and your customers' lives easier.

■ 8 ■

Usage Guidelines

THIS CHAPTER CONTAINS guidelines for using common types in publicly accessible APIs. It deals with direct usage of built-in Framework types (e.g., `Collection<T>`, serialization attributes), implementing common interfaces, and inheriting from common base classes. The last section of the chapter talks about overloading common operators.

8.1 Arrays

This section presents guidelines for using arrays in publicly accessible APIs.

✓ **DO** prefer using collections over arrays in public APIs. Section 8.3.3 provides details about how to choose between collections and arrays.

```
public class Order {
    public Collection<OrderItem> Items { get { ... } }
    ...
}
```

✗ **DO NOT** use read-only array fields. The field itself is read-only and can't be changed, but elements in the array can be changed.

This example demonstrates the pitfalls of using read-only array fields:

```
//bad code
public sealed class Path {
    public static readonly char[] InvalidPathChars =
        { '\"', '<', '>', '|'};
}
```

This allows callers to change the values in the array as follows:

```
Path.InvalidPathChars[0] = 'A';
```

Instead, you can either use a read-only collection (only if the items are immutable) or clone the array before returning it.

```
public static ReadOnlyCollection<char> GetInvalidPathChars() {
    return Array.AsReadOnly(badChars);
}

public static char[] GetInvalidPathChars() {
    return (char[])badChars.Clone();
}
```

✓ **CONSIDER** using jagged arrays instead of multidimensional arrays.

A jagged array is an array with elements that are also arrays. The arrays that make up the elements can be of different sizes, leading to less wasted space for some sets of data (e.g., sparse matrix) compared to multidimensional arrays. Furthermore, the CLR optimizes index operations on jagged arrays, so they might exhibit better runtime performance in some scenarios.

```
// jagged arrays
int[][] jaggedArray = {
    new int[] {1,2,3,4},
    new int[] {5,6,7},
    new int[] {8},
    new int[] {9}
};
```

```
// multidimensional arrays
int [,] multiDimArray = {
    {1,2,3,4},
    {5,6,7,0},
    {8,0,0,0},
    {9,0,0,0}
};
```

> **■ BRAD ABRAMS** In general, I have found that usage of non-SZ (one dimension, zero lower bound) arrays in mainstream public APIs is very rare. Their usage should be constrained to problem areas that inherently lend themselves to multidimensional cases (such as matrix multiplication). All other usages should prefer defining a custom data structure or passing multiple arrays.

8.2 Attributes

System.Attribute is a base class used to define custom attributes. The following is an example of a custom attribute:

```
[AttributeUsage(...)]
public class NameAttribute : Attribute {
  public NameAttribute (string userName) {..} // required argument
  public string UserName { get{..} }
  public int Age { get{..} set{..} } // optional argument
}
```

Attributes are annotations that can be added to programming elements such as assemblies, types, members, and parameters. They are stored in the metadata of the assembly and can be accessed at runtime using the reflection APIs. For example, the Framework defines the ObsoleteAttribute, which can be applied to a type or a member to indicate that the type or member has been deprecated.

Attributes can have one or more properties that carry additional data related to the attribute. For example, ObsoleteAttribute could carry additional information about the release in which a type or a member got deprecated and the description of the new APIs replacing the obsolete API.

Some properties of an attribute must be specified when the attribute is applied. These are referred to as the required properties or required arguments, because they are represented as positional constructor parameters. For example, the `ConditionString` property of the `ConditionalAttribute` is a required property.

```
public static class Trace {
    [Conditional("TRACE")]
    public static void WriteLine(string message) { ... }
}
```

Properties that do not necessarily have to be specified when the attribute is applied are called optional properties (or optional arguments). They are represented by settable properties. Compilers provide special syntax to set these properties when an attribute is applied. For example, the `AttributeUsageAttribute.Inherited` property represents an optional argument.

```
[AttributeUsage(AttributeTargets.All,Inherited = false)]
public class SomeAttribute : Attribute {
}
```

The following guidelines are aimed at designing custom attributes.

✓ **DO** name custom attribute classes with the suffix "Attribute."

```
public class ObsoleteAttribute : Attribute { ... }
```

✓ **DO** apply the `AttributeUsageAttribute` to custom attributes.

```
[AttributeUsage(...)]
public class ObsoleteAttribute{}
```

✓ **DO** provide settable properties for optional arguments.

```
public class NameAttribute : Attribute {
  ...
    public int Age { get{..} set{..} } // optional argument
}
```

✓ **DO** provide get-only properties for required arguments.

✓ **DO** provide constructor parameters to initialize properties corresponding to required arguments. Each parameter should have the same name (although with different casing) as the corresponding property.

```
[AttributeUsage(...)]
public class NameAttribute : Attribute {
    public NameAttribute(string userName){..} // required argument
    public string UserName { get{..} } // required argument
    ...
}
```

> **KRZYSZTOF CWALINA** This guideline applies equally to case-sensitive and case-insensitive languages. For example, this is how the attribute would look if defined using case-insensitive VB.NET:
>
> ```
> Public Class FooAttribute
>     Dim nameValue As String
>     Public Sub New(ByVal name As String)
>         nameValue = name
>     End Sub
>
>     Public ReadOnly Property Name() As String
>         Get
>             Return nameValue
>         End Get
>     End Property
> End Class
> ```

✗ **AVOID** providing constructor parameters to initialize properties corresponding to the optional arguments.

In other words, do not have properties that can be set with both a constructor and a setter. This guideline makes very explicit which arguments are optional and which are required, and avoids having two ways of doing the same thing.

✗ **AVOID** overloading custom attribute constructors.

Having only one constructor clearly communicates to the user which arguments are required and which are optional.

✔ **DO** seal custom attribute classes, if possible. This makes the look-up for the attribute faster.

```
public sealed class NameAttribute : Attribute { ... }
```

> ▪▪ **JASON CLARK**   In the exception section, I cautioned against the reuse of somebody else's exception type. Here I am going to do the same for custom attributes. Reuse of somebody else's custom attribute, unless it means exactly the same thing, puts your mutual clients in the awkward position of having to choose between avoiding your API and applying the co-opted attribute, which involves the risk of unexpected or expected (but undesirable) side effects from the original code that used the attribute.

The next section offers guidelines for designing collections.

8.3 **Collections**

Any type designed specifically to manipulate a group of objects having some common characteristic can be considered a collection. It is almost always appropriate for such types to implement IEnumerable or IEnumerable<T>, so in this section we only consider types implementing one or both of those interfaces to be collections.

✗ **DO NOT** use weakly typed collections in public APIs.

The type of all return values and parameters representing collection items should be the exact item type, not any of its base types (this applies only to public members of the collection). For example, a collection storing Components should not have a public Add method that takes object or a public indexer returning IComponent.

```
// bad design
public class ComponentDesigner {
   public IList Components { get { ... } }
   ...
}
// good design
public class ComponentDesigner {
   public Collection<Component> Components { get { ... } }
   ...
}
```

✗ **DO NOT** use `ArrayList` or `List<T>` in public APIs.

These types are data structures designed to be used in internal implementation, not in public APIs. `List<T>` is optimized for performance and power at the cost of cleanness of the APIs and flexibility. For example, if you return `List<T>`, you will not ever be able to receive notifications when client code modifies the collection. Also, `List<T>` exposes many members, such as `BinarySearch`, that are not useful or applicable in many scenarios. Sections 8.3.1 and 8.3.2 describe types (abstractions) designed specifically for use in public APIs.

```
// bad design
public class Order {
    public List<OrderItem> Items { get { ... } }
    ...
}
// good design
public class Order {
    public Collection<OrderItem> Items { get { ... } }
    ...
}
```

✗ **DO NOT** use `Hashtable` or `Dictionary<TKey,TValue>` in public APIs.

These types are data structures designed to be used in internal implementation. Public APIs should use `IDictionary`, `IDictionary <TKey, TValue>`, or a custom type implementing one or both of the interfaces.

✗ **DO NOT** use `IEnumerator<T>`, `IEnumerator`, or any other type that implements either of these interfaces, except as the return type of a `GetEnumerator` method.

> ▪ **ANTHONY MOORE** I've seen a lot of violations of this guideline ever since LINQ has been available. The review body made an explicit decision that LINQ should not change this guideline. Your callers can end up with a clumsy object model if they choose not to use LINQ or use a language that does not support it.

Types returning enumerators from methods other than `GetEnumerator` cannot be used with the `foreach` statement.

✗ **DO NOT** implement both `IEnumerator<T>` and `IEnumerable<T>` on the same type. The same applies to the nongeneric interfaces `IEnumerator` and `IEnumerable`.

In other words, a type should be either a collection or an enumerator, but not both.

> ■ **ANTHONY MOORE**   In design meetings, we would often describe this set of guidelines with the statement that you should "require the weakest thing you need, and return the strongest thing you have."
>
> A nonobvious example that people sometimes miss is "out" parameters, which are really more like return values than input parameters and thus work a little better with the stronger typed objects.
>
> A less clear case is properties on return values on interfaces or abstract base types. In this case, they are both input and output. These usually work better with the weak types because they leave more options to the implementation.

8.3.1 Collection Parameters

This section describes guidelines for using collections as parameters.

✓ **DO** use the least-specialized type possible as a parameter type. Most members taking collections as parameters use the `IEnumerable<T>` interface.

```
public void PrintNames(IEnumerable<string> names){
    foreach(string name in names){
        Console.WriteLine(name);
    }
}
```

✗ **AVOID** using `ICollection<T>` or `ICollection` as a parameter just to access the `Count` property.

Instead, consider using `IEnumerable<T>` or `IEnumerable` and dynamically checking whether the object implements `ICollection<T>` or `ICollection`.

```
public List<T>(IEnumerable<T> collection){
    // check if it implements ICollection
    ICollection<T> col = collection as ICollection<T>;
    if(col!=null){
        this.Capacity = collection.Count;
    }

    foreach(T item in collection){
        Add(item);
    }
}
```

8.3.2 Collection Properties and Return Values

This section offers guidelines for returning collections from methods and from property getters.

✗ **DO NOT** provide settable collection properties.

Users can replace the contents of the collection by clearing the collection first and then adding the new contents. If replacing the whole collection is a common scenario, consider providing the AddRange method on the collection.

```
// bad design
public class Order {
    public Collection<OrderItem> Items { get { ... } set { ... } }
    ...
}
// good design
public class Order {
    public Collection<OrderItem> Items { get { ... } }
    ...
}
```

✓ **DO** use Collection<T> or a subclass of Collection<T> for properties or return values representing read/write collections.

```
public Collection<Session> Sessions { get; }
```

If Collection<T> does not meet some requirement (e.g., the collection must not implement IList), use a custom collection by implementing IEnumerable<T>, ICollection<T>, or IList<T>.

✓ **DO** use ReadOnlyCollection<T>, a subclass of ReadOnlyCollection<T>, or in rare cases IEnumerable<T> for properties or return values representing read-only collections.

```
public ReadOnlyCollection<Session> Sessions { get; }
```

In general, prefer ReadOnlyCollection<T>. If it does not meet some requirement (e.g., the collection must not implement IList), use a custom collection by implementing IEnumerable<T>, ICollection<T>, or IList<T>. If you do implement a custom read-only collection, implement ICollection<T>.ReadOnly to return false.

```
public class SessionCollection : IList<Session> {

    bool ICollection<Session>.IsReadOnly { get { return false; } }
    ...
}
```

In cases where you are sure that the only scenario you will ever want to support is forward-only iteration, you can simply use IEnumerable<T>.

▪▪ **CHRIS SELLS**   One of my favorite implementations of IEnumerable<T> is sometimes known as a generator. A generator is an iterator class or method that generates collection members on the fly, which is really useful when you'd prefer not to precompute something and then buffer it simply for convenient access. For example, the following is a generator method that computes as many numbers from the Fibonacci sequence as you care to ask for wrapped in an IEnumerable for easy access via **foreach** or for passing to methods that take IEnumerable as input:

```
class FibonacciGenerator{
  public static IEnumerable<long> GetSequence(int count){
    long fib1 = 0;
    long fib2 = 1;
```

```
      yield return fib1;
       yield return fib2; // assume they want at least 2, else what
       //fun are they?
      while(--count!= 1) {
        long fib3 = fib1 + fib2;
        yield return fib3;
        fib1 = fib2;
        fib2 = fib3;
      }
    }
  }
  class Program {
    static void Main() {
      foreach(long fib in FibonacciGenerator.GetSequence(100)){
        Console.WriteLine(fib);
    }
    }
  }
```

✔ **CONSIDER** using subclasses of generic base collections instead of using the collections directly.

This allows for a better name and for adding helper members that are not present on the base collection types. This is especially applicable to high-level APIs.

```
public TraceSourceCollection : Collection<TraceSource> {
    // optional helper method
    public void FlushAll {
        foreach(TraceSource source in this){
            source.Flush();
        }
    }
    // another common helper
    public void AddSource(string sourceName){
        Add(new TraceSource(sourceName));
    }
}
```

✓ **CONSIDER** returning a subclass of `Collection<T>` or `ReadOnly-Collection<T>` from very commonly used methods and properties.

```
public class ListItemCollection : Collection<ListItem> {}
public class ListBox {
    public ListItemCollection Items { get; }
}
public class XmlAttributeCollection : ReadOnlyCollection<XmlAttribute> {}
public class XmlNode {
    public XmlAttributeCollection Attributes { get; }
}
```

This will make it possible for you to add helper methods or change the collection implementation in the future.

✓ **CONSIDER** using a keyed collection if the items stored in the collection have unique keys (names, IDs, etc.). Keyed collections are collections that can be indexed by both an integer and a key and are usually implemented by inheriting from `KeyedCollection<TKey,TItem>`.

For example, a collection of files in a directory could be represented as a subclass of `KeyedCollection<string,FileInfo>` where `string` is the filename. Users of the collection could then index the collection using filenames.

```
public class FileInfoCollection : KeyedCollection<string,FileInfo> {
    ...
}

public class Directory {
    public Directory(string root);
    public FileInfoCollection GetFiles();
}
```

Keyed collections usually have larger memory footprints and should not be used if the memory overhead outweighs the benefits of having the keys.

✗ **DO NOT** return null values from collection properties or from methods returning collections. Return an empty collection or an empty array instead.

Users of collection properties often assume that the following code will always work:

```
IEnumerable<string> list = GetList();
foreach(string name in list){
    ...
}
```

The general rule is that null and empty (0 item) collections or arrays should be treated the same.

8.3.2.1 Snapshots Versus Live Collections

Collections representing a state at some point in time are called snapshot collections. For example, a collection containing rows returned from a database query would be a snapshot. Collections that always represent the current state are called live collections. For example, a collection of ComboBox items is a live collection.

✗ **DO NOT** return snapshot collections from properties. Properties should return live collections.

```
public class Directory {
  public Directory(string root);
  public IEnumerable<FileInfo> Files { get {...} } //live collection
}
```

Property getters should be very lightweight operations. Returning a snapshot requires creating a copy of an internal collection in an O(n) operation.

✓ **DO** use either a snapshot collection or a live IEnumerable<T> (or its sub-type) to represent collections that are volatile (i.e., that can change without explicitly modifying the collection).

In general, all collections representing a shared resource (e.g., files in a directory) are volatile. Such collections are very difficult or impossible to implement as live collections unless the implementation is simply a forward-only enumerator.

```
public class Directory {
    public Directory(string root);
  public IEnumerable<FileInfo> Files { get; } // live
      // or
  public FileInfoCollection GetFiles(); // snapshot
}
```

8.3.3 Choosing Between Arrays and Collections

Framework designers often need to choose whether to use an array or a collection. These two alternative approaches have very similar usage but somewhat different performance characteristics, usability, and versioning implications.

✓ **DO** prefer collections over arrays.

Collections provide more control over contents, can evolve over time, and are more usable. In addition, using arrays for read-only scenarios is discouraged because the cost of cloning the array is prohibitive. Usability studies have shown that some developers feel more comfortable using collection-based APIs.

However, if you are developing low-level APIs, it might be better to use arrays for read-write scenarios. Arrays have a smaller memory footprint, which helps reduce the working set, and access to elements in an array is faster because it is optimized by the runtime.

✓ **CONSIDER** using arrays in low-level APIs to minimize memory consumption and maximize performance.

✓ **DO** use byte arrays instead of collections of bytes.

```
// bad design
public Collection<byte> ReadBytes() { ... }

// good design
public byte[] ReadBytes() { ... }
```

✗ **DO NOT** use arrays for properties if the property would have to return a new array (e.g., a copy of an internal array) every time the property getter is called.

This ensures that users will not write the following inefficient code:

```
//bad design
for(int index=0; index< customer.Orders.Length; index++) {
   Console.WriteLine(customer.Orders[i]);
}
```

The next section goes into the guidelines for implementing custom collections.

8.3.4 Implementing Custom Collections

In implementing custom collections, it is a good idea to follow these guidelines.

✓ **CONSIDER** inheriting from Collection<T>, ReadOnlyCollection<T>, or KeyedCollection<TKey,TItem> when designing new collections.

```
public class OrderCollection : Collection<Order> {
   protected override void InsertItem(int index, Order item) {
      ...
   }
}
```

✓ **DO** implement IEnumerable<T> when designing new collections. Consider implementing ICollection<T> or even IList<T> where it makes sense.

```
public class TextDecorationCollection : IList<TextDecoration> ... {
   ...
}
```

When implementing such custom collection, follow the API pattern established by Collection<T> and ReadOnlyCollection<T> as closely as possible. That is, implement the same members explicitly, name the parameters like these two collections name them, and so on. In other words, make your custom collection different from these two collections only when you have a very good reason to.

✓ **CONSIDER** implementing nongeneric collection interfaces (ILisT and ICollection) if the collection will often be passed to APIs taking these interfaces as input.

```
public class OrderCollection : IList<Order>, ILIst {
   ...
}
```

✗ **AVOID** implementing collection interfaces on types with complex APIs unrelated to the concept of a collection.

In other words, a collection should be a simple type used to store, access, and manipulate items, and not much more.

✗ **DO NOT** inherit from nongeneric base collections such as CollectionBase. Use Collection<T>, ReadOnlyCollection<T>, and KeyedCollection<TKey,TItem> instead.

8.3.4.1 Naming Custom Collections

Collections (types that implement IEnumerable) are created mainly for two reasons: (1) to create a new data structure with structure-specific operations and often different performance characteristics than existing data structures (e.g., List<T>, LinkedList<T>, Stack<T>), and (2) to create a specialized collection for holding a specific set of items (e.g., StringCollection). Data structures are most often used in the internal implementation of applications and libraries. Specialized collections are mainly to be exposed in APIs (as property and parameter types).

✓ **DO** use the "Dictionary" suffix in names of abstractions implementing IDictionary or IDictionary<TKey,TValue>.

✓ **DO** use the "Collection" suffix in names of types implementing IEnumerable (or any of its descendants) and representing a list of items.

```
public class OrderCollection : IEnumerable<Order> { ... }
public class CustomerCollection : ICollection<Customer> { ... }
public class AddressCollection : IList<Address> { ... }
```

✓ **DO** use the appropriate data structure name for custom data structures.

```
public class LinkedList<T> : IEnumerable<T> ,... { ... }
public class Stack<T> : ICollection<Customer> { ... }
```

✗ **AVOID** using any suffixes implying particular implementation, such as "LinkedList" or "Hashtable," in names of collection abstractions.

✓ **CONSIDER** prefixing collection names with the name of the item type. For example, a collection storing items of type Address (implementing IEnumerable<Address>) should be named AddressCollection. If the item type is an interface, the "I" prefix of the item type can be omitted. Thus, a collection of IDisposable items can be called Disposable-Collection.

✓ **CONSIDER** using the "ReadOnly" prefix in names of read-only collections if a corresponding writeable collection might be added or already exists in the framework.

For example, a read-only collection of strings should be called Read-OnlyStringCollection.

8.4 DateTime and DateTimeOffset

The .NET Framework 3.5 introduced a new type for representing a point in time called DateTimeOffset. The type is similar to the DateTime structure, which should be familiar to most users of the .NET Framework. DateTimeOffset stores similar data to DateTime but adds information about the offset from the GMT time and so is a more precise representation of a point in time.

■ **ANTHONY MOORE** This was one of the hardest types to name in the history of the Base Class Libraries. The way to think about it is Date+Time+Offset. However, it confuses people because at first glance it looks the type of just the offset piece. There were many other options discussed, but they were seen to have problems even worse than this.

The following listing shows the main properties of the `DateTime` and `DateTimeOffset`:

```
public struct DateTime {

    public DateTime Date { get; }
    public DateTimeKind Kind { get; }
    public DayOfWeek DayOfWeek { get; }
    public int Day { get; }
    public int DayOfYear { get; }
    public int Hour { get; }
    public int Millisecond { get; }
    public int Minute { get; }
    public int Month { get; }
    public int Second { get; }
    public int Year { get; }
    public long Ticks { get; }
    public TimeSpan TimeOfDay { get; }

    ...

}

public struct DateTimeOffset {

    public DateTime Date { get; }
    public DateTime DateTime { get; }
    public DateTime LocalDateTime { get; }
    public DateTime UtcDateTime { get; }
    public DayOfWeek DayOfWeek { get; }
    public int Day { get; }
    public int DayOfYear { get; }
    public int Hour { get; }
    public int Millisecond { get; }
    public int Minute { get; }
    public int Month { get; }
    public int Second { get; }
    public int Year { get; }
    public long Ticks { get; }
    public long UtcTicks { get; }
    public TimeSpan Offset { get; }
    public TimeSpan TimeOfDay { get; }

    ...

}
```

✔ **DO** use `DateTimeOffset` whenever you are referring to an exact point in time. For example, use it to calculate "now," transaction times, file change times, logging event times, and so on. If the time zone is not known, use it with UTC. These usages are much more common than the scenarios where `DateTime` is preferred, so this should be considered the default.

✓ **DO** use `DateTime` for any cases where the absolute point in time does not apply, such as store opening times that apply across time zones.

✓ **DO** use `DateTime` when the time zone either is not known or is sometimes not known. This may happen in cases where it comes from a legacy data source.

✗ **DO NOT** use `DateTimeKind` if `DateTimeOffset` can be used instead.

`DateTimeKind` is an enum stored in `DateTime` to indicate whether the instance represents UTC, local time, or unspecified time zone.

✓ **DO** use `DateTime` with a 00:00:00 time component rather than `Date-TimeOffset` to represent whole dates, such as a date of birth.

✓ **DO** use `TimeSpan` to represent times of day without a date.

> ▪▪ **ANTHONY MOORE** We have considered adding Date and Time types in future releases of the Framework. Although the idea is not off the table completely, we are concerned that such additions will complicate the Framework without providing enough value to offset the negatives.

8.5 ICloneable

The `ICloneable` interface contains a single `Clone` method, which creates a copy of the current object.

```
public interface ICloneable {
    object Clone();
}
```

There are two general ways to implement cloning, as either deep-copy or shallow-copy. Deep-copy copies the cloned object and all objects referenced by the object, recursively, until all objects in the graph are copied. A shallow-copy copies only a part of the object graph.

Because the contract of ICloneable does not specify the type of clone implementation required to satisfy the contract, different classes have different implementations of the interface. Consumers cannot rely on ICloneable to let them know whether an object is deep-copied or not. Therefore, we recommend that ICloneable not be implemented.

> ■■ **KRZYSZTOF CWALINA**   The moral of the story is that you should never ship an interface if you don't have both implementations and consumers of the interface. In the case of ICloneable, we did not have consumers when we shipped it. I searched the Framework sources and could not find even one place where we take ICloneable as a parameter.

✗ **DO NOT** implement ICloneable.

✗ **DO NOT** use ICloneable in public APIs.

✓ **CONSIDER** defining the Clone method on types that need a cloning mechanism. Ensure that the documentation clearly states whether it is a deep- or shallow-copy.

```
public class Customer {
    public Customer Clone();
    ...
}
```

8.6 IComparable<T> **and** IEquatable<T>

IComparable<T> and IEquatable<T> can be implemented by types that support either equality or order comparison. IComparable<T> specifies ordering (less than, equals, greater than) and is used mainly for sorting. IEquatable<T> specifies equality and is used mainly for look-up.

```
public interface IComparable<T> {
    // returns a negative integer if this is less than other
    // returns 0 if this and other are equal
    // returns a positive integer if this is greater than other
    public int CompareTo(T other);
}
```

```
public interface IEquatable<T> {
    public bool Equals(T other);
}
```

✓ **DO** implement IEquatable<T> on value types.

The Object.Equals method on value types causes boxing, and its default implementation is not very efficient because it uses reflection. IEquatable<T>.Equals can offer much better performance and can be implemented so that it does not cause boxing.

```
public struct Int32 : IEquatable<Int32> {
    public bool Equals(Int32 other){ ... }
}
```

✓ **DO** follow the same guidelines as for overriding Object.Equals when implementing IEquatable<T>.Equals.

See section 8.7.1 for detailed guidelines on overriding Object.Equals.

✓ **DO** override Object.Equals whenever implementing IEquatable<T>.

Both overloads of the Equals method should have exactly the same semantics.

```
public struct PositiveInt32 : IEquatable<PositiveInt32> {
    public bool Equals(PositiveInt32 other) { ... }
    public override bool Equals(object obj){
        if (!obj is PositiveInt32) return false;
        return Equals((PositiveInt32)obj);
    }
}
```

✓ **CONSIDER** overloading operator== and operator!= whenever implementing IEquatable<T>.

```
public struct Decimal : IEquatable<Decimal>, ... {
    public bool Equals(Decimal other){ ... }
    public static bool operator==(Decimal x, Decimal y) {
        return x.Equals(y);
    }
    public static bool operator!=(Decimal x, Decimal y) {
        return !x.Equals(y);
    }
}
```

See section 8.10 for more details about implementing the equality operators.

✓ **DO** implement IEquatable<T> anytime you implement IComparable<T>.

Note that the reverse is not true, and not all types can support ordering.

```
public struct Decimal : IComparable<Decimal>, IEquatable<Decimal> {
    ...
}
```

✓ **CONSIDER** overloading comparison operators (<, >,<=, >=) whenever you implement IComparable<T>.

```
public struct Decimal : IComparable< Decimal >, ... {
    public int CompareTo(Decimal other){ ... }
    public static bool operator<(Decimal x, Decimal y) {
        return x.CompareTo(y)<0;
    }
    public static bool operator>(Decimal x, Decimal y) {
        return x.CompareTo(y)>0;
    }
    ...
}
```

See section 5.6 for details on when to overload operators.

8.7 IDisposable

IDisposable is known as the Dispose Pattern and is discussed in section 9.3.

8.8 Nullable<T>

Nullable<T> is a simple type added to the .NET Framework 2.0. The type is designed to be able to represent value types with "null" values.

```
Nullable<int> x = null;
Nullable<int> y = 5;
Console.WriteLine(x == null); // prints true
Console.WriteLine(y == null); // prints false
```

Note that C# provides special support for Nullable<T> in the form of language aliases for nullable types, lifted operators, and the new coalescing operator.

```
int? x = null; // alias for Nullable<int>
long? d = x; // calls cast operator from Int32 to Int64
Console.WriteLine(d??10); // coalescing; prints 10 because d == null
```

✓ **CONSIDER** using Nullable<T> to represent values that might not be present (i.e., optional values). For example, use it when returning a strongly typed record from a database with a property representing an optional table column.

✗ **DO NOT** use Nullable<T> unless you would use a reference type in a similar manner, taking advantage of the fact that reference type values can be null.

For example, you would not use null to represent optional parameters.

```
// bad design
public class Foo {
    public Foo(string name, int? id);
}

// good design
public class Foo {
    public Foo(string name, int id);
    public Foo(string name);
}
```

✗ **AVOID** using Nullable<bool> to represent a general three-state value.

Nullable<bool> should only be used to represent truly optional Boolean values: true, false, and not available. If you simply want to represent three states (e.g., yes, no, cancel), consider using an enum.

✗ **AVOID** using System.DBNull. Prefer Nullable<T> instead.

> ▪▪ **PABLO CASTRO** `Nullable<T>` is in general a better representation of optional database values. One thing to consider though is that while `Nullable<T>` gives you the ability to represent null values, you don't get database null operational semantics. Specifically, you don't get null propagation through operators and functions. If you deeply care about the propagation semantics, consider sticking with `DBNull`.

8.9 Object

`System.Object` has several members that are very commonly overridden. The following sections describe when and how to override these members.

8.9.1 Object.Equals

The default implementation of `Object.Equals` on value types returns true if all fields of the values being compared compare themselves as equal. We call such equality the value equality. The implementation uses reflection to access the fields and because of that it is often unacceptably inefficient and needs to be overridden.

The default implementation of `Object.Equals` on reference types returns true if the two references being compared point to the same object. We call such equality the reference equality. Some reference types override the default implementation to provide value equality semantics. For example, the value of a string is based on the characters of the string, and so the `Equals` method of the `String` class returns true for any two string instances that contain exactly the same characters in the same order.

The following guidelines describe when and how to override the default behavior of the `Object.Equals` method.

✓ **DO** comply with the contract defined for `Object.Equals` when overriding the method.

For convenience, the contract taken directly from the `System.Object` documentation is provided here.

- `x.Equals(x)` returns true.
- `x.Equals(y)` returns the same value as `y.Equals(x)`.
- If `(x.Equals(y) && y.Equals(z))` returns true, then `x.Equals(z)` returns true.

- Successive invocations of x.Equals(y) return the same value as long as the objects x and y are not modified.
- x.Equals(null) returns false.

✓ **DO** override GetHashCode whenever you override Equals.

The contracts of Equals and GetHashCode are interdependent. For more information, see section 8.7.2 on implementing GetHashCode.

✓ **CONSIDER** implementing IEquatable<T> whenever overriding Object. Equals.

✗ **DO NOT** throw exceptions from Equals.

Two objects should either be equal or not. So, for example, even if the argument passed to Equals is null, returning false is better than throwing an exception.

8.9.1.1 Equals on Value Types

✓ **DO** override Equals on value types.

The default implementation uses reflection to access and compare all the fields and because of that is often unacceptably inefficient.

✓ **DO** provide an overload of Equals taking the value type parameter by implementing IEquatable<T>.

This provides a way to compare two value types without boxing the parameter passed to Equals.

```
public struct MyStruct {
    public bool Equals (MyStruct value) { ... }
    ...
}
```

8.9.1.2 Equals on Reference Types

✓ **CONSIDER** overriding Equals to provide value equality if a reference type represents a value. For example, you might want to override Equals in reference types representing numbers or other mathematical entities.

✗ DO NOT implement value equality on mutable reference types.

Reference types that implement value equality (e.g., `System.String`) should be immutable. Mutable reference types with value equality can, for example, be "lost" as hashtables when their value (and so the hashcode) changes.

8.9.2 `Object.GetHashCode`

A hash function is used to generate a number (hash code) that corresponds to the identity of an object that is determined by an associated implementation of equality. Hash codes are used by hashtables and it is important to understand how hashtables work to be able to implement hash functions properly.

✓ DO override `GetHashCode` if you override `Object.Equals`.

This guarantees that two objects considered equal have the same hash code. The following guidelines provide more information.

✓ DO ensure that if the `Object.Equals` method returns true for any two objects, `GetHashCode` returns the same value for these objects.

Types that do not follow this guideline will not work correctly when used as hashtable keys.

> **■ CHRISTOPHER BRUMME** This means that if `obj1.Equals(obj2)` returns true, both of the objects should have the same hash code. If the objects aren't equal, they might or might not have the same hash code. Strictly speaking, all objects could have a hash code of 1. This would really be terrible from a performance point of view when looking up such items in a hashtable, of course.

✓ DO make every effort to ensure that `GetHashCode` generates a random distribution of numbers for all objects of a type.

This will minimize hashtable collisions, which degrade performance.

For example, two strings return the same hash code if they represent the same string value, as defined by the `String.Equals` implementation. Also, the method uses all the characters in the string to generate reasonably randomly distributed output, even when the input is clustered in certain ranges (e.g., many users could have strings that contain only the lower 128 ASCII characters, even though a string can contain any of the 65,535 Unicode characters).

✓ **DO** ensure that GetHashCode returns exactly the same value regardless of any changes that are made to the object.

Note that there are several related guidelines throughout the book. In particular, there are guidelines advising against mutable value types and against mutable reference types implementing value equality. See sections 8.9.1.2 and 4.7.

✗ **AVOID** throwing exceptions from GetHashCode.

> ■ **BRIAN PEPIN** This has tripped me up more than once: Make sure GetHashCode always returns the same value across the lifetime of an instance. Remember that hash codes are used to identify "buckets" in most hashtable implementations. If an object's "bucket" changes, a hashtable may not be able to find your object. These can be very hard bugs to find, so get it right the first time.

8.9.3 Object.ToString

The Object.ToString method is intended to be used for general display and debugging purposes. The default implementation simply provides the object type name. The default implementation is not very useful, and it is recommended that the method be overridden.

✓ **DO** override ToString whenever an interesting human-readable string can be returned.

The default implementation is not very useful, and a custom implementation can almost always provide more value.

> ■ **CHRIS SELLS** I consider ToString an especially dangerous method to provide for UI-generic types, because it's likely to be implemented with some specific UI in mind, making it useless for other UI needs. To avoid tempting myself in this way, I prefer to make my ToString output as geeky as possible to emphasize that the only "humans" that should ever see the output are "developer humans" (a subspecies all their own).

BRIAN PEPIN   I tend to be very careful with ToString. I treat it as a diagnostic API and seldom use it for presentation to users unless I know exactly how it works. A few months ago I was working with the source code to Expression Blend and had an instance of an object that represented a value converted to a string. There was no obvious API to return the string, but what do you know, ToString had just what I needed! It turned out I was wrong: ToString was returning debugging information that looked just like the value I wanted most of the time. Other times, however, it returned different diagnostic information and broke my code. The moral is use ToString only for diagnostics and define a separate method for end-user presentation.

VANCE MORRISON   The most important value of ToString is that the debugger uses it as the default way of displaying the object. This is really valuable and is well worth doing. Sadly, all too often we don't do this and the debuggability of our code suffers. In my own code, for nontrivial types, I found that writing something that looked like an XML fragment was quite useful (it is unambiguous, and programmers understand its syntax).

✓ **DO** try to keep the string returned from ToString short.

The debugger uses ToString to get a textual representation of an object to be shown to the developer. If the string is longer than the debugger can display (typically less than one screen length), the debugging experience is hindered.

CHRISTOPHE NASARRE   In term of debugging experience, you should decorate your type with DebuggerDisplayAttribute in addition to overriding ToString for that particular purpose.

✓ **CONSIDER** returning a unique string associated with the instance.

✓ **DO** prefer a friendly name over a unique but not readable ID.

✓ **DO** string formatting based on the current thread culture when returning culture-dependent information.

> ■ **CHRISTOPHE NASARRE** To be more explicit, use the `CultureInfo` instance returned by a thread's `CurrentCulture` property to format any numeric or date, and the one returned by `CurrentUICulture` to look up any resource. People are often confused between the two properties.

✓ **DO** provide overload `ToString(string format)`, or implement `IFormattable`, if the string returned from `ToString()` is culture sensitive or there are various ways to format the string. For example, `DateTime` provides the overload and implements `IFormattable`.

✗ **DO NOT** return an empty string or null from `ToString`.

✗ **AVOID** throwing exceptions from `ToString`.

✓ **DO** ensure that `ToString` has no observable side effects.

One reason for this is that `ToString` is called by debuggers during debugging, and such side effects can make debugging difficult.

✓ **DO** report security-sensitive information through an override of `ToString` only after demanding an appropriate permission. If the permission demand fails, return a string excluding the security-sensitive information.

> ■ **RICO MARIANI** Do not store the results of `ToString` in any generally accessible data structure unless that data structure suitably secures the string from untrusted code. This advice applies to all strings, but because exception strings frequently contain sensitive information (such as file paths), I reiterate the advice here.

✓ **CONSIDER** having the output of `ToString` be a valid input for any parsing methods on this type.

For example, the string returned from `DateTime.ToString` can be successfully parsed using `DateTime.Parse`.

```
DateTime now = DateTime.Now;
DateTime parsed = DateTime.Parse(now.ToString());
```

8.10 **Serialization**

Serialization is the process of converting an object into a format that can be readily persisted or transported. For example, you can serialize an object, transport it over the Internet using HTTP, and deserialized it at the destination machine.

The .NET Framework offers three main serialization technologies optimized for various serialization scenarios. Table 8-1 lists these technologies and the main Framework types related to these technologies.

TABLE 8.1: .NET Framework Serialization Technologies

Technology Name	Main Types	Scenarios
Data Contract Serialization	DataContractAttribute DataMemberAttribute DataContractSerializer NetDataContractSerializer DataContractJsonSerializer ISerializable	General persistence Web Services JSON
XML Serialization	XmlSerializer	XML format with full control over the shape of the XML
Runtime Serialization (Binary and SOAP)	SerializableAttribute ISerializable BinaryFormatter SoapFormatter	.NET Remoting

When you design new types, you should decide which, if any, of these technologies those types need to support. The following guidelines describe how to make that choice and how to provide such support. Please note that these guidelines are not trying to help you choose what serialization technology you should use in the implementation of your application or library. Such guidelines are not directly related to API design and thus are not within the scope of this book.

✓ **DO** think about serialization when you design new types.

Serialization is an important design consideration for any type, because programs might need to persist or transmit instances of the type.

8.10.1 Choosing the Right Serialization Technology to Support

Any given type can support none, one, or more of the serialization technologies.

✓ **CONSIDER** supporting Data Contract Serialization if instances of your type might need to be persisted or used in Web Services.

See section 8.10.2 for details on supporting Data Contract Serialization.

✓ **CONSIDER** supporting the XML Serialization instead of or in addition to Data Contract Serialization if you need more control over the XML format that is produced when the type is serialized.

This may be necessary in some interoperability scenarios where you need to use an XML construct that is not supported by Data Contract Serialization, for example, to produce XML attributes. See section 8.10.3 for details on supporting XML Serialization.

✓ **CONSIDER** supporting the Runtime Serialization if instances of your type need to travel across .NET Remoting boundaries.

See section 8.10.4 for details on supporting Runtime Serialization.

✗ **AVOID** supporting Runtime Serialization or XML Serialization just for general persistence reasons. Prefer Data Contract Serialization instead.

8.10.2 **Supporting Data Contract Serialization**

Types can support Data Contract Serialization by applying the Data-ContractAttribute to the type and the DataMemberAttribute to the members (fields and properties) of the type.

```
[DataContract]
class Person {

    [DataMember]string lastName;
    [DataMember]string FirstName;

    public Person(string firstName; string lastName){ ... }

    public string LastName {
        get { return lastName; }
    }
    public string FirstName {
        get { return firstName; }
    }
}
```

✓ **CONSIDER** marking data members of your type public if the type can be used in partial trust.

In full trust, Data Contract serializers can serialize and deserialize nonpublic types and members, but only public members can be serialized and deserialized in partial trust.

✓ **DO** implement a getter and setter on all properties that have Data-MemberAttribute. Data Contract serializers require both the getter and the setter for the type to be considered serializable.[1] If the type won't be used in partial trust, one or both of the property accessors can be nonpublic.

```
[DataContract]
class Person {

    string lastName;
    string firstName;

    public Person(string firstName, string lastName){
        this.lastName = lastName;
        this.firstName = firstName;
    }
```

_____

1. In .NET Framework 3.5 SP1, some collection properties can be get-only.

```
    [DataMember]
    public string LastName {
        get { return lastName; }
        private set { lastName = value; }

    }

    [DataMember]
    public string FirstName {
        get { return firstName; }
        private set { firstName = value; }
    }
}
```

✓ **CONSIDER** using the serialization callbacks for initialization of deserialized instances.

Constructors are not called[2] when objects are deserialized. Therefore, any logic that executes during normal construction needs to be implemented as one of the serialization callbacks.

```
[DataContract]
class Person {

    [DataMember] string lastName;
    [DataMember] string firstName;
    string fullName;

    public Person(string firstName, string lastName){
        this.lastName = lastName;
        this.firstName = firstName;
        fullName = firstName + " " + lastName;
    }

    public string FullName {
        get { return fullName; }
    }

    [OnDeserialized]
    void OnDeserialized(StreamingContext context) {
        fullName = firstName + " " + lastName;
    }
}
```

---

2. There are exceptions to the rule. Constructors of collections marked with `CollectionData-ContractAttribute` are called during deserialization.

`OnDeserializedAttribute` is the most commonly used callback attribute. The other attributes in the family are `OnDeserializingAttribute`, `OnSeralizingAttribute`, and `OnSerializedAttribute`. They can be used to mark callbacks that get executed before deserialization, before serialization, and finally, after serialization, respectively.

✓ **CONSIDER** using the `KnownTypeAttribute` to indicate concrete types that should be used when deserializing a complex object graph.

For example, if a type of a deserialized data member is represented by an abstract class, the serializer will need the Known Type information to decide what concrete type to instantiate and assign to the member. If the Known Type is not specified using the attribute, it will need to be passed to the serializer explicitly (you can do it by passing Known Types to the serializer constructor) or it will need to be specified in the configuration file.

```
[KnownType(typeof(USAddress))]
[DataContract]
class Person {

    [DataMember] string fullName;
    [DataMember] Address address; // Address is abstract

    public Person(string fullName, Address address){
        this.fullName = fullName;
        this.address = address;
    }

    public string FullName {
        get { return fullName; }
    }
}


[DataContract]
public abstract class Address {
    public abstract string FullAddress { get; }
}

[DataContract]
public class USAddress : Address {

    [DataMember] public string Street { get; set; }
    [DataMember] public string City { get; set; }
    [DataMember] public string State { get; set; }
    [DataMember] public string ZipCode { get; set; }
```

```
      public override string FullAddress { get {
      return Street + "\n" + City + ", " + State + " " + ZipCode; }
      }
  }
```

In cases where the list of Known Types is not known statically (when the Person class is compiled), the KnownTypeAttribute can also point to a method that returns a list of Known Types at runtime.

✓ **DO** consider backward and forward compatibility when creating or changing serializable types.

Keep in mind that serialized streams of future versions of your type can be deserialized into the current version of the type, and vice versa.

Make sure you understand that data members, even private and internal, cannot change their names, types, or even their order in future versions of the type unless special care is taken to preserve the contract using explicit parameters to the data contract attributes.

Test compatibility of serialization when making changes to serializable types. Try deserializing the new version into an old version, and vice versa.

✓ **CONSIDER** implementing IExtensibleDataObject to allow round-tripping between different versions of the type.

The interface allows the serializer to ensure that no data is lost during round-tripping. The IExtensibleDataObject.ExtensionData property is used to store any data from the future version of the type that is unknown to the current version, and so it cannot store it in its data members. When the current version is subsequently serialized and deserialized into a future version, the additional data will be available in the serialized stream.

```
  [DataContract]
  class Person : IExtensibleDataObject {

    [DataMember] string fullName;

    public Person(string fullName){
      this.fullName = fullName;
    }
```

```
public string FullName {
    get { return fullName; }
}

ExtensionDataObject serializationData;
ExtensionDataObject IExtensibleDataObject.ExtensionData {
    get { return serializationData; }
    set { serializationData = value; }
}
}
```

8.10.3 Supporting XML Serialization

Data Contract Serialization is the main (default) serialization technology in the .NET Framework, but there are serialization scenarios that Data Contract Serialization does not support. For example, it does not give you full control over the shape of XML produced or consumed by the serializer. If such fine control is required, XML Serialization has to be used, and you need to design your types to support this serialization technology.

✗ **AVOID** designing your types specifically for XML Serialization, unless you have a very strong reason to control the shape of the XML produced. This serialization technology has been superseded by the Data Contract Serialization discussed in the previous section.

In other words, don't apply attributes from System.Xml.Serialization namespace to new types, unless you know that the type will be used with XML Serialization. The following example shows how System.Xml.Serialization can be used to control the shape of the XML produced.

```
public class Address {
    [XmlAttribute] // serialize as XML attribute, instead of an element
    public string Name { get { return "John Smith"; } set { } }

    [XmlElement(ElementName = "StreetLine")] // explicitly name element
    public string Street = "1 Some Street";
    ...
}
```

✓ **CONSIDER** implementing the IXmlSerializable interface if you want even more control over the shape of the serialized XML than what's offered by applying the XML Serialization attributes. Two methods of the interface, `ReadXml` and `WriteXml`, allow you to fully control the serialized XML stream. You can also control the XML schema that gets generated for the type by applying the `XmlSchemaProviderAttribute`.

8.10.4 Supporting Runtime Serialization

Runtime Serialization is a technology used by .NET Remoting. If you think your types will be transported using .NET Remoting, you need to make sure they support Runtime Serialization.

The basic support for Runtime Serialization can be provided by applying the `SerializableAttribute`, and more advanced scenarios involve implementing a simple Runtime Serializable Pattern (implement `ISerializable` and provide serialization constructor).

✓ **CONSIDER** supporting Runtime Serialization if your types will be used with .NET Remoting. For example, the `System.AddIn` namespace uses .NET Remoting, and so all types exchanged between `System.AddIn` add-ins need to support Runtime Serialization.

```
[Serializable]
public class Person {
   ...
}
```

✓ **CONSIDER** implementing the Runtime Serializable Pattern if you want complete control over the serialization process. For example, if you want to transform data as it gets serialized or deserialized.

The pattern is very simple. All you need to do is implement the `ISerializable` interface and provide a special constructor that is used when the object is deserialized.

```
[Serializable]
public class Person : ISerializable {
    string fullName;

    public Person() { }
    protected Person(SerializationInfo info, StreamingContext context) {
        if (info == null) throw new System.ArgumentNullException("info");
        fullName = (string)info.GetValue("name", typeof(string));
    }
```

```
    [SecurityPermission(
    SecurityAction.LinkDemand,
    Flags = SecurityPermissionFlag.SerializationFormatter)
]
    void ISerializable.GetObjectData(SerializationInfo info,
            StreamingContext context) {
        if (info == null) throw new System.ArgumentNullException("info");
        info.AddValue("name", fullName);
    }

    public string FullName {
        get { return fullName; }
        set { fullName = value; }
    }
}
```

✓ **DO** make the serialization constructor protected and provide two parameters typed and named exactly as shown in the sample here.

```
[Serializable]
public class Person : ISerializable {
    protected Person(SerializationInfo info, StreamingContext context) {
        ...
    }
}
```

✓ **DO** implement the ISerializable members explicitly.

```
[Serializable]
public class Person : ISerializable {
    void ISerializable.GetObjectData(...) {
        ...
    }
}
```

✓ **DO** apply a link demand to ISerializable.GetObjectData implementation. This ensures that only fully trusted core and the Runtime Serializer have access to the member.

```
[Serializable]
public class Person : ISerializable {
    [SecurityPermission(
    SecurityAction.LinkDemand,
    Flags = SecurityPermissionFlag.SerializationFormatter)
]
```

```
    void ISerializable.GetObjectData(...) {
        ...
    }
}
```

8.11 Uri

System.Uri is a type that can be used to represent uniform resource identifiers (URIs). These concepts can also be represented using strings. Some of the most important guidelines in this section are intended to help you choose between System.Uri and System.String for representing URIs.

✓ **DO** use System.Uri to represent URI and URL data.

This applies to parameter types, property types, and return value types.

```
public class Navigator {
    public Navigator(Uri initialLocation);
    public Uri CurrentLocation { get; }
    public Uri NavigateTo(Uri location);
}
```

▪▫ **MARK ALCAZAR**   System.Uri is a much safer and richer way of representing URIs. Extensive manipulation of URI-related data using plain strings has been shown to cause many security and correctness problems.

✓ **CONSIDER** providing string-based overloads for most commonly used members with System.Uri parameters.

In cases where the usage pattern of taking a string from a user will be common enough, you should consider adding a convenience overload accepting a string. The string-based overload should be implemented in terms of the Uri-based overload.

```
public class Navigator {
    public void NavigateTo(Uri location);
    public void NavigateTo(string location) {
        NavigateTo (new Uri(location));
    }
}
```

✗ **DO NOT** automatically overload all `Uri`-based members with a version that accepts a string.

Generally, `Uri`-based APIs are preferred. String-based overloads are meant to be helpers for the most common scenarios. Therefore, you should not automatically provide string-based overloads for all variants of the `Uri`-based members. Be selective and provide such helpers just for the most commonly used variants.

```
public class Navigator {
    public void NavigateTo(Uri location);
    public void NavigateTo(Uri location, NavigationMode mode);
    public void NavigateTo(string location);
}
```

8.11.1 `System.Uri` Implementation Guidelines

The guidelines in this section help with the implementation of code using `System.Uri`.

✓ **DO** call the `Uri`-based overloads, if available.

✗ **DO NOT** store URI/URL data in a string.

When you accept a URI/URL input as a string, you should convert the string to `System.Uri` and store the instance of `System.Uri`.

```
public class SomeResource {
    Uri location;
    public SomeResource(string location) {
        this.location = new Uri(location);
    }
    public SomeResource(Uri location){
        this.location = location;
    }
}
```

8.12 `System.Xml` Usage

This section talks about usage of several types residing in `System.Xml` namespaces that can be used to represent XML data.

✗ **DO NOT** use XmlNode or XmlDocument to represent XML data. Favor using instances of IXPathNavigable, XmlReader, XmlWriter, or subtypes of XNode instead. XmlNode and XmlDocument are not designed for exposing in public APIs.

```
// bad design
public class ServerConfiguration {
   ...
   public XmlDocument ConfigurationData { get { ... } }
}
// good design
public class ServerConfiguration {
   ...
   public IXPathNavigable ConfigurationData { get { ... } }
}
```

✓ **DO** use XmlReader, IXPathNavigable, or subtypes of XNode as input or output of members that accept or return XML.

Use these abstractions instead of XmlDocument, XmlNode, or XPath-Document, because this decouples the methods from specific implementations of an in-memory XML document and allows them to work with virtual XML data sources that expose XNode, XmlReader, or XPath-Navigator.

✗ **DO NOT** subclass XmlDocument if you want to create a type representing an XML view of an underlying object model or data source.

This guideline means that XmlDataDocument is an example of what not to do.

■■ **DARE OBASANJO**   There are several problems with implementations like the XmlDataDocument. One is inefficiency. Because XmlNodes need to be distinct objects, such implementations result in large memory consumption. The second problem is that the data model of the DataSet does not map 1:1 with that of XML. There are all sorts of edge cases when one does things like insert comments, PIs, or CDATA sections into an XmlDataDocument.

Implementing a custom XPathNavigator gets around the inefficiency problems because the navigator is a cursor; there is no need to create objects for each node in the tree. It also reduces the Data/XML impedance mismatch. Because the main goal of XmlDataDocument was so users could either write out the DataSet as XML or query it with XPath, there is no need to support editability via the DOM. Second, the simpler data model of the XPath-Navigator leads to fewer edge cases in mapping your data model to XML.

8.13 Equality Operators

This section discusses overloading equality operators and refers to operator== and operator!= as equality operators.

✗ **DO NOT** overload one of the equality operators and not the other.

It is very surprising to developers when they discover that a type overloads just one of the operators.

✓ **DO** ensure that Object.Equals and the equality operators have exactly the same semantics and similar performance characteristics.

This often means that Object.Equals needs to be overridden when the equality operators are overloaded.

```
public struct PositiveInt32 : IEquatable<PositiveInt32> {
    public bool Equals(PositiveInt32 other) { ... }
    public override bool Equals(object obj) { ... }
    public static bool operator==(PositiveInt32 x, PositiveInt32 y){
        return x.Equals(y);
    }
    public static bool operator!=(PositiveInt32 x, PositiveInt32 y){
        return !x.Equals(y);
    }
    ...
}
```

✗ **AVOID** throwing exceptions from equality operators.

For example, return false if one of the arguments is null instead of throwing NullReferenceException.

8.13.1 Equality Operators on Value Types

✓ **DO** overload the equality operators on value types, if equality is meaningful.

In most programming languages, there is no default implementation of `operator==` for value types.

8.13.2 Equality Operators on Reference Types

✗ **AVOID** overloading equality operators on mutable reference types.

Many languages have built-in equality operators for reference types. The built-in operators usually implement the reference equality, and many developers are surprised when the default behavior is changed to the value equality.

This problem is mitigated for immutable reference types because immutability makes it much harder to notice the difference between reference equality and value equality.

✗ **AVOID** overloading equality operators on reference types if the implementation would be significantly slower than that of reference equality.

The next chapter discusses a set of design patterns used in the design of the .NET Framework that we feel will be of help to other framework designers.

9
Common Design Patterns

THERE ARE NUMEROUS books on software patterns, pattern languages, and antipatterns that address the very broad subject of patterns. Thus, this chapter provides guidelines and discussion related to a very limited set of patterns that are used frequently in the design of the .NET Framework APIs.

9.1 Aggregate Components

Many feature areas might benefit from one or more façade types that act as simplified views over more complex but also more powerful APIs. A façade that supports component-oriented design (see section 9.1.1) is called an aggregate component.

An aggregate component ties multiple lower-level factored types into a higher-level component to support common scenarios. An example might be an e-mail component that ties together Simple Mail Transfer Protocol (SMTP), sockets, encodings, and so on. It is important for an aggregate component to provide a higher abstraction level rather than just a different way of doing things.

Providing simplified high-level operations is crucial for those developers who do not want to learn the whole extent of the functionality provided by the feature and just need to get their (often very simple) tasks done.

> ■■ **KRZYSZTOF CWALINA** `System.Net.WebClient` is an example of an aggregate component. It provides an API for simple scenarios in the `System.Net` namespace. Other examples of such components include `System.Messaging.MessageQueue`, `System.IO.SerialPort`, and `System.Diagnostics.EventLog`.

Aggregate components, as high-level APIs, should be implemented so they magically work without the user being aware of sometimes complicated things happening underneath. We often refer to this concept as It-Just-Works. For example, the `EventLog` component hides the fact that a log has a read handle and a write handle that need to be opened. As far as the user is concerned, the component can be instantiated, properties can be set, and log events can be written.

Sometimes a bit more transparency is required. We recommend more transparency for operations if the user would be required to take an explicit action as a result of an operation. For example, implicitly opening a file and then requiring the user to explicitly close it is probably taking the principle of It-Just-Works a bit too far.

> ■■ **KRZYSZTOF CWALINA** An important API design principle is that complexity should be either completely hidden (or very close to completely) or not hidden at all. The worst thing you can do is design an API that looks simple but as developers start to use it, they discover (usually the hard way) that it is not.

It is often possible to design clever solutions that hide even those complexities. For example, reading a file can be implemented as a single operation that opens a file, reads its content, and closes it, thus shielding the user from all the complexities related to opening and closing the file handles.

```
string[] lines = File.ReadAllLines(@"c:\foo.txt");
```

Users of aggregate components should not be required to implement any interfaces, modify any configuration files, and so on. Framework designers should ship default implementations for all interfaces they declare. All configuration settings should be optional and backed by sensible defaults. Tools and IDE features should be considered for all common development tasks that are required beyond writing simple lines of code. In other words, framework designers should provide full end-to-end solutions, not just the APIs.

> ■ **KRZYSZTOF CWALINA** The `System.ServiceProcess` namespace greatly simplifies development of Windows Service applications. The API would be more successful with a wider range of developers if writing a service relied on hooking up event handlers instead of requiring the developer to override methods.

Aggregate components frequently integrate with Visual Studio designers by implementing `IComponent` or deriving from one of the UI Element classes).

The next section describes component-oriented design, an important concept in the design of high-level APIs, particularly in the design of aggregate components.

9.1.1 Component-Oriented Design

Component-oriented design is a design in which APIs are exposed as types, with constructors, properties, methods, and events. It actually has more to do with the way the API is used than with the mere inclusions of the constructors, methods, properties, and events. The usage model for component-oriented design follows a pattern of instantiating a type with a default or relatively simple constructor, setting some instance properties, and then calling simple instance methods. We call such pattern the Create-Set-Call Pattern.

```vbnet
' VB.NET sample code
' Instantiate
Dim t As New T()

' Set properties/options
t.P1 = v1
t.P2 = v2
t.P3 = v3
```

```
' Call methods and optionally change options between calls
t.M1()
' t.P3 = v4
t.M2()
```

A concrete example showing the Create-Set-Call usage pattern would look like the following:

```
' Instantiate
Dim queue As New MessageQueue()

' Set properties
queue.Path = queuePath
queue.EncryptionRequired = EncryptionRequired.Body
queue.Formatter = New BinaryMessageFormatter()

' Call methods
queue.Send("Hello World")
queue.Close()
```

It is very important that all aggregate components support this pattern. The pattern is something that users of aggregate components expect and for which tools such as Intellisense and designers are optimized.

> ■ **STEVEN CLARKE**   We have investigated this design pattern extensively in our usability labs. Our observations highlighted just how critical this pattern is for some developers. Without it, reading, writing, and debugging code can be much more difficult, because it can be more difficult to learn about the purpose of each parameter that a method takes.

One of the problems with component-oriented design is that it sometimes results in types that can have modes and invalid states. For example, a default constructor allows users to instantiate a MessageQueue component without providing a valid path. Also, properties, which can be set optionally and independently, sometimes cannot enforce consistent and atomic changes to the state of the object. The benefits of component-oriented design often outweigh these drawbacks for mainline scenario APIs, such as aggregate components, where usability is the top priority.

Also, some of the problems can and should be mitigated with proper error reporting. When users call methods that are not valid in the current state of the object, an InvalidOperationException should be thrown. The exception's message should clearly explain what properties need to be changed to get the object into a valid state.

> ▪▪ **STEVEN CLARKE**   Following this pattern means that it is very easy to learn about how to use the API through usage, rather than having to resort to documentation.

Often, API designers try to design types so objects cannot exist in an invalid state. This is accomplished by having all required settings as parameters to the constructor, having get-only properties for settings that cannot be changed after instantiation, and breaking functionality into separate types so that properties and methods do not overlap. This approach is strongly recommended for factored types (see section 9.1.2) but does not work for aggregate components. For aggregate components, we recommend relying on clear exceptions for communicating invalid states to the user. The exceptions should be thrown when an operation is being performed, not when the component is initialized (i.e., when the constructor is called or the property is being set). This is important for avoiding situations in which the invalid state is temporary and gets "fixed" in a subsequent line of code.

```
var workingSet = new PerformanceCounter();
workingSet.Instance = process.ProcessName;
// exception is not thrown here despite that the counter is in an
// invalid state (counter is not specified).

workingSet.Counter = "Working Set"; // state is "fixed" here!
workingSet.Category = "Process";

Debug.WriteLine(workingSet.NextValue());
```

> ▪▪ **CHRISTOPHE NASARRE**   It is not recommended to define a class with the opposite pattern: Create-Call-Get. For example, don't define a `Session` class that provides a `Login` method that pops up a dialog in which the end user enters his credential. The `Get` properties for the user name, for example, are valid for use only after the call to `Login`. Instead, you should implement the `Login` method to return another type that contains the credential details. It is even worse if the class provides other methods that depend on methods to be called in specific order, such as `GetSessionInfo`, only if the `Login` method has already been called.

An aggregate component is a façade based on component-oriented design with the following additional requirements:

- **Constructors:** An aggregate component should have a default constructor.
- **Constructors:** All constructor parameters correspond to and initialize properties.
- **Properties:** Most properties have getters and setters.
- **Properties:** All properties have sensible defaults.
- **Methods:** Methods do not take parameters if the parameters specify options that stay constant across method calls (in main scenarios). Such options should be specified using properties.
- **Events:** Methods do not take delegates as parameters. All callbacks are implemented in terms of events.

9.1.2 Factored Types

As described in the preceding section, an aggregate component provides shortcuts for most common high-level operations and is usually implemented as a façade over a set of more complex but also richer types. We call these types factored types.

Factored types should not have modes and should have very clear lifetimes. An aggregate component might provide access to its internal factored types through some properties or methods. Users would access the internal factored types in advanced scenarios or in scenarios where integration with different parts of the system is required. The following example shows an aggregate component (`SerialPort`) exposing its internal factored type (a serial port `Stream`) through the `BaseStream` property.

```
var port = new SerialPort("COM1");
port.Open();
GZipStream compressed;
compressed = new GZipStream(port.BaseStream, CompressionMode.Compress);
compressed.Write(data, 0, data.Length);
port.Close();
```

> ▪▪ **PHIL HAACK**   Since Factored Types have an explicit lifetime, it proba-
> bly makes good sense to implement the `IDisposable` interface so that
> developers can make use of the `using` statement. The code sample here
> could then be refactored to:
>
> ```
> using(SerialPort port = new SerialPort("COM1")) {
>   port.Open();
>   GZipStream compressed;
>   compressed = new GZipStream(port.BaseStream,
>     CompressionMode.Compress);
>   compressed.Write(data, 0, data.Length);
> }
> ```

9.1.3 Aggregate Component Guidelines

The following guidelines provide guidance for designing aggregate
components.

✓ **CONSIDER** providing aggregate components for commonly used feature areas.

Aggregate components provide high-level functionality and are starting points for exploring given technology. They should provide shortcuts for common operations and add significant value over what is
already provided by factored types. They should not simply duplicate
the functionality. Many main scenario code samples should start with
an instantiation of an aggregate component.

> ▪▪ **KRZYSZTOF CWALINA**   An easy trick to increase visibility of an aggre-
> gate component is to choose the most "attractive" name for the component
> and less attractive names for the corresponding factored types. For exam-
> ple, a name representing a well-known system entity like `File` will attract
> more attention than `StreamReader`.

✓ **DO** model high-level concepts (physical objects) rather than system-
level tasks with aggregate components.

For example, the components should model files, directories, and
drives, not streams, formatters, or comparers.

✓ **DO** increase visibility of aggregate components by giving them names that correspond to well-known entities of the system, such as `Message-Queue`, `Process`, or `EventLog`.

✓ **DO** design aggregate components so they can be used after very simple initialization. If some initialization is necessary, the exception resulting from not having the component initialized should clearly explain what needs to be done.

✗ **DO NOT** require the users of aggregate components to explicitly instantiate multiple objects in a single scenario.

Simple tasks should be done with just one object. The next best thing is to start with one object that in turn creates other supporting objects. Your top five scenario samples showing aggregate component usage should not have more than one new statement.

```
var queue = new MessageQueue();
queue.Path = ...;
queue.Send("Hello World");
```

> ▪ **KRZYSZTOF CWALINA**   Book publishers say that the number of copies a book will sell is inversely proportional to the number of equations in the book. The API designer version of this law is that the number of customers who will use your API is inversely proportional to the number of new statements in your simple scenarios.

✓ **DO** make sure aggregate components support the Create-Set-Call usage pattern, where developers expect to be able to implement most scenarios by instantiating the component, setting its properties, and calling simple methods.

✓ **DO** provide a default or a very simple constructor for all aggregate components.

```
public class MessageQueue {
    public MessageQueue() { ... }
    public MessageQueue(string path) { ... }
}
```

✓ **DO** provide properties with getters and setters corresponding to all parameters of aggregate component constructors.

It should always be possible to use the default constructor and then set some properties instead of calling a parameterized constructor.

```
public class MessageQueue {
    public MessageQueue() { ... }
    public MessageQueue(string path) { ... }

    public string Path { get { ... } set { ... } }
}
```

✓ **DO** use events instead of delegate-based APIs in aggregate components.

Aggregate components are optimized for ease of use, and events are much easier to use than APIs using delegates. See section 5.4, for more details.

✓ **CONSIDER** using events instead of virtual members that need to be overridden.

✗ **DO NOT** require users of aggregate components to inherit, override methods, or implement any interfaces in common scenarios.

Components should mostly rely on properties and composition as the means of modifying their behavior.

✗ **DO NOT** require users of aggregate components to do anything besides writing code in common scenarios. For example, users should not have to configure components in the configuration file, generate any resource files, and so on.

✓ **CONSIDER** making changes to aggregate components' modes automatic.

For example, a single instance of MessageQueue can be used to send and receive messages, but the user should not be aware that mode switching is occurring.

✗ **DO NOT** design factored types that have modes.

Factored types should have a well-defined life span scoped to a single mode. For example, instances of `Stream` can either read or write, and an instantiated stream is already opened.

✓ **CONSIDER** integrating your aggregate components with Visual Studio designers.

Integration allows placing the component on the Visual Studio Toolbox and adds support for drag and drop, property grid, event hookup, and so on. The integration is simple and can be done by implementing `IComponent` or inheriting from a type implementing the interface, such as `Component` or `Control`.

✓ **CONSIDER** separating aggregate components and factored types into different assemblies.

This allows the component to aggregate arbitrary functionality provided by factored types without circular dependencies.

✓ **CONSIDER** exposing access to internal factored types of an aggregate component.

Factored types are ideal for integrating different feature areas. For example, the `SerialPort` component exposes access to its stream, thus allowing integration with reusable APIs, such as compression APIs that operate on streams.

9.2 The Async Patterns

The .NET Framework uses two different API patterns to model asynchronous APIs: the so-called Classic Async Pattern (a.k.a. Async Pattern) and a newer Event-Based Async Pattern (a.k.a. Async Pattern for Components). This section describes details of these two patterns as well as how to choose between them when designing asynchronous APIs.

9.2.1 Choosing Between the Async Patterns

This section discusses the criteria for choosing the appropriate pattern for implementing asynchronous APIs. The main difference between the patterns is that the Event-Based Async Pattern is optimized for usability and integration with visual designers; the other is optimized for power and small surface area.

> ■ **STEVEN CLARKE** This was clearly called out during our usability studies on this pattern. Most participants in our study could use the event-based pattern successfully without reading any documentation. On the other hand, developers who are unfamiliar with the Classic Async Pattern will have a more difficult time without spending time reading documentation.
>
> While it's not the case that usability in the context of an API means the ability to use that API without reading documentation, for some users APIs that support learning by doing are preferable to those that don't.

The Classic Async Pattern offers a powerful and flexible programming model but is lacking when it comes to ease of use, especially when applied to components supporting graphical designers. The main reasons for usability differences between the patterns are the following:

- The Classic Async Pattern callbacks are executed on an arbitrary thread as opposed to a thread appropriate for the application model (for example, the UI thread for Windows Forms applications).
- There is currently no Visual Studio support for using the Classic Async Pattern, because it is delegate-based rather than event-based. Visual Studio provides extensive support for defining and hooking up event handlers, and the Event-Based Async Pattern takes full advantage of this support.

> ■ **GREG SCHECHTER** Also, even if visual designers aren't used, the VB.NET code editor combined with `WithEvents` provides much greater support for implementing and connecting event handlers than it does for delegates.

✓ **DO** implement the Event-Based Async Pattern if your type is a component supporting visual designers (i.e., if the type implements `IComponent`).

✔ **DO** implement the Classic Async Pattern if you must support wait handles.

The main reason to support wait handles is to be able to initiate multiple asynchronous operations simultaneously and then wait for the completion of one or all of the operations.

✔ **CONSIDER** implementing the Event-Based Async Pattern if you are designing higher-level APIs. For example, aggregate components (see section 9.2.4) should implement this pattern.

✔ **CONSIDER** implementing the Classic Async Pattern for low-level APIs where usability is less important than power, memory consumption, flexibility, and small surface area.

> ■ **JOE DUFFY** This decision is ultimately very simple to me. If you are developing a type meant to be consumed by other library or framework developers, you should use the Classic Async Pattern. They will appreciate the flexibility. If you are developing a type meant to be consumed by application developers, you should almost always prefer the Event-Based Async Pattern. They will appreciate the simplicity and Visual Studio integration.

✗ **AVOID** implementing both patterns at the same time on a single type or even on a single set of related types.

Components that implement both patterns may be confusing to some users. For example, for one synchronous method SomeMethod, there will be four asynchronous operations.

```
SomeMethod
SomeMethodAsync
BeginSomeMethod
EndSomeMethod
SomeMethodCompleted
```

9.2.2 Classic Async Pattern

The Classic Async Pattern is a naming, method signature, and behavioral convention for providing APIs that can be used to execute asynchronous operations. The main elements of the Async Pattern include the following:

- The `Begin` method, which initiates an asynchronous operation.
- The `End` method, which completes an asynchronous operation.
- The `IAsyncResult` object, which is returned from the `Begin` method and is essentially a token representing a single asynchronous operation. It contains methods and properties providing access to some basic information about the operation.
- An async callback, which is a user-supplied method that is passed to the `Begin` method and is called when the asynchronous operation is completed.
- The `State` object, which is a user-provided state that can be passed to the `Begin` method, is then passed to the async callback. This state is commonly used to pass caller-specific data to the async callback.

The following guidelines spell out conventions related to the API design part of the Classic Async Pattern. The guidelines do not go into the details of implementing the pattern.

Note that the guidelines assume that a method implementing a synchronous version of the operation already exists. It is quite common that an asynchronous operation is provided together with a synchronous counterpart, but it is not an absolute requirement.

✓ **DO** use the following convention for defining APIs for asynchronous operations. Given a synchronous method named `Operation`, provide `BeginOperation` and `EndOperation` methods with the following signatures (note that the out params are optional):

```
// synchronous method
public <return> Operation(<parameters>,<out params>)
// async pattern methods
public IAsyncResult BeginOperation(<parameters>, AsyncCallback callback,
object state)
public <return> EndOperation(IAsyncResult asyncResult, <out params>)
```

As an example, `System.IO.Stream` defines a synchronous Read method and the `BeginRead` and `EndRead` methods.

```
public int Read(byte[] buffer, int offset, int count)
public IAsyncResult BeginRead(byte[] buffer, int offset, int count,
    AsyncCallback callback, object state)
public int EndRead(IAsyncResult asyncResult)
```

✓ **DO** ensure that the return type of the `Begin` method implements `IAsyncResult`.

✓ **DO** ensure that any by-value and `ref` parameters of the synchronous method are represented as by-value parameters of the `Begin` method. `Out` parameters of the synchronous methods should not show in the signature of the `Begin` method.

✓ **DO** ensure that the return type of the `End` method is the same as the return type of the synchronous method.

```
public abstract class Stream {
    public int Read(byte[] buffer, int offset, int count)
    public int EndRead(IAsyncResult asyncResult)
}
```

✓ **DO** ensure that any out and `ref` parameters of the synchronous method are represented as out parameters of the `End` method. By-value parameters of the synchronous methods should not show in the signature of the `End` method.

✗ **DO NOT** continue the asynchronous operation if the `Begin` method throws an exception.

This method should throw if it needs to indicate the asynchronous operation could not be started. The async callback should not be called after this method throws.

✓ **DO** notify the caller that the asynchronous operation completed via all of the following mechanisms in this order:

- Set `IAsyncResult.IsCompleted` to true.
- Signal the wait handle returned from `IAsyncResult.AsyncWaitHandle`.
- Call the async callback.

> ■ **JOE DUFFY** This callback should never be transferred to a specific thread. It is all right to queue a work item to the thread pool for invocation so as not to reuse the current callstack at the time the operation completes. This can be

particularly useful if the operation completed synchronously. But you should specifically not try to do anything with `SynchronizationContext`, Windows Forms' `Control.Invoke`, Windows Presentation Foundation's Dispatcher, etc. to marshal the callback to another thread. One of the great things about the Classic Async Pattern is that it is consistent in this regard. If you find yourself needing to do this kind of marshaling, it's an indication you ought to consider using the Event-Based Async Pattern instead.

✓ **DO** throw exceptions from the `End` method to indicate that the asynchronous operation could not complete successfully.

This allows a deterministic place to catch those exceptions.

✓ **DO** complete all remaining work synchronously once the `End` method is called.

In other words, the `End` method blocks until the operation completes and then returns.

✓ **CONSIDER** throwing an `InvalidOperationException` if the `End` method is called with the same `IAsyncResult` twice, or if the `IAsyncResult` was returned from an unrelated `Begin` method.

✓ **DO** set `IAsyncResult.CompletedSynchronously` to true if and only if the async callback will be run on the thread that called `Begin`.

■ BRIAN GRUNKEMEYER The point of the `CompletedSynchronously` property is not to report the underlying details of the asynchronous operation, but instead to help the async callback deal with potential stack overflows. Some callers might want to call the `Begin` method again from within their callback, passing in the callback again as to the nested `Begin`. This can lead to stack overflows if the underlying operation executes synchronously and the callback is called on that same thread. By checking this property, the callback can tell whether it is running at some arbitrary stack depth on a user thread or at the base of a thread pool thread.

Yes, I know, the name might have been poorly chosen. Alternate names could have been something like `CallbackRunningOnThreadpoolThread` or `CallbackCanContinueCallingBeginMethodName`.

9.2.3 **Classic Async Pattern Basic Implementation Example**

The following sample shows a basic implementation of the Async Pattern. This particular implementation is for illustrative purposes only. Although the implementation is useful for understanding the general pattern, it is unlikely to produce the optimum performance in exposing asynchronous operations because it utilizes the asynchronous functionality built into delegates. This uses the remoting layer and so is not optimum in terms of performance and resource consumption.

```csharp
public class FiboCalculator {
    delegate void Callback(int count,ICollection<decimal> series);
    private Callback callback = new Callback(GetFibo);

    // Starts the process of generating a series and returns
    public IAsyncResult BeginGetFibo(
        int count,
        ICollection<decimal> series,
        AsyncCallback callback,
        object state)
    {
        return this.callback.BeginInvoke(count,series,callback,state);
    }

    // Blocks until the process of generating a series completes
    public void EndGetFibo(IAsyncResult asyncResult) {
        this.callback.EndInvoke(asyncResult);
    }

    // Generate a series of the first count Fibonacci numbers
    public static void GetFibo(
        int count, ICollection<decimal> series)
    {
        for (int i = 0; i < count; i++) {
            decimal d = GetFiboCore(i);
            lock (series) {
                series.Add(d);
            }
        }
    }

    // Return the Nth Fibonacci number
    static decimal GetFiboCore(int n){
        if (n < 0) throw new ArgumentException("n must be > 0");
        if (n == 0 || n == 1) return 1;
        return GetFiboCore(n-1) + GetFiboCore(n-2);
    }
}
```

> ■ **CHRISTOPHER BRUMME** A better way to implement this pattern is to provide `Begin` and `End` methods that use `ThreadPool.QueueUserWorkItem` under the covers. Essentially, you are avoiding all the interpretive overhead of remoting messages by writing the methods that put your state into a work item and then getting your state back out of the work item. This is pretty easy to do, and the performance should be much better than when using asynchronous delegates.

> ■ **BRIAN GRUNKEMEYER** To implement the async design pattern using asynchronous I/O, look at `System.Threading.Overlapped` and `System.Threading.Threadpool.BindHandle`. `BindHandle` internally binds a handle to a Win32 I/O completion port, which is the most performant mechanism in the operating system to handle asynchronous I/O, allowing the operating system to throttle I/O threads as needed. Use the `Overlapped` class to provide a `NativeOverlapped*`, which you can then pass to Win32 methods taking an `LPOVERLAPPED`. Make sure any buffers you use for your asynchronous I/O operation are passed to `Overlapped.Pack` or `UnsafePack`, or you will corrupt memory if an application domain unload happens while your asynchronous I/O operation is in flight.

9.2.4 Event-Based Async Pattern

Usually, asynchronous APIs are offered in addition to synchronous APIs. The following step-by-step guide for defining asynchronous APIs assumes the synchronous versions already exist, but it is important to keep in mind that the synchronous methods need not even be present if the component just wants to expose asynchronous API.

9.2.4.1 Defining Asynchronous Methods

Define an asynchronous method for each synchronous method that you want to provide an asynchronous version for. The asynchronous method should return void and take the same parameters as the synchronous method (see section 5.8.3 for handling out and ref parameters). The name of the method should be built by appending the "Async" suffix to the name of the synchronous method.

Optionally, define an overload of the asynchronous method with an additional object parameter called "userState." Do this if the API supports multiple concurrent invocations of the asynchronous operation, in which case the userState will be delivered back to the event handler to distinguish between the invocations.

For example, given the following synchronous method:

```
public class SomeType {
    public SomeReturnType Method(string arg1, string arg2);
}
```

The following asynchronous methods should be added:

```
public class SomeType {
    public void MethodAsync(string arg1, string arg2);

    // optional
    public void MethodAsync(string arg1, string arg2, object userState);

    public SomeReturnType Method(string arg1, string arg2);
}
```

✔ **DO** ensure that if your component defines the asynchronous method without the userState parameter, any attempt to invoke the method before the prior invocation has completed will result in an Invalid-OperationException being raised.

For each asynchronous method, also define the following event:

```
public class SomeType {
    public event EventHandler<MethodCompleteEventArgs> MethodCompleted;

    public void MethodAsync(string arg1, string arg2);
    public void MethodAsync(string arg1, string arg2, object userState);
    public SomeReturnType Method(string arg1, string arg2);
}
```

✔ **DO** ensure you invoke event handlers on the proper thread. This is one of the main benefits of using the Event-Based Async Pattern over the Classic Async Pattern.

It is critical that event handlers get invoked on the proper thread for the given application model. The Framework provides a mechanism, `AsyncOperationManager`, to do this easily and consistently. The mechanism allows components to be used equally well across all application models.

✓ **DO** ensure that you always invoke the event handler, on successful completion, on an error, or on cancellation. Applications should not be put in a situation where they indefinitely wait for something that doesn't happen. An exception to this, of course, is if the actual asynchronous operation itself never starts or completes.

```
public class MethodCompletedEventArgs : AsyncCompletedEventArgs {
    public SomeReturnType Result { get; }
}
```

✓ **DO** ensure that accessing a property[1] of the event arguments class of a failed asynchronous operation results in an exception being thrown. In other words, if there was an error completing the task, the results shouldn't be accessible.

✗ **DO NOT** define new event handlers or event argument types for void methods. Use `AsyncCompletedEventArgs`, `AsyncCompletedEventHandler`, or `EventHandler<AsyncCompletedEventArg>` instead.

9.2.5 Supporting `Out` and `Ref` Parameters

The above examples are based on synchronous methods that take only input parameters; out and `ref` parameters are not dealt with. Although the use of out and `ref` is discouraged in general, sometimes they are unavoidable.

Given a synchronous method with `out` parameters, the asynchronous version of the method should omit the parameters from its signature. Instead, the parameters should be exposed as get-only properties of the `EventArgs` class. The names and types of the properties should be the same as the names and types of the parameters.

`Ref` parameters to the synchronous method should appear as input parameters of asynchronous version, and as get-only properties of the

---

1. This refers only to properties carrying the results of the asynchronous operation, not to properties carrying the error information, for example.

EventArgs class. The names and types of the properties should be the same as the names and types of the parameters.

For example, given the following synchronous method:

```
public string Method(object arg1, ref int arg2, out long arg3)
```

The asynchronous version would look like the following:

```
public void MethodAsync(object arg1, int arg2);

public class MethodCompletedEventArgs : AsyncCompletedEventArgs {
    public string Result { get; }
    public int Arg2 { get; }
    public long Arg3 { get; }
}
```

9.2.6 Supporting Cancellation

The pattern can optionally support cancellation of pending operations. Cancellation should be exposed through a CancelAsync method.

If the asynchronous operations support multiple outstanding operations, that is, if the asynchronous methods take parameter userState, the cancellation method should also take a parameter userState. Otherwise, the method does not take any parameters.

```
public class SomeType {

    public void CancelAsync(object userState);
    // or public void CancelAsync();
    // if multiple outstanding requests are not supported

    public SomeReturnType Method(string arg1, string arg2);
    public void MethodAsync(string arg1, string arg2);
    public void MethodAsync(string arg1, string arg2, object userState);
    public event MethodCompletedEventHandler MethodCompleted;
}
```

✓ **DO** ensure that in the case of cancellation, you set the Cancelled property of the event arguments class to true, and that any attempt to access the result raises an InvalidOperationException stating that the operation was cancelled.

✓ **DO** ignore calls to the cancellation method if the particular operation cannot be cancelled, instead of raising an exception. The reason for this is that in general a component cannot know whether an operation is truly cancelable at any given time and cannot know whether a previously issued cancellation has succeeded. However, the application will always know when a cancellation succeeded, because it is indicated by the Cancelled property of the event arguments class.

9.2.7 Supporting Progress Reporting

It is frequently desired and feasible to provide progress reporting during an asynchronous operation. The following section describes APIs for such support.

If an asynchronous operation needs to support progress reporting, add an additional event, named `ProgressChanged`, to be raised by the asynchronous operation.

```
public class SomeType {

    public event EventHandler<ProgressChangedEventArgs> ProgressChanged;

    public void CancelAsync(object userState);
    public SomeReturnType Method(string arg1, string arg2);
    public void MethodAsync(string arg1, string arg2);
    public void MethodAsync(string arg1, string arg2, object userState);
    public event MethodCompletedEventHandler MethodCompleted;
}
```

`ProgressChangedEventArgs` parameter, passed to the handler, carries an integer-valued progress indicator that is expected to be between 0 and 100.

```
// this is a standard type defined by the Framework
public class ProgressChangedEventArgs : EventArgs {
    public ProgressChangedEventArgs(int progressPercentage,
                                    object userState);
    public object UserState { get; }
    public int ProgressPercentage { get; }
}
```

Note that in most cases there is only one `ProgressChanged` event for the component, regardless of the number of asynchronous operations. Clients are expected to use the `userState` object that was passed in to the operations to distinguish between progress updates on multiple concurrent operations.

There may be situations where multiple operations support progress, and they each return a different indicator for that progress. In that case, a single `ProgressChanged` event is no longer appropriate, and the implementer may consider supporting multiple `ProgressChanged` events as the situation dictates. In such case the specific progress events should be called `<MethodName>ProgressChanged`.

The basic implementation of progress reporting uses the `Progress-ChangedEventArgs` class and the `EventHandler<ProgressChangedEventArgs>` delegate. Optionally, if a more domain-specific progress indicator is desired (for example, number of bytes read), a subclass of `Progress-ChangedEventArgs` can be defined and used.

> ■■ **GREG SCHECHTER** One could argue that a floating-point value between 0.0 and 1.0 would be more appropriate as `ProgressPercentage`. An integer range was chosen because it maps well to the progress control, which also uses the integer range from 0 to 100.

✓ **DO** ensure that, if you implement a `ProgressChanged` event, there are no such events raised for a particular asynchronous operation after that operation's completed event has been raised.

> ■■ **GREG SCHECHTER** If you're dispatching progress and completion events from the same thread, ensure that no progress events occur after the operation has completed. If they're coming from different threads, you may not be able to do this without compromising concurrency, and thus it likely shouldn't be pursued in those situations.

✓ **DO** ensure that, if the standard `ProgressChangedEventArgs` is being used, the `ProgressPercentage` can always be interpreted as a percentage (it does not need to necessarily be an accurate percentage, but it does need to represent a percentage). If your progress reporting metric must be something different, then a subclass of `ProgressChangedEventArgs` is more appropriate, and you should leave the `ProgressPercentage` property at 0.

> ■ **CHRIS SELLS**   Please make progress reporting move forward, if for no other reason than my family makes fun of me when they see a progress report going backwards, as if it's my fault. Personally, I've implemented several progress percentage algorithms and while I often can't get the timing to be smooth through all stages of an operation, at least they always move forward. In fact, I think you'd have to work extra hard to make them move backwards.

9.2.8 Supporting Incremental Results

Occasionally, asynchronous operations can return incremental results periodically, prior to being complete. There are a number of different options that can be used to support this scenario, based on the constraints.

If the component supports multiple asynchronous operations, each capable of returning incremental results, these incremental results should all have the same type.

✓ **DO** raise this `ProgressChanged` event when there is an incremental result to report back.

✓ **DO** extend the `ProgressChangedEventArgs` to carry the incremental result data, and define a `ProgressChanged` event with this extended data.

If the multiple asynchronous operations return a different type of data, the following approach should be used.

✓ **DO** separate out your incremental result reporting from your progress reporting.

✔ **DO** define a separate `<MethodName>ProgressChanged` event with appropriate event arguments for each asynchronous operation to handle that operation's incremental result data.

> ▪ **CHRIS SELLS** I find the `System.ComponentModel.Background-`
> `Worker` component to be a simple way to implement the Event-Based
> Async Pattern if you'd like help. It's also an excellent example of such an
> implementation.

9.3 **Dependency Properties**

A dependency property (DP) is a regular property that stores its value in a property store instead of storing it in a type variable (field), for example.

An attached dependency property is a kind of dependency property modeled as static Get and Set methods representing "properties" describing relationships between objects and their containers (e.g., the position of a `Button` object on a `Panel` container).

This section describes when this might be useful and guidelines related to the design of such properties.

✔ **DO** provide the dependency properties, if you need the properties to support WPF features such as styling, triggers, data binding, animations, dynamic resources, and inheritance.

In the following example, the `TextButton.Text` property is a dependency property supporting WPF style triggers.

```
<Style TargetType="TextButton">
   <Setter Property="Text" Value="Move here and click" />
   <Style.Triggers>
      <Trigger Property="IsMouseOver" Value="True">
         <Setter Property="Text" Value="Now click" />
      </Trigger>
   </Style.Triggers>
</Style>
```

… and here's an example using the property with data binding:

```
<TextButton Text="{Binding FirstName}" />
```

9.3.1 Dependency Property Design

The following guidelines describe details of dependency property design.

✓ **DO** inherit from `DependencyObject`, or one of its subtypes, when implementing dependency properties. The type provides a very efficient implementation of a property store and automatically supports WPF data binding.

✓ **DO** provide a regular CLR property and public static read-only field storing an instance of `System.Windows.DependencyProperty` for each dependency property.

```
public class TextButton : DependencyObject {

    public string Text {
       get { return (string)this.GetValue(TextProperty); }
       set { this.SetValue(TextProperty,value); }
    }

    public static readonly DependencyProperty TextProperty =
       DependencyProperty.Register("Text",typeof(string),typeof(TextButton));
}
```

✓ **DO** implement dependency properties by calling instance methods `DependencyObject.GetValue` and `DependencyObject.SetValue`.

```
public class TextButton : DependencyObject {

    public string Text {
       get { return (string)this.GetValue(TextProperty); }
       set { this.SetValue(TextProperty,value); }
    }

    public static readonly DependencyProperty TextProperty = ...
}
```

✓ **DO** name the dependency property static field by suffixing the name of the property with "Property."

The first parameter to the `DependencyProperty.Register` method should be the name of the wrapper property.

```
public class TextButton : DependencyObject {

    public static readonly DependencyProperty TextProperty =
        DependencyProperty.Register("Text",typeof(string),typeof(
        TextButton));
}
```

✗ **DO NOT** set default values of dependency properties explicitly in code; set them in metadata instead.

If you set a property default explicitly, you might prevent that property from being set by some implicit means, such as a styling.

```
public class TextButton : DependencyObject {

    public TextButton(){
        // do not set DP default values explicitly
            Text = String.Empty;  // this is bad!
    }

    public static readonly DependencyProperty TextProperty =
        DependencyProperty.Register(
            "Text",
            typeof(string),
            typeof(TextButton),
            new PropertyMetadata(String.Empty) // this is good!
        );
}
```

✗ **DO NOT** put code in the property accessors other than the standard code to access the static field.

That code won't execute if the property is set by implicit means, such as a styling, because styling uses the static field directly.

```
public string Text {
    get { return (string)GetValue(TextProperty); }
    set {
        SetValue(TextProperty, value);
        DoWorkOnTextChanged(); // this is bad!
    }
}
```

✗ **DO NOT** use dependency properties to store secure data. Even private dependency properties can be accessed publicly.

```
public class BadType : DependencyObject {
    // do not do this! It's not secure!
    private static readonly DependencyProperty SecretProperty =
        DependencyProperty.Register("Secret",typeof(string),typeof(
        BadType));


    public BadType() {
        SetValue(SecretProperty,"password");
    }
}

static void Main(){
    var b = new BadType();
        var enumerator = b.GetLocalValueEnumerator();
        while (enumerator.MoveNext()) {
            Console.WriteLine("{0}={1}",
            enumerator.Current.Property,
            enumerator.Current.Value
        );
    }
}
```

9.3.2 Attached Dependency Property Design

Dependency properties described in the preceding section represent intrinsic properties of the declaring type; for example, the Text property is a property of TextButton, which declares it. A special kind of dependency property is the attached dependency property. The dependency property guidelines apply to attached dependency properties as well, but there are some additional guidelines to consider when implementing attached dependency properties, and this section describes these special considerations.

Attached dependency properties represent properties that are defined on one type but that can be set on an object of another type.

CHRISTOPHE NASARRE This is close to what you would achieve with a PropertyExtender in Windows Forms.

A classic example of an attached property is the `Grid.Column` property. The property represents Button's (not Grid's) column position, but it is only relevant if the Button is contained in a Grid, and so it's "attached" to Buttons by Grids.

```
<Grid>
    <Grid.ColumnDefinitions>
        <ColumnDefinition />
        <ColumnDefinition />
    </Grid.ColumnDefinitions>

    <Button Grid.Column="0">Click</Button>
    <Button Grid.Column="1">Clack</Button>
</Grid>
```

The definition of an attached property looks mostly like that of a regular dependency property, except that the accessors are represented by static Get and Set methods:

```
public class Grid {

    public static int GetColumn(DependencyObject obj) {
        return (int)obj.GetValue(ColumnProperty);
    }

    public static void SetColumn(DependencyObject obj, int value) {
        obj.SetValue(ColumnProperty,value);
    }

    public static readonly DependencyProperty ColumnProperty =
        DependencyProperty.RegisterAttached(
            "Column",
            typeof(int),
            typeof(Grid)
    );
}
```

9.3.3 Dependency Property Validation

Properties often implement what is called validation. Validation logic executes when an attempt is made to change the value of a property. The following example shows the typical validation code ensuring that a property is not ever set to null.

```
public string Text {
    set {
        if (value==null) {
            throw new ArgumentNullException("value",...);
        }
    }
}
```

Unfortunately dependency property accessors cannot contain arbitrary validation code, as described in section 9.3.3. Instead, dependency property validation logic needs to be specified during property registration.

✗ **DO NOT** put dependency property validation logic in the property's accessors. Instead, pass a validation callback to `DependencyProperty.Register` method.

```
public static readonly DependencyProperty TextProperty =
    DependencyProperty.Register(
        "Text",
        typeof(string),
        typeof(TextButton),
        new PropertyMetadata(String.Empty),
        delegate(object value) { return value != null; } // validation
    );
```

9.3.4 Dependency Property Change Notifications

Similarly to validation logic described in the previous section, dependency property accessors should not have custom code that would be normally used to trigger property change notification events because these accessors are not called from XAML generated code.

```
public string Text {
    set {
        if(this.text!=value){
            this.text = value;
        }
        OnTextChanged();  // bad
    }
}
```

✗ DO NOT implement change notification logic in dependency property accessors. Dependency properties have a built-in change notifications feature that must be used by supplying a change notification callback to the `PropertyMetadata`.

```
public static readonly DependencyProperty TextProperty =
    DependencyProperty.Register(
        "Text",
        typeof(string),
        typeof(TextButton),
        new PropertyMetadata(
            String.Empty,
            delegate(DependencyObject e,DependencyPropertyChangedEventArgs
    args){
                // property changed
                ...
            }
        )
    );
```

9.3.5 Dependency Property Value Coercion

Property coercion takes place when the value given to a property setter is modified by the setter before the property store is actually modified. The following example shows simple coercion logic.

```
public string Text {
    set {
        if (value == null){ value = String.Empty; }
        this.text = value;
    }
}
```

Similarly to validation and change notification logic described in the previous sections, dependency properties must specify coercion logic during property registration, not directly in the property accessor.

✗ DO NOT implement coercion logic in dependency property accessors. Dependency properties have a built-in coercion feature, and it can be used by supplying a coercion callback to the `PropertyMetadata`.

```
public static readonly DependencyProperty NameProperty =
    DependencyProperty.Register("Name", typeof(string), typeof(WpfType),
        new PropertyMetadata(
        String.Empty,
        delegate(DependencyObject e, DependencyPropertyChangedEventArgs args) {
                // change notification callback
        },
        delegate(DependencyObject e, object value) {
        if (value == null) value = String.Empty; // coercion
        return value;
        }
    )
);
```

9.4 Dispose Pattern

All programs acquire one or more system resources, such as memory, system handles, or database connections, during the course of their execution. Developers have to be careful when using such system resources, because they must be released after they have been acquired and used.

The CLR provides support for automatic memory management. Managed memory (memory allocated using the C# operator new) does not need to be explicitly released. It is released automatically by the garbage collector (GC). This frees developers from the tedious and difficult task of releasing memory and has been one of the main reasons for the unprecedented productivity afforded by the .NET Framework.

Unfortunately, managed memory is just one of many types of system resources. Resources other than managed memory still need to be released explicitly and are referred to as unmanaged resources. The GC was specifically not designed to manage such unmanaged resources, which means that the responsibility for managing unmanaged resources lies in the hands of the developers.

The CLR provides some help in releasing unmanaged resources. System.Object declares a virtual method Finalize (also called the finalizer) that is called by the GC before the object's memory is reclaimed by the GC and can be overridden to release unmanaged resources. Types that override the finalizer are referred to as finalizable types.

Although finalizers are effective in some cleanup scenarios, they have two significant drawbacks:

- The finalizer is called when the GC detects that an object is eligible for collection. This happens at some undetermined period of time after the resource is not needed anymore. The delay between when the developer could or would like to release the resource and the time when the resource is actually released by the finalizer might be unacceptable in programs that acquire many scarce resources (resources that can be easily exhausted) or in cases in which resources are costly to keep in use (e.g., large unmanaged memory buffers).

- When the CLR needs to call a finalizer, it must postpone collection of the object's memory until the next round of garbage collection (the finalizers run between collections). This means that the object's memory (and all objects it refers to) will not be released for a longer period of time.

Therefore, relying exclusively on finalizers might not be appropriate in many scenarios when it is important to reclaim unmanaged resources as quickly as possible, when dealing with scarce resources, or in highly performant scenarios in which the added GC overhead of finalization is unacceptable.

The Framework provides the `System.IDisposable` interface that should be implemented to provide the developer a manual way to release unmanaged resources as soon as they are not needed. It also provides the `GC.SuppressFinalize` method that can tell the GC that an object was manually disposed of and does not need to be finalized anymore, in which case the object's memory can be reclaimed earlier. Types that implement the `IDisposable` interface are referred to as disposable types.

▪▪ **BRIAN PEPIN** The idea behind `Dispose` is that you call it to release scarce or unmanaged resources. We've designed it so if you don't call `Dispose`, the object will finalize and release the resource anyway. It's great that we'll clean up eventually for you, but in reality you probably have a bug if you're not disposing of an object when you're done with it. The exception here is when you're sharing an object with other code. For example, Windows Forms controls that have an `ImageList` property never dispose of the `ImageList`, because they don't know if it is being used by other controls.

JOE DUFFY   The advice I would like to give people is roughly as follows. When a type implements `IDisposable`, and ownership is obvious, you should do your best to call `Dispose` when you are done with the object. But if ownership becomes tricky (because the object is referenced from multiple places or shared across threads, for example), neglecting to call `Dispose` will do no harm. This is along the lines of what Brian says above. Unfortunately, there are a few instances in the .NET Framework where failure to call `Dispose` can lead to surprising behavior. `FileStream`, for example, will keep the file handle open until finalization time. If that handle was opened in write-exclusive mode, nobody else on the machine will be able to open the file until the finalizer runs. Moreover, the contents written won't be flushed to disk until then. This is a nondeterministic event, and it is terrible to rely on it for correctness.

The Dispose Pattern is intended to standardize the usage and implementation of finalizers and the `IDisposable` interface.

The main motivation for the pattern is to reduce the complexity of the implementation of the `Finalize` and the `Dispose` methods. The complexity stems from the fact that the methods share some but not all code paths (the differences are described later in the chapter). In addition, there are historical reasons for some elements of the pattern related to the evolution of language support for deterministic resource management.

✓ **DO** implement the Basic Dispose Pattern on types containing instances of disposable types. See section 9.4.1 for details on the basic pattern.

If a type is responsible for the lifetime of other disposable objects, developers need a way to dispose of them, too. Using the container's `Dispose` method is a convenient way to make this possible.

✓ **DO** implement the Basic Dispose Pattern and provide a finalizer on types holding resources that need to be freed explicitly and that do not have finalizers.

For example, the pattern should be implemented on types storing unmanaged memory buffers. Section 9.4.2 discusses guidelines related to implementing finalizers.

✓ **CONSIDER** implementing the Basic Dispose Pattern on classes that themselves don't hold unmanaged resources or disposable objects but are likely to have subtypes that do.

A great example of this is the System.IO.Stream class. Although it is an abstract base class that doesn't hold any resources, most of its subclasses do and because of this, it implements this pattern.

9.4.1 Basic Dispose Pattern

The basic implementation of the pattern involves implementing the System.IDisposable interface and declaring the Dispose(bool) method that implements all resource cleanup logic to be shared between the Dispose method and the optional finalizer. Please note that this section does not discuss providing a finalizer. Finalizers are extensions to this basic pattern and are discussed in section 9.4.2.

The following example shows a simple implementation of the basic pattern:

```
public class DisposableResourceHolder : IDisposable {

    private SafeHandle resource; // handle to a resource

    public DisposableResourceHolder(){
        this.resource = ... // allocates the resource
    }

    public void Dispose(){
        Dispose(true);
        GC.SuppressFinalize(this);
    }
```

```
    protected virtual void Dispose(bool disposing){
        if (disposing){
            if (resource!= null) resource.Dispose();
        }
    }
}
```

> **HERB SUTTER** If using C++, simply write the usual destructor (~T())
> and the compiler will automatically generate all of the machinery described
> later in this section. In the rare cases in which you do want to write a final-
> izer (!T()) as well, the recommended way to share code is to put as much
> of the work into the finalizer as the finalizer is able to handle (e.g., the final-
> izer cannot reliably touch other objects, so don't put code in there that needs
> to use other objects), put the rest in the destructor, and have your destructor
> call your finalizer explicitly.

The Boolean parameter disposing indicates whether the method was invoked from the IDisposable.Dispose implementation or from the finalizer. The Dispose(bool) implementation should check the parameter before accessing other reference objects (e.g., the resource field in the preceding sample). Such objects should only be accessed when the method is called from the IDisposable.Dispose implementation (when the disposing parameter is equal to true). If the method is invoked from the finalizer (disposing is false), other objects should not be accessed. The reason is that objects are finalized in an unpredictable order and so they, or any of their dependencies, might already have been finalized.

Also, this section applies to classes with a base that does not already implement the Dispose Pattern. If you are inheriting from a class that already implements the pattern, simply override the Dispose(bool) method to provide additional resource cleanup logic.

✓ **DO** declare a protected virtual void Dispose(bool disposing) method to centralize all logic related to releasing unmanaged resources.

All resource cleanup should occur in this method. The method is called from both the finalizer and the IDisposable.Dispose method. The parameter will be false if being invoked from inside a finalizer. It should be used to ensure any code running during finalization is not accessing other finalizable objects. Details of implementing finalizers are described in section 9.4.2.

```
protected virtual void Dispose(bool disposing){
    if (disposing){
        if (resource!= null) resource.Dispose();
    }
}
```

JEFFREY RICHTER The idea here is that `Dispose(bool)` knows whether it is being called to do explicit cleanup (the Boolean is true) versus being called due to a garbage collection (the Boolean is false). This distinction is useful because, when being disposed explicitly, the `Dispose(bool)` method can safely execute code using reference type fields that refer to other objects knowing for sure that these other objects have not been finalized. When the Boolean is false, the `Dispose(Boolean)` method should not execute code that refers to reference type fields because those objects might have already been finalized.

JOE DUFFY Jeff's comment might seem incorrect at first glance—that is, can't you safely access reference type objects that aren't finalizable? The answer is yes, if and only if you are certain that the object doesn't rely on the finalizable state itself! This is a nontrivial thing to figure out and is subject to change from release to release. Unless you're 100 percent certain, perhaps because you own the type in question, just avoid doing it.

✓ **DO** implement the `IDisposable` interface by simply calling `Dispose(true)` followed by `GC.SuppressFinalize(this)`.

The call to `SuppressFinalize` should only occur if `Dispose(true)` executes successfully.

```
public void Dispose(){
    Dispose(true);
    GC.SuppressFinalize(this);
}
```

> **BRAD ABRAMS** We had a fair amount of debate about the relative ordering of calls in the `Dispose()` method. We opted for the ordering where `SuppressFinalize` is called after `Dispose(bool)`. It ensures that `GC.SuppressFinalize()` only gets called if the `Dispose` operation completes successfully.

> **JEFFREY RICHTER** I, too, wrestled back and forth with the order of these calls. Originally, I felt that `SuppressFinalize` should be called prior to `Dispose`. My thinking was this: If `Dispose` throws an exception then, it will throw the same exception when `Finalize` is called and there is no benefit to this, and the second exception should be prevented. However, I have since changed my mind and I now agree with this guideline that `SuppressFinalize` should be called after `Finalize`. The reason is that `Dispose()` calls `Dispose(true)`, which might throw, but when `Finalize` is called later, `Dispose(false)` is called. This might be a different code path than before, and it would be good if this different code path executed. In addition, the different code path might not throw the exception.

✗ **DO NOT** make the parameterless `Dispose` method virtual.

The `Dispose(bool)` method is the one that should be overridden by subclasses.

```
// bad design
public class DisposableResourceHolder : IDisposable {
    public virtual void Dispose(){ ... }
    protected virtual void Dispose(bool disposing){ ... }
}

// good design
public class DisposableResourceHolder : IDisposable {
    public void Dispose(){ ... }
    protected virtual void Dispose(bool disposing){ ... }
}
```

> **BRIAN PEPIN** If you look hard enough, there are still places in the Framework where we don't follow this pattern. By the time we finalized the `Dispose` pattern, quite a bit of the Framework had already been written. Although we scrubbed everything to the best of our ability, a few things still slipped through the cracks.

✗ **DO NOT** declare any overloads of the `Dispose` method other than `Dispose()` and `Dispose(bool)`.

`Dispose` should be considered a reserved word to help codify this pattern and prevent confusion among implementers, users, and compilers. Some languages might choose to automatically implement this pattern on certain types.

✓ **DO** allow the `Dispose(bool)` method to be called more than once. The method might choose to do nothing after the first call.

```
public class DisposableResourceHolder : IDisposable {

    bool disposed = false;

    protected virtual void Dispose(bool disposing){
        if(disposed) return;
        // cleanup
        ...
        disposed = true;
    }
}
```

✗ **AVOID** throwing an exception from within `Dispose(bool)` except under critical situations where the containing process has been corrupted (leaks, inconsistent shared state, etc.).

Users expect that a call to `Dispose` will not raise an exception. For example, consider the manual try-finally in this snippet:

```
TextReader tr = new StreamReader(File.OpenRead("foo.txt"));
try {
    // do some stuff
}
finally {
    tr.Dispose();
    // more stuff
}
```

If `Dispose` could raise an exception, further finally-block cleanup logic will not execute. To work around this, the user would need to wrap every call to Dispose (within the finally block!) in a try block, which leads to very complex cleanup handlers. If executing a Dispose(bool disposing) method, never throw an exception if disposing is false. Doing so will terminate the process if executing inside a finalizer context.

✓ **DO** throw an ObjectDisposedException from any member that cannot be used after the object has been disposed of.

```
public class DisposableResourceHolder : IDisposable {
    bool disposed = false;
    SafeHandle resource; // handle to a resource

    public void DoSomething(){
        if(disposed) throw new ObjectDisposedException(...);
        // now call some native methods using the resource
        ...
    }
    protected virtual void Dispose(bool disposing){
        if(disposed) return;
        // cleanup
        ...
        disposed = true;
    }
}
```

✓ **CONSIDER** providing method Close(), in addition to the Dispose(), if close is standard terminology in the area.

When doing so, it is important that you make the Close implementation identical to Dispose and consider implementing the IDisposable. Dispose method explicitly. See section 5.1.2, on implementing interfaces explicitly.

```
public class Stream : IDisposable {
    IDisposable.Dispose(){
        Close();
    }
    public void Close(){
        Dispose(true);
        GC.SuppressFinalize(this);
    }
}
```

> **■ JEFF PROSISE** Implementing `Close` and `Dispose` so that they're semantically equivalent helps avoid a lot of confusion. More than once, I've had developers tell me that you shouldn't instantiate a `SqlConnection` in a `using` statement because the resultant code will call `Dispose` but not `Close`. In reality, it's fine to combine `using` and `SqlConnection` because `SqlConnection.Dispose` calls `SqlConnection.Close`.

9.4.2 Finalizable Types

Finalizable types are types that extend the Basic Dispose Pattern by overriding the finalizer and providing finalization code path in the `Dispose(bool)` method.

Finalizers are notoriously difficult to implement correctly, primarily because you cannot make certain (normally valid) assumptions about the state of the system during their execution. The following guidelines should be taken into careful consideration.

Note that some of the guidelines apply not just to the `Finalize` method, but to any code called from a finalizer. In the case of the Basic Dispose Pattern previously defined, this means logic that executes inside `Dispose(bool disposing)` when the disposing parameter is false.

If the base class already is finalizable and implements the Basic Dispose Pattern, you should not override `Finalize` again. You should instead just override the `Dispose(bool)` method to provide additional resource cleanup logic.

> **■ HERB SUTTER** You really don't want to write a finalizer if you can help it. Besides problems already noted earlier in this chapter, writing a finalizer on a type makes that type more expensive to use even if the finalizer is never called. For example, allocating a finalizable object is more expensive because it must also be put on a list of finalizable objects. This cost can't be avoided, even if the object immediately suppresses finalization during its construction (as when creating a managed object semantically on the stack in C++).

The following code shows an example of a finalizable type:

```
public class ComplexResourceHolder : IDisposable {

    private IntPtr buffer; // unmanaged memory buffer
    private SafeHandle resource; // disposable handle to a resource

    public ComplexResourceHolder(){
        this.buffer = ... // allocates memory
        this.resource = ... // allocates the resource
    }

    protected virtual void Dispose(bool disposing){
            ReleaseBuffer(buffer); // release unmanaged memory
        if (disposing){ // release other disposable objects
            if (resource!= null) resource.Dispose();
        }
    }

    ~ ComplexResourceHolder(){
        Dispose(false);
    }

    public void Dispose(){
        Dispose(true);
        GC.SuppressFinalize(this);
    }
}
```

✗ **AVOID** making types finalizable.

Carefully consider any case in which you think a finalizer is needed. There is a real cost associated with instances with finalizers, from both a performance and code complexity standpoint. Prefer using resource wrappers such as `SafeHandle` to encapsulate unmanaged resources where possible, in which case a finalizer becomes unnecessary because the wrapper is responsible for its own resource cleanup.

> ■ **CHRIS SELLS** Of course, if you're implementing your own managed wrappers around unmanaged resources, those will need to implement the finalizable type pattern.

■■ **BRIAN GRUNKEMEYER** If you're writing a wrapper class for an OS resource such as handles or memory, please consider `SafeHandle`. That will handle all of the tricky reliability and security problems associated with guaranteeing resources get freed eventually and in a threadsafe manner. Additionally, it will usually mean you don't need to write a finalizer on your own type. You should still implement `IDisposable`, though.

■■ **JOE DUFFY** The extra cost of a finalizer object arises in three specific places. First, at allocation time the object must be registered with the GC as being finalizable. This makes just creating an object more expensive. Second, when such an object is found to be unreachable, it must be moved to a special to-be-finalized queue. This actually causes the object to be promoted to the next GC generation. Third, the finalizer thread needs to spend time processing the to-be-finalized queue and executing finalizers on the objects within it. There is only a single finalizer thread, so having too many finalizable objects can actually cause scalability problems. On a heavily loaded server, you may find that one processor spends 100 percent of its time just running finalizers.

■■ **VANCE MORRISON** Wrapping unmanaged resources is pretty much the ONLY reason to have a finalizer. If you are wrapping an unmanaged resource, ideally that should be the only thing the class does, and there is a good chance you should be subclassing `SafeHandle` to do it. Thus, "ordinary" types should not have finalizers.

✗ **DO NOT** make value types finalizable.

Only reference types actually get finalized by the CLR, and thus any attempt to place a finalizer on a value type will be ignored. The C# and C++ compilers enforce this rule.

✓ **DO** make a type finalizable if the type is responsible for releasing an unmanaged resource that does not have its own finalizer.

When implementing the finalizer, simply call `Dispose(false)` and place all resource cleanup logic inside the `Dispose(bool disposing)` method.

```
public class ComplexResourceHolder : IDisposable {

    ~ ComplexResourceHolder(){
        Dispose(false);
    }

    protected virtual void Dispose(bool disposing){
        ...
    }
}
```

✔ **DO** implement the Basic Dispose Pattern on every finalizable type. See section 9.4.1 for details on the basic pattern.

This gives users of the type a means to explicitly perform deterministic cleanup of those same resources for which the finalizer is responsible.

▪ **JEFFREY RICHTER**   This guideline is very important and should always be followed, without exception. Without this guideline, a user of a type can't control the resource properly.

▪ **HERB SUTTER**   Languages ought to warn on this case. If you have a finalizer, you want a destructor (`Dispose`).

✗ **DO NOT** access any finalizable objects in the finalizer code path, because there is significant risk that they will have already been finalized.

For example, a finalizable object A that has a reference to another finalizable object B cannot reliably use B in A's finalizer, or vice versa. Finalizers are called in a random order (short of a weak ordering guarantee for critical finalization).

Also, be aware that objects stored in static variables will get collected at certain points during an application domain unload or while exiting the process. Accessing a static variable that refers to a finalizable object (or calling a static method that might use values stored in static variables) might not be safe if `Environment.HasShutdownStarted` returns true.

> ▪▪ **JEFFREY RICHTER**   Note that it is OK to touch unboxed value type fields.

✓ **DO** make your `Finalize` method protected.

C#, C++, and VB.NET developers do not need to worry about this, because the compilers help to enforce this guideline.

✗ **DO NOT** let exceptions escape from the finalizer logic, except for system-critical failures.

If an exception is thrown from a finalizer, the CLR will shut down the entire process (as of .NET Framework version 2.0), preventing other finalizers from executing and resources from being released in a controlled manner.

✓ **CONSIDER** creating and using a critical finalizable object (a type with a type hierarchy that contains `CriticalFinalizerObject`) for situations in which a finalizer absolutely must execute even in the face of forced application domain unloads and thread aborts.

The next section presents guidelines on how and when to use factories to create object instances.

9.5 **Factories**

The most common and consistent way to create an instance of a type is via its constructor. However, sometimes a preferable alternative is to use a factory.

A factory is an operation or collection of operations that abstract the object creation process for the users, allowing for specialized semantics and finer granularity of control over an object's instantiation. Simply put, a factory's primary purpose is to generate and provide instances of objects to callers.

There are two main groups of factories: factory methods and factory types (also called abstract factories).

File.Open and Activator.CreateInstance are examples of factory methods.

```
public class File {
    public static FileStream Open(String path, FileMode mode) { ... }
}

public static class Activator {
    public static object CreateInstance(Type type){ ... }
}
```

Factory methods often appear on the types for which instances are to be created and are typically static. Such static factory methods are often limited to creating instances of a specific type determined at the time of compilation (notice, this is true of constructors as well). This is sufficient in most scenarios, but sometimes it is necessary to return a dynamically selected subclass.

Factory types can address these scenarios. Factory types are special-purpose types with factory methods implemented as virtual (usually abstract) instance functions.

For example, consider the following scenario in which factory types inherited from StreamFactory can be used to dynamically select the actual type of the Stream:

```
public abstract class StreamFactory {
    public abstract Stream CreateStream();
}

public class FileStreamFactory: StreamFactory {
    ...
}

public class IsolatedStorageStreamFactory: StreamFactory {
    ...
}
```

✓ **DO** prefer constructors to factories, because they are generally more usable, consistent, and convenient than specialized construction mechanisms.

Factories sacrifice discoverability, usability, and consistency for implementation flexibility. For example, Intellisense will guide a user through the instantiation of a new object using its constructors but won't point users in the direction of factory methods.

> ■ **KRZYSZTOF CWALINA**   I often hear criticism that we take tool support into account when making API design decisions. To answer this, I have to say that I strongly believe that a modern framework is more than just a piece of stand-alone reusable code. It is a part of a large ecosystem of runtimes, languages, documentation packages, support networks, and finally, tools. All parts of the ecosystem must influence each other to provide an optimal solution. A modern framework designed outside of its ecosystem loses its competitive potential.

✓ **CONSIDER** using a factory if you need more control than can be provided by constructors over the creation of the instances.

For example, consider the Singleton, Builder, or other similar patterns that constrain the ways in which objects are created. A constructor is very limited in its ability to enforce rich patterns such as these, whereas a factory method can easily perform caching, throttling, and sharing of objects, for example.

> ■ **ANDERS HEJLSBERG**   The advantage of the factory pattern is that `SomeClass.GetReader` can return an object whose runtime type is derived from `SomeReader`.
>
> ```
> SomeClass c = new SomeClass(...)
> SomeReader r = c.GetReader(...);
> ```
>
> The choice of an actual runtime type can be based on state in the `SomeClass` instance as well as arguments passed to `GetReader`. Say, for example, that a `SomeClass` can represent a local file or a URL. `GetReader` could then return instances of either `FileReader` or `UrlReader`, both of which are derived from `SomeReader`. The folks building the managed `XmlReader` and `XmlWriter` switched from constructors in .NET 1.1 to a factory pattern in .NET 2.0 for exactly this reason. Another advantage of the factory pattern is that `GetReader` isn't required to return a fresh instance—it could cache objects and return previously allocated instances.

The advantages of the constructor pattern are simplicity and the extensibility argument given previously. Most users find the constructor pattern simpler and more discoverable because they are used to objects being created by constructors. The disadvantage is that you can't dynamically decide the runtime type of what you return, nor can you return a previously allocated instance. If you are confident you will never need these capabilities, then constructors are probably the better choice. Simplicity is always a good thing.

In short: Factory patterns give you more degrees of freedom, but constructors are simpler for the user.

Now, pick your poison ;-)

✓ **DO** use a factory in cases where a developer might not know which type to construct, such as when coding against a base type or interface.

A factory can often use parameters and other context-based information to make this decision for the user.

```
public class Type {
    // this factory returns instances of various types including:
    // PropertyInfo, ConstructorInfo, MethodInfo, etc.
    MemberInfo[] GetMember(string name);
}
```

✓ **CONSIDER** using a factory if having a named method is the only way to make the operation self-explanatory.

Constructors cannot have names, and sometimes using a constructor lacks sufficient context to inform a developer of an operation's semantics. For example, consider:

```
public String(char c, int count);
```

This operation generates a string of repeated characters. Its semantics would have been clearer if a static factory was provided instead, because the method name makes the operation self-explanatory, as in this example:

```
public static String Repeat(char c, int count);
```

> **BRAD ABRAMS**   This is, in fact, the pattern we use for the same concept in `ArrayList`.

✓ **DO** use a factory for conversion-style operations.

For example, consider the standard `Parse` method available on the primitive value types.

```
int i = int.Parse("35");
DateTime d = DateTime.Parse("10/10/1999");
```

The semantics of the `Parse` operation is such that information is converted from one representation of the value into another. In fact, it doesn't feel like we are constructing a new instance at all, but rather rehydrating one from an existing state (the string). The `System.Convert` class exposes many such static factory methods that take a value type in one representation and convert it to an instance of a different value type, retaining the same logical state in the process. Constructors have a very rigid contract with callers: A unique instance of a specific type will be created, initialized, and returned.

✓ **DO** prefer implementing factory operations as methods rather than properties.

✓ **DO** return created instances as method return values, not as `out` parameters.

> **KRZYSZTOF CWALINA**   Methods implementing the Try-Parse Pattern (see section 7.5.2) are factory methods that return created instances through `out` parameters. This is unfortunate, but using the return value for the Boolean is the best way to implement the pattern. This is an example showing that sometimes even **Do** and **Do not** guidelines need to be broken.

✓ **CONSIDER** naming factory methods by concatenating `Create` and the name of the type being created.

For example, consider naming a factory method that creates buttons `CreateButton`. In some cases, a domain-specific name can be used, as in `File.Open`.

✓ **CONSIDER** naming factory types by concatenating the name of the type being created and `Factory`. For example, consider naming a factory type that creates `Control` objects `ControlFactory`.

The next section discusses when and how to design abstractions that might or might not support some features.

9.6 LINQ Support

Writing applications that interact with data sources, such as databases, XML documents, or Web Services, was made easier in the .NET Framework 3.5 with the addition of a set of features collectively referred to as LINQ (Language-Integrated Query). The following sections provide a very brief overview of LINQ and list guidelines for designing APIs related to LINQ support, including the so-called Query Pattern.

9.6.1 Overview of LINQ

Quite often, programming requires processing over sets of values. Examples include extracting the list of the most recently added books from a database of products, finding the e-mail address of a person in a directory service such as Active Directory, transforming parts of an XML document to HTML to allow for Web publishing, or something as frequent as looking up a value in a hashtable. LINQ allows for a uniform language-integrated programming model for querying datasets, independent of the technology used to store that data.

> ▪ **RICO MARIANI** Like everything else, there are good and bad ways to use these patterns. The Entity Framework and LINQ to SQL offer good examples of how you can provide rich query semantics and still get very good performance using strong typing and by offering query compilation.
>   The Pit of Success notion is very important in LINQ implementations. I've seen some cases where the code that runs as a result of using a LINQ pattern is simply terrible in comparison to what you would write the conventional way. That's really not good enough—EF and LINQ to SQL let you write it nicely, and you get high-quality database interactions. That's what to aim for.

In terms of concrete language features and libraries, LINQ is embodied as:

- A specification of the notion of extension methods. These are described in detail in section 5.6.
- Lambda expressions, a language feature for defining anonymous delegates.
- New types representing generic delegates to functions and procedures: `Func<...>` and `Action<...>`.
- Representation of a delay-compiled delegate, the `Expression<...>` family of types.
- A definition of a new interface, `System.Linq.IQueryable<T>`.
- The Query Pattern, a specification of a set of methods a type must provide in order to be considered as a LINQ provider. A reference implementation of the pattern can be found in `System.Linq.Enumerable` class. Details of the pattern will be discussed later in this chapter.
- Query Expressions, an extension to language syntax allowing for queries to be expressed in an alternative, SQL-like format.

```
//using extension methods:
var names = set.Where(x => x.Age>20).Select(x=>x.Name);

//using SQL-like syntax:
var names = from x in set where x.Age>20 select x.Name;
```

■ MIRCEA TROFIN The interplay between these features is the following: Any `IEnumerable` can be queried upon using the LINQ extension methods, most of which require one or more lambda expressions as parameters; this leads to an in-memory generic evaluation of the queries. For cases where the set of data is not in memory (e.g., in a database) and/or queries may be optimized, the set of data is presented as an `IQueryable`. If lambda expressions are given as parameters, they are transformed by the compiler to `Expression<...>` objects. The implementation of `IQueryable` is responsible for processing said expressions. For example, the implementation of an `IQueryable` representing a database table would translate Expression objects to SQL queries.

9.6.2 Ways of Implementing LINQ Support

There are three ways by which a type can support LINQ queries:

- The type can implement `IEnumerable<T>` (or an interface derived from it).
- The type can implement `IQueryable<T>`.
- The type can implement the Query Pattern.

The following sections will help you choose the right method of supporting LINQ.

9.6.3 Supporting LINQ through `IEnumerable<T>`

✓ **DO** implement `IEnumerable<T>` to enable basic LINQ support.

Such basic support should be sufficient for most in-memory datasets. The basic LINQ support will use the extension methods on `IEnumerable<T>` provided in the .NET Framework. For example, simply define as follows:

```
public class RangeOfInt32s : IEnumerable<int> {
    public IEnumerator<int> GetEnumerator() {...}
    IEnumerator IEnumerable.GetEnumerator() {...}
}
```

Doing so allows for the following code, despite the fact that `RangeOfInt32s` did not implement a `Where` method:

```
var a = new RangeOfInt32s();
var b = a.Where(x => x>10);
```

RICO MARIANI Keeping in mind that you'll get your same enumeration semantics, and putting a LINQ façade on them does not make them execute any faster or use less memory.

✓ **CONSIDER** implementing `ICollection<T>` to improve performance of query operators.

For example, the `System.Linq.Enumerable.Count` method's default implementation simply iterates over the collection. Specific collection types can optimize their implementation of this method, since they often offer an `O(1)` - complexity mechanism for finding the size of the collection.

✓ **CONSIDER** supporting selected methods of `System.Linq.Enumerable` or the Query Pattern (see section 9.6.5) directly on new types implementing `IEnumerable<T>` if it is desirable to override the default `System.Linq.Enumerable` implementation (e.g., for performance optimization reasons).

9.6.4 Supporting LINQ through `IQueryable<T>`

✓ **CONSIDER** implementing `IQueryable<T>` when access to the query expression, passed to members of `IQueryable`, is necessary.

When querying potentially large datasets generated by remote processes or machines, it might be beneficial to execute the query remotely. An example of such a dataset is a database, a directory service, or Web service.

✗ **DO NOT** implement `IQueryable<T>` without understanding the performance implications of doing so.

Building and interpreting expression trees is expensive, and many queries can actually get slower when `IQueryable<T>` is implemented.

The trade-off is acceptable in the LINQ to SQL case, since the alternative overhead of performing queries in memory would have been far greater than the transformation of the expression to an SQL statement and the delegation of the query processing to the database server.

✓ **DO** throw `NotSupportedException` from `IQueryable<T>` methods that cannot be logically supported by your data source.

For example, imagine representing a media stream (e.g., an Internet radio stream) as an `IQueryable<byte>`. The `Count` method is not logically supported—the stream can be considered as infinite, and so the `Count` method should throw `NotSupportedException`.

9.6.5 Supporting LINQ through the Query Pattern

The Query Pattern refers to defining the methods in Figure 9-1 without implementing the `IQueryable<T>` (or any other LINQ interface).

Please note that the notation is not meant to be valid code in any particular language but to simply present the type signature pattern.

The notation uses `S` to indicate a collection type (e.g., `IEnumerable<T>`, `ICollection<T>`), and `T` to indicate the type of elements in that collection. Additionally, we use `O<T>` to represent subtypes of `S<T>` that are ordered. For example, `S<T>` is a notation that could be substituted with `IEnumerable<int>`, `ICollection<Foo>`, or even `MyCollection` (as long as the type is an enumerable type).

The first parameter of all the methods in the pattern (marked with `this`) is the type of the object the method is applied to. The notation uses extension-method-like syntax, but the methods can be implemented as extension methods or as member methods; in the latter case the first parameter should be omitted, of course, and the `this` pointer should be used.

Also, anywhere `Func<...>` is being used, pattern implementations may substitute `Expression<Func<...>>` for it. You can find guidelines later that describe when that is preferable.

```
S<T> Where(this S<T>, Func<T,bool>)

S<T2> Select(this S<T1>, Func<T1,T2>)
S<T3> SelectMany(this S<T1>, Func<T1,S<T2>>, Func<T1,T2,T3>)
S<T2> SelectMany(this S<T1>, Func<T1,S<T2>>)

O<T> OrderBy(this S<T>, Func<T,K>), where K is IComparable
O<T> ThenBy(this O<T>, Func<T,K>), where K is IComparable

S<T> Union(this S<T>, S<T>)
S<T> Take(this S<T>, int)
S<T> Skip(this S<T>, int)
S<T> SkipWhile(this S<T>, Func<T,bool>)

S<T3> Join(this S<T1>, S<T2>, Func<T1,K1>, Func<T2,K2>,
Func<T1,T2,T3>)

T ElementAt(this S<T>,int)
```

FIGURE 9-1: Query Pattern Method Signatures

✔ **DO** implement the Query Pattern as instance members on the new type, if the members make sense on the type even outside of the context of LINQ. Otherwise, implement them as extension methods.

For example, instead of the following:

```
public class MyDataSet<T>:IEnumerable<T>{...}
...
public static class MyDataSetExtensions{
    public static MyDataSet<T> Where(this MyDataSet<T> data, Func<T,bool>
query){...}
}
```

Prefer the following, because it's completely natural for datasets to support Where methods:

```
public class MyDataSet<T>:IEnumerable<T>{
    public MyDataSet<T> Where(Func<T,bool> query){...}
        ...
}
```

✔ **DO** implement IEnumerable<T> on types implementing the Query Pattern.

✔ **CONSIDER** designing the LINQ operators to return domain-specific enumerable types. Essentially, one is free to return anything from a Select query method; however, the expectation is that the query result type should be at least enumerable.

This allows the implementation to control which query methods get executed when they are chained. Otherwise, consider a user-defined type MyType, which implements IEnumerable<T>. MyType has an optimized Count method defined, but the return type of the Where method is IEnumerable<T>. In the example here, the optimization is lost after the Where method is called; the method returns IEnumerable<T>, and so the built-in Enumerable.Count method is called, instead of the optimized one defined on MyType.

```
var result = myInstance.Where(query).Count();
```

✗ **AVOID** implementing just a part of the Query Pattern if fallback to the basic `IEnumerable<T>` implementations is undesirable.

For example, consider a user-defined type `MyType`, which implements `IEnumerable<T>`. `MyType` has an optimized `Count` method defined but does not have `Where`. In the example here, the optimization is lost after the `Where` method is called; the method returns `IEnumerable<T>`, and so the built-in `Enumerable.Count` method is called, instead of the optimized one defined on `MyType`.

```
var result = myInstance.Where(query).Count();
```

✓ **DO** represent ordered sequences as a separate type, from its unordered counterpart. Such types should define `ThenBy` method.

This follows the current pattern in the `LINQ to Objects` implementation and allows for early (compile-time) detection of errors such as applying `ThenBy` to an unordered sequence.

For example, the Framework provides the `IOrderedEnumerable<T>` type, which is returned by `OrderBy`. The `ThenBy` extension method is defined for this type, and not for `IEnumerable<T>`.

✓ **DO** defer execution of query operator implementations. The expected behavior of most of the Query Pattern members is that they simply construct a new object which, upon enumeration, produces the elements of the set that match the query.

The following methods are exceptions to this rule: `All`, `Any`, `Average`, `Contains`, `Count`, `ElementAt`, `Empty`, `First`, `FirstOrDefault`, `Last`, `LastOrDefault`, `Max`, `Min`, `Single`, `Sum`.

In the example here, the expectation is that the time necessary for evaluating the second line will be independent from the size or nature (e.g., in-memory or remote server) of `set1`. The general expectation is that this line simply prepares `set2`, delaying the determination of its composition to the time of its enumeration.

```
var set1 = ...
var set2 = set1.Select(x => x.SomeInt32Property);
foreach(int number in set2){...} // this is when actual work happens
```

✓ **DO** place query extensions methods in a "Linq" subnamespace of the main namespace. For example, extension methods for System.Data features reside in System.Data.Linq namespace.

✓ **DO** use Expression<Func<...>> as a parameter instead of Func<...> when it is necessary to inspect the query. See section 9.6.5 for more details.

As discussed earlier, interacting with an SQL database is already done through IQueryable<T> (and therefore expressions) rather than IEnumerable<T>, since this gives an opportunity to translate lambda expressions to SQL expressions.

An alternative reason for using expressions is performing optimizations. For example, a sorted list can implement look-up (Where clauses) with binary search, which can be much more efficient than the standard IEnumerable<T> or IQueryable<T> implementations.

9.7 Optional Feature Pattern

When designing an abstraction, you might want to allow cases in which some implementations of the abstraction support a feature or a behavior, whereas other implementations do not. For example, stream implementations can support reading, writing, seeking, or any combination thereof.

One way to model these requirements is to provide a base class with APIs for all nonoptional features and a set of interfaces for the optional features. The interfaces are implemented only if the feature is actually supported by a concrete implementation. The following example shows one of many ways to model the stream abstraction using such an approach.

```
// framework APIs
public abstract class Stream {
    public abstract void Close();
    public abstract int Position { get; }
}
public interface IInputStream {
    byte[] Read(int numberOfBytes);
}
```

```
public interface IOutputStream {
   void Write(byte[] bytes);
}
public interface ISeekableStream {
   void Seek(int position);
}
public interface IFiniteStream {
   int Length { get; }
   bool EndOfStream { get; }
}

// concrete stream
public class FileStream : Stream, IOutputStream, IInputStream,
ISeekableStream, IFiniteStream {
   ...
}

// usage
void OverwriteAt(IOutputStream stream, int position, byte[] bytes){
   // do dynamic cast to see if the stream is seekable
   ISeekableStream seekable = stream as ISeekableStream;
   if(seekable==null){
      throw new NotSupportedException(...);
   }
   seekable.Seek(position);
   stream.Write(bytes);
}
```

You will notice the .NET Framework's System.IO namespace does not follow this model, and with good reason. Such factored design requires adding many types to the framework, which increases general complexity. Also, using optional features exposed through interfaces often requires dynamic casts, and that in turn results in usability problems.

KRZYSZTOF CWALINA Sometimes framework designers provide interfaces for common combinations of optional interfaces. For example, the OverwriteAt method would not have to use the dynamic cast if the framework design provided ISeekableOutputStream. The problem with this approach is that it results in an explosion of the number of different interfaces for all combinations.

Sometimes the benefits of factored design are worth the drawbacks, but often they are not. It is easy to overestimate the benefits and underestimate the drawbacks. For example, the factorization did not help the developer who wrote the OverwriteAt method avoid runtime exceptions (the main reason for factorization). It is our experience that many designs incorrectly err on the side of too much factorization.

The Optional Feature Pattern provides an alternative to excessive factorization. It has drawbacks of its own but should be considered as an alternative to the factored design described previously. The pattern provides a mechanism for discovering whether the particular instance supports a feature through a query API and uses the features by accessing optionally supported members directly through the base abstraction.

```csharp
// framework APIs
public abstract class Stream {
    public abstract void Close();
    public abstract int Position { get; }

    public virtual bool CanWrite { get { return false; } }
    public virtual void Write(byte[] bytes){
        throw new NotSupportedException(...);
    }

    public virtual bool CanSeek { get { return false; } }
    public virtual void Seek(int position){
        throw new NotSupportedException(...);
    }
    ... // other options
}

// concrete stream
public class FileStream : Stream {
    public override bool CanSeek { get { return true; } }
    public override void Seek(int position) { ... }
    ...
}

// usage
void OverwriteAt(Stream stream, int position, byte[] bytes){
    if(!stream.CanSeek || !stream.CanWrite){
        throw new NotSupportedException(...);
    }
    stream.Seek(position);
    stream.Write(bytes);
}
```

In fact, the `System.IO.Stream` class uses this design approach. Some abstractions might choose to use a combination of factoring and the Optional Feature Pattern. For example, the Framework collection interfaces are factored into indexable and nonindexable collections (`IList<T>` and `ICollection<T>`), but they use the Optional Feature Pattern to differentiate between read-only and read-write collections (`ICollection<T>`. `IsReadOnly` property).

✓ **CONSIDER** using the Optional Feature Pattern for optional features in abstractions.

The pattern minimizes the complexity of the framework and improves usability by making dynamic casts unnecessary.

> ■ **STEVE STARCK** If your expectation is that only a very small percentage of classes deriving from the base class or interface would actually implement the optional feature or behavior, using interface-based design might be better. There is no real need to add additional members to all derived classes when only one of them provides the feature or behavior. Also, factored design is preferred in cases when the number of combinations of the optional features is small and the compile-time safety afforded by factorization is important.

✓ **DO** provide a simple Boolean property that clients can use to determine whether an optional feature is supported.

```
public abstract class Stream {
    public virtual bool CanSeek { get { return false; } }
    public virtual void Seek(int position){ ... }
}
```

Code that consumes the abstract base class can query this property at runtime to determine whether it can use the optional feature.

```
if(stream.CanSeek){
    stream.Seek(position);
}
```

✓ **DO** use virtual methods on the base class that throw `NotSupported-Exception` to define optional features.

```
public abstract class Stream {
    public virtual bool CanSeek { get { return false; } }
    public virtual void Seek(int position){
        throw new NotSupportedException(...);
    }
}
```

The method can be overridden by subclasses to provide support for the optional feature. The exception should clearly communicate to the user that the feature is optional and which property the user should query to determine if the feature is supported.

9.8 Simulating Covariance

Different constructed types don't have a common root type. For example, there would not be a common representation of `IEnumerable<string>` and `IEnumerable<object>` if not for a pattern implemented by `IEnumerable<T>` called Simulated Covariance. This section describes the details of the pattern.

Generics is a very powerful type system feature added to the .NET Framework 2.0. It allows creation of so-called parameterized types. For example, `List<T>` is such a type and it represents a list of objects of type T. The T is specified at the time when the instance of the list is created.

```
var names = new List<string>();
names.Add("John Smith");
names.Add("Mary Johnson");
```

Such generic data structures have many benefits over their nongeneric counterparts. But they also have some—sometimes surprising—limitations. For example, some users expect that a `List<string>` can be cast to `List<object>`, just as a `String` can be cast to `Object`. But unfortunately, the following code won't even compile.

```
List<string> names = new List<string>();
List<object> objects = names; // this won't compile
```

There is a very good reason for this limitation, and that is to allow for full strong typing. For example, if you could cast `List<string>` to a `List<object>` the following incorrect code would compile, but the program would fail at runtime.

```
static void Main(){
    var names = new List<string>();

    // this of course does not compile, but if it did
    // the whole program would compile, but would be incorrect as it
    // attempts to add arbitrary objects to a list of strings.
    AddObjects((List<object>)names);

    string name = names[0]; // how could this work?
}

// this would (and does) compile just fine.
static void AddObjects(List<object> list){
    list.Add(new object()); // it's a list of strings, really. Should we throw?
    list.Add(new Button());
}
```

Unfortunately, this limitation can also be undesired in some scenarios. For example, let's consider the following type:

```
public class CountedReference<T> {
    public CountedReference(T value);
    public T Value { get; }
    public int Count { get; }
    public void AddReference();
    public void ReleaseReference();
}
```

There is nothing wrong with casting a `CountedReference<string>` to `CountedReference<object>`, as in the following example.

```
var reference = new CountedReference<string>(...);
CountedReference<object> obj = reference; // this won't compile
```

In general, having a way to represent any instance of this generic type is very useful.

```
// what type should ??? be?
// CountedReference<object> would be nice but it won't work
static void PrintValue(??? anyCountedReference){
    Console.WriteLine(anyCountedReference.Value);
}
```

> ■■ **KRZYSZTOF CWALINA**   Of course, `PrintValue` could be a generic method taking `CountedReference<T>` as the parameter.
>
> ```
> static void PrintValue<T>(CountedReference<T> any){
>     Console.WriteLine(any.Value);
> }
> ```
>
> This would be a fine solution in many cases. But it does not work as a general solution and might have negative performance implications. For example, the trick does not work for properties. If a property needed to be typed as "any reference," you could not use `CountedReference<T>` as the type of the property. In addition, generic methods might have undesirable performance implications. If such generic methods are called with many differently sized type arguments, the runtime will generate a new method for every argument size. This might introduce unacceptable memory consumption overhead.

Unfortunately, unless `CountedReference<T>` implemented the Simulated Covariance Pattern described next, the only common representation of all `CountedReference<T>` instances would be `System.Object`. But `System.Object` is too limiting and would not allow the `PrintValue` method to access the `Value` property.

The reason that casting to `CountedReference<object>` is just fine, but casting to `List<object>` can cause all sorts of problems, is that in case of `CountedReference<object>`, the object appears only in the output position (the return type of `Value` property). In the case of `List<object>`, the object represents both output and input types. For example, `object` is the type of the input to the `Add` method.

```
// T does not appear as input to any members except the constructor
public class CountedReference<T> {
    public CountedReference(T value);
    public T Value { get; }
    public int Count { get; }
    public void AddReference();
    public void ReleaseReference();
}

// T does appear as input to members of List<T>
public class List<T> {
    public void Add(T item); // T is an input here
    public T this[int index]{
    get;
    set; // T is actually an input here
}
}
```

In other words, we say that in CountedReference<T>, the T is at covariant positions (outputs). In List<T>, the T is at covariant and contravariant (inputs) positions.

To solve the problem of not having a common type representing the root of all constructions of a generic type, you can implement what's called the Simulated Covariance Pattern.

Consider a generic type (class or interface) and its dependencies described in the code fragment that follows.

```
public class Foo<T> {
    public T Property1 { get; }
    public T Property2 { set; }
    public T Property3 { get; set; }
    public void Method1(T arg1);
    public T Method2();
    public T Method3(T arg);
    public Type1<T> GetMethod1();
    public Type2<T> GetMethod2();
}
public class Type1<T> {
    public T Property { get; }
}
public class Type2<T> {
    public T Property { get; set; }
}
```

Create a new interface (root type) with all members containing a T at contravariant positions removed. In addition, feel free to remove all members that might not make sense in the context of the trimmed-down type.

```
public interface IFoo<out T> {
    T Property1 { get; }
    T Property3 { get; } // setter removed
    T Method2();
    Type1<T> GetMethod1();
    IType2<T> GetMethod2(); // note that the return type changed
}
public interface IType2<T> {
    T Property { get; } // setter removed
}
```

The generic type should then implement the interface explicitly and "add back" the strongly typed members (using T instead of object) to its public API surface.

```
public class Foo<T> : IFoo<object> {
    public T Property1 { get; }
    public T Property2 { set; }
    public T Property3 { get; set;}
    public void Method1(T arg1);
    public T Method2();
    public T Method3(T arg);
    public Type1<T> GetMethod1();
    public Type2<T> GetMethod2();

    object IFoo<object>.Property1 { get; }
    object IFoo<object>.Property3 { get; }
    object IFoo<object>.Method2() { return null; }
    Type1<object> IFoo<object>.GetMethod1();
    IType2<object> IFoo<object>.GetMethod2();
}

public class Type2<T> : IType2<object> {
    public T Property { get; set; }
    object IType2<object>.Property { get; }
}
```

Now, all constructed instantiations of Foo<T> have a common root type IFoo<object>.

```
var foos = new List<IFoo<object>>();
foos.Add(new Foo<int>());
foos.Add(new Foo<string>());
```

```
...
foreach(IFoo<object> foo in foos){
   Console.WriteLine(foo.Property1);
   Console.WriteLine(foo.GetMethod2().Property);
}
```

In the case of the simple `CountedReference<T>`, the code would look like the following:

```
public interface ICountedReference<out T> {
   T Value { get; }
   int Count { get; }
   void AddReference();
   void ReleaseReference();
}

public class CountedReference<T> : ICountedReference<object> {
   public CountedReference(T value) {...}
   public T Value { get { ... } }
   public int Count { get { ... } }
   public void AddReference(){...}
   public void ReleaseReference(){...}

   object ICountedReference<object>.Value { get { return Value; } }
}
```

✓ **CONSIDER** using the Simulated Covariance Pattern if there is a need to have a representation for all instantiations of a generic type.

The pattern should not be used frivolously, because it results in additional types in the framework and can makes the existing types more complex.

✓ **DO** ensure that the implementation of the root's members is equivalent to the implementation of the corresponding generic type members.

There should not be an observable difference between calling a member on the root type and calling the corresponding member on the generic type. In many cases, the members of the root are implemented by calling members on the generic type.

```
public class Foo<T> : IFoo<object> {

   public T Property3 { get { ... } set { ... } }
   object IFoo<object>.Property3 { get { return Property3; } }
   ...
}
```

✓ **CONSIDER** using an abstract class instead of an interface to represent the root.

This might sometimes be a better option, because interfaces are more difficult to evolve (see section 4.3). On the other hand, there are some problems with using abstract classes for the root. Abstract class members cannot be implemented explicitly and the subtypes need to use the new modifier. This makes it tricky to implement the root's members by delegating to the generic type members.

✓ **CONSIDER** using a nongeneric root type if such type is already available.

For example, List<T> implements IEnumerable for the purpose of simulating covariance.

9.9 Template Method

The Template Method Pattern is a very well-known pattern described in much greater detail in many sources, such as the classic book *Design Patterns* by Gamma et al. Its intent is to outline an algorithm in an operation. The Template Method Pattern allows subclasses to retain the algorithm's structure while permitting redefinition of certain steps of the algorithm. We are including a simple description of this pattern here, because it is one of the most commonly used patterns in API frameworks.

The most common variation of the pattern consists of one or more non-virtual (usually public) members that are implemented by calling one or more protected virtual members.

```
public Control{
  public void SetBounds(int x, int y, int width, int height){
    ...
    SetBoundsCore (...);
  }

  public void SetBounds(int x, int y, int width, int
  height, BoundsSpecified specified){
    ...
    SetBoundsCore (...);
  }
```

```
    protected virtual void SetBoundsCore(int x, int y, int width, int
    height, BoundsSpecified specified){
        // Do the real work here.
    }
}
```

The goal of the pattern is to control extensibility. In the preceding example, the extensibility is centralized to a single method (a common mistake is to make more than one overload virtual). This helps to ensure that the semantics of the overloads stay consistent, because the overloads cannot be overridden independently.

Also, public virtual members basically give up all control over what happens when the member is called. This pattern is a way for the base class designer to enforce some structure of the calls that happen in the member. The nonvirtual public methods can ensure that certain code executes before or after the calls to virtual members and that the virtual members execute in a fixed order.

As a framework convention, the protected virtual methods participating in the Template Method Pattern should use the suffix "Core."

✗ **AVOID** making public members virtual.

If a design requires virtual members, follow the template pattern and create a protected virtual member that the public member calls. This practice provides more controlled extensibility.

✓ **CONSIDER** using the Template Method Pattern to provide more controlled extensibility.

In this pattern, all extensibility points are provided through protected virtual members that are called from nonvirtual members.

✓ **CONSIDER** naming protected virtual members that provide extensibility points for nonvirtual members by suffixing the nonvirtual member name with "Core."

```
    public void SetBounds(...){
       ...
       SetBoundsCore (...);
    }
    protected virtual void SetBoundsCore(...){ ... }
```

> ■ **BRIAN PEPIN**   I like to take the template pattern one step further and implement all argument checking in the nonvirtual public method. This way I can stop garbage entering methods that were possibly overridden by another developer, and it helps to enforce a little more of the API contract across implementations.

The next section goes into designing APIs that need to support timeouts.

9.10 Timeouts

Timeouts occur when an operation returns before its completion because the maximum time allocated for the operation (timeout time) has elapsed. The user often specifies the timeout time. For example, it might take a form of a parameter to a method call.

```
server.PerformOperation(timeout);
```

An alternative approach is to use a property.

```
server.Timeout = timeout;
server.PerformOperation();
```

The following short list of guidelines describes best practices for the design of APIs that need to support timeouts.

✓ **DO** prefer method parameters as the mechanism for users to provide timeout time.

Method parameters are favored over properties because they make the association between the operation and the timeout much more apparent. The property-based approach might be better if the type is designed to be a component used with visual designers.

✓ **DO** prefer using TimeSpan to represent timeout time.

Historically, timeouts have been represented by integers. Integer timeouts can be hard to use for the following reasons:

- It is not obvious what the unit of the timeout is.
- It is difficult to translate units of time into the commonly used millisecond. (How many milliseconds are in 15 minutes?)

Often, a better approach is to use TimeSpan as the timeout type. TimeSpan solves the preceding problems.

```
class Server {
    void PerformOperation(TimeSpan timeout){
        ...
    }
}

var server = new Server();
server.PerformOperation(new TimeSpan(0,15,0));
```

Integer timeouts are acceptable if:

- The parameter or property name can describe the unit of time used by the operation, for example, if a parameter can be called milliseconds without making an otherwise self-describing API cryptic.
- The most commonly used value is small enough that users won't have to use calculators to determine the value, for example, if the unit is milliseconds and the commonly used timeout is less than 1 second.

✓ **DO** throw System.TimeoutException when a timeout elapses.

Timeout equal to TimeSpan(0) means that the operation should throw if it cannot complete immediately. If the timeout equals TimeSpan.MaxValue, the operation should wait forever without timing out. Operations are not required to support either of these values, but they should throw an InvalidArgumentException if an unsupported timeout value is specified.

If a timeout expires and the System.TimeoutException is thrown, the server class should cancel the underlying operation.

In the case of an asynchronous operation with a timeout, the callback should be called and an exception thrown when the results of the operation are first accessed.

```
void OnReceiveCompleted(Object source, ReceiveCompletedEventArgs
asyncResult){
    MessageQueue queue = (MessageQueue)source;
    // the following line will throw if BeginReceive has timed out
    Message message = queue.EndReceive(asyncResult.AsyncResult);
    Console.WriteLine("Message: " + (string)message.Body);
    queue.BeginReceive(new TimeSpan(1,0,0));
}
```

For more information on timeouts and asynchronous operation, see section 9.2.

✗ **DO NOT** return error codes to indicate timeout expiration.

Expiration of a timeout means the operation could not complete successfully and thus should be treated and handled as any other runtime error (see Chapter 7).

9.11 **XAML Readable Types**

XAML is an XML format used by WPF (and other technologies) to represent object graphs. The following guidelines describe design considerations for ensuring that your types can be created using XAML readers.

✓ **CONSIDER** providing the default constructor if you want a type to work with XAML.

For example, consider the following XAML markup:

```
<Person Name="John" Age="22" />
```

It is equivalent to the following C# code:

```
new Person() { Name = "John", Age = 22 };
```

Consequently, for this code to work, the Person class needs to have a default constructor. Markup extensions, discussed in the next guideline in this section, are an alternative way of enabling XAML.

> **CHRIS SELLS** In my opinion, this one should really be a DO, not a CONSIDER. If you're designing a new type to support XAML, it's far preferable to do it with a default constructor than with markup extensions or type converters.

✔ **DO** provide markup extension if you want an immutable type to work with XAML readers.

Consider the following immutable type:

```
public class Person {
    public Person(string name, int age){
        this.name = name;
        this.age = age;
    }
    public string Name { get { return name; } }
    public int Age { get { return age; } }

    string name;
    int age;
}
```

Properties of such type cannot be set using XAML markup, because the reader does not know how to initialize the properties using the parameterized constructor. Markup extensions address the problem.

```
[MarkupExtensionReturnType(typeof(Person))]
public class PersonExtension : MarkupExtension {
    public string Name { get; set; }
    public int Age { get; set; }

    public override object ProvideValue(IServiceProvider serviceProvider){
        return new Person(this.Name,this.Age);
    }
}
```

Keep in mind that immutable types cannot be written using XAML writers.

✗ **AVOID** defining new type converters unless the conversion is natural and intuitive. In general, limit type converter usage to the ones already provided by the .NET Framework.

Type converters are used to convert a value from a string to the appropriate type. They're used by XAML infrastructure and in other places, such as graphical designers. For example, the string "#FFFF0000" in the following markup gets converted to an instance of a red `Brush` thanks to the type converter associated with the `Rectangle.Fill` property.

```
<Rectangle Fill="#FFFF0000"/>
```

But type converters can be defined too liberally. For example, the Brush type converter should not support specifying gradient brushes, as shown in the following hypothetical example.

```
<Rectangle Fill="HorizontalGradient White Red" />
```

Such converters define new "minilanguages," which add complexity to the system.

✓ **CONSIDER** applying the `ContentPropertyAttribute` to enable convenient XAML syntax for the most commonly used property.

```
[ContentProperty("Image")]
public class Button {
    public object Image { get; set; }
}
```

The following XAML syntax would work without the attribute:

```
<Button>
    <Button.Image>
        <Image Source="foo.jpg"
    </Button.Image>
</Button>
```

The attribute makes the following much more readable syntax possible.

```
<Button>
    <Image Source="foo.jpg"
</Button>
```

9.12 **And in the End...**

The process of creating a great framework is demanding. It requires dedication, knowledge, practice, and a lot of hard work. But in the end, it can be one of the most fulfilling jobs software engineers ever get to do. Large system frameworks can enable millions to build software that was not possible before. Application extensibility frameworks can turn simple applications into powerful platforms and make them shine. Finally, reusable component frameworks can inspire and enable developers to take their applications beyond the ordinary. When you create a framework like that, please let us know. We would like to congratulate you.

A

C# Coding Style Conventions

Unlike the Framework Design Guidelines, these coding style conventions are not required and should be treated as a set of suggestions. The reason we don't insist on following these coding conventions is that they have no direct effect on the end user of the framework.

There are many coding style conventions, each with its own history and philosophy. The conventions described here have the following goals:

- The conventions must be something real developers use. To accomplish this goal, we reviewed sources written by the .NET Framework developers and rejected any conventions that were proposed but are not used widely in code contributing to the Framework.

- The conventions are optimized for brevity, within reason. We feel it's generally useful to fit more lines of code in a small space, to minimize lines running past the end of the screen or wrapping, and to maximize the density of code (no empty lines), as long as the code readability is not compromised.

- The conventions are simple. We don't think coding conventions need to spell out every single detail of every single formatting option. Such complicated conventions are difficult to follow and don't add much value on top of a small set of core conventions.

A.1 General Style Conventions

A.1.1 Brace Usage

✓ **DO** place the opening brace at the end of the preceding statement.

```
if(someExpression){
    DoSomething();
}
```

✓ **DO** align the closing brace with the beginning of the line containing the corresponding opening brace unless closing a single-statement-block.

```
if(someExpression){
    DoSomething();
}
```

✓ **DO** place the closing brace at the beginning of a new line.

```
if(someExpression){
    DoSomething();
}
```

✓ **CONSIDER** single-statement-blocks that have braces that begin and end on the same line. Property accessors often use this style.

```
public int Foo{
    get{ return foo; }
    set{ foo = value; }
}
```

✓ **CONSIDER** single accessor properties having all brackets on the same line.

```
public int Foo{ get{ return foo; } }
```

✓ **DO** place the closing brace on its own line unless followed by an `else`, `else if`, or `while` statement.

```
if(someExpression){
   do{
      DoSomething();
   } while(someOtherCondition);
}
```

✗ **AVOID** omitting braces, even if the language allows it.

Braces should not be considered optional. Even for single-statement-blocks, you should use braces. This increases code readability and maintainability.

```
for(int i=0; i<100; i++){ DoSomething(i); }
```

There are very limited cases when omitting braces might be acceptable, such as when adding a new statement after an existing single-line statement is either impossible or extremely rare. For example, it is meaningless to add a statement after a `throw` statement:

```
if(someExpression) throw new ArgumentOutOfRangeException(...);
```

Another exception to the rule is braces in case statements. These braces can be omitted, because the `case` and `break` statements indicate the beginning and the start of the block.

```
case 0:
   DoSomething();
break;
```

A.1.2 Space Usage

✓ **DO** use one space after the opening and before the closing braces.

```
public int Foo{ get{ return foo; } }
```

✗ **AVOID** using spaces before the opening braces.

```
Preferred: if(someExpression){
Acceptable: if(someExpression) {
```

✔ **DO** use a single space after a comma between parameters.

```
Right: public void Foo(char bar, int x, int y)
Wrong: public void Foo(char bar,int x,int y)
```

✘ **AVOID** using space between arguments.

```
Preferred:  Foo(myChar,0,1)
Acceptable: Foo(myChar, 0, 1)
```

✘ **AVOID** using spaces after the opening or before the closing parentheses.

```
Preferred:  Foo(myChar,0,1)
Acceptable: Foo( myChar,0,1 )
```

✘ **DO NOT** use spaces between a member name and opening parenthesis.

```
Right: Foo()
Wrong: Foo ()
```

✘ **DO NOT** use spaces after or before the brackets.

```
Right: x = dataArray[index];
Wrong: x = dataArray[ index ];
```

✘ **DO NOT** use spaces before flow control statements.

```
Right: while(x==y)
Wrong: while (x==y)
```

✘ **AVOID** using spaces before and after binary operators.

```
Preferred:  if(x==y){ ... }
Acceptable: if(x == y){ ... }
```

✘ **DO NOT** use spaces before or after unary operators.

```
Right: if(!y){ ... }
Wrong: if(! y){ ... }
```

A.1.3 Indent Usage

✓ **DO** use 4 consecutive space characters for indents.

✗ **DO NOT** use the tab character for indents.

✓ **DO** indent contents of code blocks.

```
if(someExpression){
    DoSomething();
}
```

✓ **DO** indent case blocks even if not using braces.

```
switch(someExpression){
  case 0:
      DoSomething();
  break;
      ...
}
```

A.1.4 Other

✓ **CONSIDER** using the var keyword whenever the resulting type of the variable is obvious. Avoid using it if it decreases readability.

```
var names = new List<string>(); // good usage of var

string source = GetSource();
var tokens = source.Split(' '); // ok; most developers know String.Split

var id = GetId(); // probably not good; it's not clear what the type of id is
```

A.2 Naming Conventions

In general, we recommend following the Framework Design Guidelines for naming identifiers. However, there are some additional conventions and exceptions to using the Framework Design Guidelines for naming internal and private identifiers.

✓ **DO** follow the Framework Design Guidelines for naming identifiers, except for naming private and internal fields.

✓ **DO** use PascalCasing for namespace, type, and member names, except for internal and private fields.

✓ **DO** use camelCasing for private and internal fields.

✓ **DO** use camelCasing for local variables.

✓ **DO** use camelCasing for parameters.

✗ **DO NOT** use Hungarian notation (i.e., do not encode the type of a variable in its name).

✗ **AVOID** prefixing local variables.

✓ **DO** use C# aliases instead of Framework type names.

For example, use `int` instead of `Int32` and `object` instead of `Object`.

A.3 Comments

Comments should be used to describe the intent, algorithmic overview, and logical flow. It would be ideal, if from reading the comments alone, someone other than the author could understand the function's behavior and purpose. Although there are no minimum comment requirements and certainly some very small routines need no commenting at all, it is desirable for most routines to have comments reflecting the programmer's intent and approach.

✗ **DO NOT** use comments unless they describe something not obvious to someone other than the developer who wrote the code.

✗ **AVOID** multiline syntax (/* ... */) for comments. The single-line syntax (// ...) is preferred even when a comment spans multiple lines.

```
// Implements a variable-size list that uses an array of objects
// to store the elements. A List has a capacity, which is the
// allocated length of the internal array. As elements are added
// to a List, the capacity of the List is automatically increased
// as required by reallocating the internal array.
//
```

```
public class List<T> : IList<T>, IList {
    ...
}
```

✗ DO NOT place comments at the end of a line unless the comment is very short.

```
//Avoid
public class ArrayList {
    private int count; // -1 indicates uninitialized array
}
```

A.4 **File Organization**

✗ DO NOT have more than one public type in a source file, unless they differ only in the number of generic parameters or one is nested in the other.

Multiple internal types in one file are allowed.

✓ DO name the source file with the name of the public type it contains.

For example, String class should be in String.cs file and List<T> class should be in List.cs file.

✓ DO organize the directory hierarchy just like the namespace hierarchy.

For example, the source file for System.Collections.Generic.List<T> should be in the System\Collections\Generic directory.

✓ CONSIDER grouping members into the following sections in the specified order:

- All fields
- All constructors
- Public and protected properties
- Methods
- Events
- All explicit interface implementations
- Internal members

- Private members
- All nested types

✓ **DO** use #region blocks around not publicly callable and explicit interface implementation groups.

```
#region internal members
...
#endregion
#region private members
...
#endregion
```

> ■ **VANCE MORRISON**   I find this guideline to be surprisingly useful. I now get highly annoyed if I can't collapse the class and quickly see just the public surface of the class.

✓ **CONSIDER** organizing members of each group in alphabetical order.

✓ **CONSIDER** organizing overloads from the simplest to the most complex.

✓ **DO** place the using directives outside the namespace declaration.

```
using System;

namespace System.Collections{
    ...
}
```

■ B ■

Using FxCop to Enforce the Framework Design Guidelines

Sheridan Harrison and David Kean

FXCOP IS A tool that analyzes managed assemblies and reports issues when an assembly does not conform to one or more Framework Design Guidelines. After presenting a brief introduction to FxCop and how it has evolved over time, this appendix discusses FxCop rules that enforce each set of guidelines.

> ■ **MIKE FANNING**   Over the past several years, FxCop has also expanded into a general correctness checker for managed code implementations. Although its original (and still primary) purpose is programmatic enforcement of the Framework Design Guidelines, we will continue to extend its general analysis capabilities in the future.

B.1 **What Is FxCop?**

FxCop analyzes compiled managed code and evaluates its adherence to various Framework Design Guidelines and best practices. FxCop also alerts you to unexpected consequences of certain design decisions. The rules that FxCop uses to evaluate managed code have evolved over time and capture the knowledge and expertise of top .NET Framework developers. In addition to being a crucial part of the development lifecycle, FxCop is also an excellent way for those who are new to the Framework Design Guidelines to learn the core guidelines simply by writing code and using FxCop to identify issues with names, design, and performance, among others. While using FxCop is not a substitute for reading and understanding all of the guidelines that are applicable to your development project, FxCop provides a big productivity boost by teaching you what is expected in well-designed frameworks.

While most people who know of and use FxCop think of it as an item in the developer's toolkit, FxCop is useful in any discipline that includes coding. For example, technical writers can use FxCop to ensure that the code examples in their documentation adhere to the Framework Design Guidelines. Software testers can use FxCop to check libraries and applications for security vulnerabilities and performance issues.

B.2 **The Evolution of FxCop**

FxCop started out at Microsoft as an internal tool. It was developed when the creators of the Framework Design Guidelines recognized that by programmatically analyzing the .NET Framework assemblies, many design errors could be detected and reported to the library designers. Because of its origins, the charter and vision for FxCop have always been closely aligned with the Framework Design Guidelines presented in this book. In addition to enforcing the Framework Design Guidelines, the tool grew to include other tenets of robust design, such as security and performance do's and don'ts. Teams at Microsoft began integrating it into their development projects when they recognized that by using FxCop they could identify and fix many problems early in the development cycle. Today, the FxCop team develops and supports the tool for both internal and external software developers. Now recognized as a mission-critical software development tool, FxCop has been integrated into the Visual Studio family of products under the name Visual Studio Code Analysis.

MIKE FANNING The original version of FxCop was called UrtCop and was developed by Brad and Krzysztof, among others. It was handed over to the .NET Framework 1.0 SDK development team when demands for new features outstripped the informal development process that had brought it into existence. FxCop's value and adoption across Microsoft increased so quickly that eventually the application became the sole purpose of the entire development team. FxCop was renamed from UrtCop (that is, Universal Runtime Cop) to reflect a larger purpose to ensure consistency across the framework libraries. Due to the newness of managed code and the Framework Design Guidelines themselves, it's interesting to note that the development team itself broke a core guideline by not renaming the program FXCop. Fortunately, by the time this was noticed, "FxCop" had become such a recognized brand that it warranted an exception according to the Framework Design Guidelines. While we're airing dirty laundry, FxCop itself did not ship entirely FxCop-clean until version 1.32 (after nearly three years of development and 27 updates).

B.3 How Does It Work?

FxCop provides a graphical user interface (FxCop.exe) for interactive sessions on the developer's desktop and a command-line interface (FxCopcmd.exe) for automated code analysis. You must specify the managed assemblies to be analyzed and select the set of rules that are run for your assemblies. When code in the assemblies violates a rule, FxCop generates an issue message. This message includes the location of the issue, a level, certainty, and resolution. Depending on the issue, the location will be an assembly, namespace, type, or member. The level indicates the importance of the issue. The issue levels (in order from most important to least important) are: Critical Error, Error, Critical Warning, Warning, and Informational. The certainty measure estimates the probability of an issue being detected correctly. A high value means that the rule is most likely detecting a problem. A low certainty value indicates that there is a significant probability that the rule is generating a false positive. The resolution provides detailed information on what FxCop detected and how to fix it.

The following sections highlight some of the FxCop rules that help to enforce the Framework Design Guidelines. Refer to the FxCop documentation for a detailed description of the complete set of rules shipping with FxCop.

> **■ MIKE FANNING**   The freeware version of FxCop is currently available for download at http://msdn.microsoft.com/.

B.4 FxCop Guideline Coverage

B.4.1 FxCop Rules for the Naming Guidelines

FxCop enforces naming guidelines using rules in the naming rules category. There are naming rules to ensure that casing, spelling, prefixes, and suffixes are correct and consistent with the Framework Design Guidelines for identifiers. There are also FxCop naming rules that check whether enumerations, types, members, and parameters are well named.

FxCop uses a dictionary to check the spelling of words used in names. The FxCop documentation gives instructions for adding words and acronyms to the FxCop dictionary.

> **■ DAVID KEAN**   While most of FxCop's naming and design roles fire only against externally visible type and members (both public and protected), there is a little-known option to change this in both FxCop and Visual Studio 2008. Turn this on, and FxCop will start looking at the naming and design of private and internal APIs.

B.4.1.1 FxCop Rules for Capitalization Conventions

Identifiers should be cased correctly

This rule reports an error if identifiers and tokens within identifiers are not cased correctly.

This rule ensures that identifiers respect the following guidelines:

- Assembly, namespace, type, and member names are Pascal-cased.
- Parameter names are camel-cased.
- Acronyms that are less than three characters are all uppercase.
- Acronyms that are three or more characters are Pascal-cased.

FxCop assumes that part of an identifier is an acronym when it encounters two or more characters in uppercase. Note that when you change a three-letter acronym to PascalCasing, the *Identifiers should be spelled correctly* rule will report an error if the acronym is not found in the dictionary.

This rule and the Framework Design Guidelines consider "ID" to be an abbreviation for "identity" or "identifier"—not an acronym. In Pascal-cased identifiers, instances of "ID" should be changed to "Id."

Be aware that there are limitations on what this rule can accurately detect. For example, if a method name contains two short acronyms adjacent to each other, FxCop will treat them as one long acronym that is incorrectly cased. Consider a property named DBIORate, which reports a database's input/output rate. FxCop assumes DBIO is a long acronym and will suggest that it be changed to Dbio.

■ MIKE FANNING   "ID" versus "Id" has by far caused the greatest amount of developer annoyance and churn in source code at Microsoft. For at least two years, no one noticed inconsistent usage of these terms, since ID was permitted as a two-letter acronym while Id was recognized by the spell-checker. It is a tribute to the pervasive commitment to the Framework Design Guidelines at Microsoft that as many teams have spent as many hours resolving this sole issue in order to bring their projects into conformance.

B.4.1.1.1 FxCop Rules for Capitalizing Compound Words and Common Terms

Compound words should be cased correctly

This rule reports an error when an identifier contains a word that should be treated as a compound word and not as two separate words. For example, "endpoint" is a compound word and should not appear as "EndPoint" or "endPoint" when used as an identifier. The rule also detects when a pair of words is incorrectly cased as a compound word.

> ■ **MIKE FANNING**   The original lexicon used by the FxCop spell-checker was first deployed in the Microsoft Office Suite and contained (incorrectly) several computer-related terms that were strangely cased, such as Fileserver, Dropdown, and Textbox. This was noticed on deploying FxCop against the Windows Forms namespaces, which define classes (correctly) named Drop-Down and TextBox. In some cases, where no clear standard previously existed, the Framework Design Guidelines and FxCop team mined existing Microsoft code to determine a standard based on previously shipped code. FxCop also captures guidance described in a style manual developed for Microsoft documentation specialists. This guide tells us, for example, that LogOn is preferred as a term over LogIn, while SignOff should be used instead of SignOut. Keeping up with previously undetected inconsistencies is a full-time job and one of the reasons FxCop is a valuable tool, because we have the ability to update and release additional guidance several times a year.

B.4.1.1.2 FxCop Rules for Case Sensitivity

Identifiers should differ by more than case

This rule checks namespace, type, member, and parameter names. For each kind of identifier, the rule reports an error when there are multiple instances of the identifier that differ only by case. For example, FxCop will report an error if it detects a type named "DataSet" and another type named "Dataset." Note that it will not report an error if it sees a type named "DataSet" and a property named "Dataset."

B.4.1.2 FxCop Rules for General Naming Conventions

B.4.1.2.1 FxCop Rules for Word Choice

Identifiers should not contain underscores

This rule reports an error when the names chosen for assemblies, namespaces, types, members, and parameters contain underscore ("_") characters.

> **MIKE FANNING** Some versions of the Visual Studio applications designers will automatically create event handlers for controls that contain underscores, such as button1_ClickHandler. Generally speaking, these handlers do not need to be externally visible. To resolve FxCop violations against them, change the accessibility of these members to internal. Visual Studio 2005 will emit these items as private or internal by default.

Identifiers should not match keywords

This rule reports an error when it encounters identifiers that are reserved keywords in programming languages that target the Common Language Runtime (CLR). This rule does not recognize all keywords in all languages.

B.4.1.2.2 FxCop Rules for Using Abbreviations and Acronyms

Identifiers should be spelled correctly

This rule uses the Microsoft spelling checker library to verify that the words in assembly, namespace, type, member, and parameter names are correctly spelled. Refer to the FxCop documentation for instructions on how to add words to the dictionary used by this rule.

> **MIKE FANNING** All versions of FxCop up to and including 1.35 require that Microsoft Office or the Microsoft Office Proofing Tools be installed on the computer in order to run the FxCop spelling rules. Versions of FxCop 1.36 and later will install the required spellers and lexicons with the application. Note that the first release of Visual Studio 2005 Team System (which integrates FxCop in the Developer version) did not ship with the spelling rules, but these rules were added in Visual Studio 2008 Team System.

Be aware that FxCop cannot detect cases where a word in the dictionary is being used as an acronym. For example, FxCop will not report that the method name `FindPopServer()` is incorrect even though, in this example, POP is an acronym and the method name should be `FindPointOfPresenceServer()`.

B.4.1.2.3 FxCop Rules for Avoiding Language-Specific Names

Identifiers should not contain type names

This rule reports an error if the name of a member or parameter contains the name of a language-specific data type, or if the name of a parameter contains the name of a data type. For example, this rule will report a violation if a parameter is of type System.Int64 and contains the C# data type "long" in its name.

The rule can detect when certain data or language-specific type names are being used in a manner that does not violate the Framework Design Guidelines. For example, a parameter of type string named longName will not cause FxCop to report an error, even though long is a C#-specific type name. If, however, the parameter was of type Int64 or UInt64, the rule would report a violation because the parameter type and the keyword match. FxCop takes this as an indication that the C# keyword long is being used to indicate the parameter type.

Like many FxCop rules, this rule does not report errors for parameters of members that override a base class member; the rule will report the error only on the base class member.

B.4.1.2.4 FxCop Rules for Naming New Versions of Existing APIs

Identifiers should not have incorrect suffix

This naming rule reports an error when the name of a type ends in "Ex."

B.4.1.3 FxCop Rules for Names of Assemblies and DLLs

The version of FxCop provided on the companion DVD does not provide rules to enforce the guidelines for naming assemblies and DLLs.

B.4.1.4 FxCop Rules for Names of Namespaces

Type names should not match namespaces

This rule compiles a list of all of the namespaces being analyzed and the .NET Framework namespaces. Using this list, the rule compares the name of each type being analyzed to the components in each namespace name and reports an error when the type name matches a namespace name component. For example, this rule will report an error when it encounters a type named "Specialized" because that is one of the components in the "System.Collections.Specialized" namespace name.

B.4.1.5 **FxCop Rules for Names of Classes, Structs, and Interfaces**

Flags enums should have plural names

This rule reports an error if an enumeration decorated with the `System.FlagsAttribute` attribute does not end in "s","i," or "ae."

Identifiers should have correct prefix

This rule reports an error if an interface name does not begin with "I" and if the name of a generic type parameter does not begin with "T."

Identifiers should not have incorrect prefix

This rule reports an error if the name of a type uses "C" as a prefix as in "CString." The rule contains logic to detect type names that correctly begin with "C" such as `CollectionBase`.

B.4.1.5.1 **FxCop Rules for Names of Common Types**

Identifiers should have correct suffix

This rule checks for naming consistency for types that derive from certain framework types or implement certain interfaces. The following table shows the base type or interface and the suffix that should be used.

TABLE B.1: Suffixes for Common Base Types and Interfaces

Base Type or Interface	Suffix
Event handler delegate	`EventHandler`
`System.Attribute`	`Attribute`
`System.EventArgs`	`EventArgs`
`System.Exception`	`Exception`

Continues

TABLE B.1: Continued

Base Type or Interface	Suffix
System.Collections.ICollection System.Collections.Generic.ICollection<T> System.Collections.IEnumerable System.Collections.Generic.IEnumerable<T> System.Collections.IList System.Collections.Generic.IList<T>	Collection
System.Collections.IDictionary, System.Collections.Generic.IDictionary<K,V>	Dictionary
System.Collections.Queue	Collection or Queue
System.Collections.Stack	Collection or Stack
System.Data.DataSet	DataSet
System.Data.DataTable	DataTable
System.IO.Stream	Stream
System.Security.IPermission, System.Security.CodeAccessPermission	Permission
System.Security.Policy.IMembershipCondition	Condition

Identifiers should not have incorrect suffix

This rule reports an error when types that should not use the reserved suffixes (see the preceding rule in this section) do use them. This rule also checks that delegates don't end in "Delegate."

B.4.1.5.2 **FxCop Rules for Naming Enumerations**

Do not prefix enum values with type name

This rule reports an error if the name of the type is used a prefix on the names of the members of the enumeration.

Identifiers should not have incorrect suffix

To enforce correct naming of enumerations, this rule checks that enumeration names don't end in "Enum" or "Flags."

Flags enums should have plural names

This rule enforces the use of plural names for enumerations that have the `FlagsAttribute` attribute and singular names for enumerations that do not have the `FlagsAttribute` attribute.

Only `FlagsAttribute` enums should have plural names

This rule reports an error when an enumeration is not decorated with the `FlagsAttribute` attribute and ends in "s," "i," or "ae." This rule does not report an error if the enumeration name ends in one of the following special cases:

- "ss"
- "is"
- "us"
- "as"

> ■ **DAVID KEAN**   Although the last two rules did not appear in the Visual Studio 2005 Team System release, they were added in Visual Studio 2008 Team System and are enabled when running with the system culture set to an English-based culture.

B.4.1.6 FxCop Rules for Names of Type Members

B.4.1.6.1 FxCop Rules for Names of Properties

Property names should not match `Get` methods

This naming rule reports an error if the name of a method begins with "Get" and the rest of the name matches the name of a property. For example, if a type declares a method named "GetMessage()" and also declares a property named "Message," FxCop will report an error.

B.4.1.6.2 FxCop Rules for Names of Events

Declare event handlers correctly

Unlike the rules we've covered so far, which are all in the naming rules category, this is a design rule that checks the names of the parameters declared in event handlers. This rule reports an error if any one of the following conditions is true:

- The event's event handler does not have `System.Void` as its return type.
- The event's first parameter is not named "sender" or is not of type `System.Object`.
- The event's second parameter is not named "e" or is not a `System.EventArgs` type or subclass.
- The event handler has more than two parameters.

> ■ **MIKE FANNING**   It's worth noting that this convention is one of the few places in the .NET Framework where a parameter name consisting of a single letter is an acceptable identifier. This particular convention was established very early in the development of version 1.0 of the .NET Framework and was not changed, even as additional guidance recommending more informative parameter names was added.

Events should not have "Before" or "After" prefix

This naming rule reports an error when the name of an event starts with "Before" or "After."

Identifiers should have correct suffix

This rule is described in detail in section B.4.1.5.1 of this appendix. To enforce the event-naming guidelines, this rule checks that types that inherit from `System.EventArgs` end with "EventArgs."

B.4.1.6.3 **FxCop Rules for Naming Fields**

Identifiers should be cased correctly

This rule is described in detail in section B.4.1.1 of this appendix. You should be aware that this naming rule does not report a violation for publicly visible instance fields that are incorrectly cased. Instead, FxCop reports a different error because the instance field is publicly accessible.

> ■ **MIKE FANNING**   In general, FxCop tries to restrict analysis to root-cause problems. Otherwise, developers might fix issues out of order and make a change that would be entirely unnecessary if a different violation had been fixed first. For example, there is no sense in renaming a publicly visible field if the developer will eventually make it a private member.

B.4.1.7 **FxCop Rules for Naming Parameters**

Identifiers should be cased correctly

This naming rule, which is described in section B.4.1.1 of this appendix, ensures that parameters use camelCasing.

Parameter names should not match member names

This naming rule reports an error if a member has the same name as one of its parameters. When a parameter name matches the member name, it is likely that the name is not descriptive enough to be useful.

B.4.1.8 **FxCop Rules for Naming Resources**

Resource strings should be spelled correctly

This naming rule checks resource (ResX) files to ensure strings are spelled correctly. The rule reports a critical warning for each misspelled string in the resource file.

Resource string compound words should be cased correctly

This naming rule detects when a resource string contains a word that should be treated as a compound word and not as two separate words. The rule also detects when a pair of adjacent words is incorrectly cased as a compound word.

B.4.2 FxCop Rules for the Type Design Guidelines

FxCop enforces type design guidelines using rules in the naming, design, and usage rules categories. Using FxCop, you can avoid common design problems with interfaces, nested types, enumerations, and static types.

B.4.2.1 FxCop Rules for Types and Namespaces

Avoid namespaces with few types

This design rule reports a warning if a namespace contains fewer than five types. Namespaces with the following suffixes are exempt from this rule: `.Configuration`, `.Permissions`, `.Design`, and `.Interop`. The Visual Basic "My" namespace and the global namespace are also exempt.

Declare types in namespaces

This design rule reports an error when a publicly visible type is in the global namespace. A type is automatically assigned to the global namespace when it is not defined in a named namespace.

B.4.2.2 FxCop Rules for Choosing Between Class and Struct

The version of FxCop provided on the companion DVD does not provide rules to enforce the guidelines for choosing between a class and struct.

B.4.2.3 FxCop Rules for Choosing Between Class and Interface

B.4.2.3.1 FxCop Rules for Abstract Classes

Abstract types should not have constructors

This design rule reports a critical warning if an abstract type defines a public constructor.

B.4.2.3.2 FxCop Rules for Static Classes

Static holder types should be sealed

This design rule reports a critical warning if all of a type's members are static and the type is not sealed (`NotInheritable` in Visual Basic). If the compiler inserts a default public constructor in your type, this rule will not report a violation because the constructor is an instance method. To ensure that FxCop detects this issue, you must either mark the class as static if your programming language supports this, or explicitly define a private constructor.

Static holder types should not have constructors

This design rule reports an error when a public type defines only static members and has a public or protected constructor. This rule does not report errors for abstract (`MustInherit` in Visual Basic) types.

B.4.2.4 FxCop Rules for Interface Design

Avoid empty interfaces

This design rule reports a warning when an interface does not define any members. Interfaces that implement multiple interfaces are not required to define members and are exempt from this rule.

B.4.2.5 FxCop Rules for Struct Design

The version of FxCop provided on the companion DVD does not provide rules to enforce the guidelines for designing structs.

B.4.2.6 FxCop Rules for Enum Design

Do not name enum values "Reserved"

This naming rule checks enumeration values and reports an error if an enumeration contains a value named "Reserved." The rule performs the name comparison case insensitively.

Enums should have zero value

This design rule reports a critical error if any of the following are true:

- An enumeration without the `FlagsAttribute` attribute does not have a zero value.
- An enumeration with the `FlagsAttribute` attribute has a zero value, but that value is not named "None."
- An enumeration defines more than one zero value.

This rule ignores enumeration in namespaces that end with `.Interop`.

Enum storage should be Int32

This design rule reports a warning when an enumeration uses a type other than Int32 as its underlying type. To permit large bitwise combinable enumerations, enumerations with the FlagsAttribute attribute that use Int64 as the underlying type are exempt from this rule.

Only FlagsAttribute enums should have plural names

Flags enums should have plural names

These naming rules are described in detail in section B.4.1.5.2 of this appendix. They enforce the use of plural names for enumerations that have the FlagsAttribute attribute, and singular names for enumerations that do not have the FlagsAttribute attribute.

B.4.2.6.1 FxCop Rules for Designing Flags Enums

Do not mark enums with FlagsAttribute

This usage rule reports an error when an enumeration has the FlagsAttribute attribute but its values are not limited to powers of two and combinations of powers of two.

Mark enums with FlagsAttribute

This design rule checks enumeration values to determine whether they are solely powers of two and combinations of powers of two. If this is the case and the enumeration does not have the FlagsAttribute attribute, the rule reports a warning.

B.4.2.7 FxCop Rules for Nested Types

Nested types should not be visible

This design rule reports an error when a publicly visible type is nested within a publicly visible type. Types that implement the System.IEnumerator and System.IEnumerator<T> interfaces are exempt from this rule.

> ■ **DAVID KEAN** Previous versions of FxCop used to also fire on protected nested types. This was changed in FxCop 1.36 to reflect guidelines around subclassing and other advanced customization scenarios.

B.4.3 **FxCop Rules for Member Design**

B.4.3.1 **FxCop Rules for General Member Design Guidelines**

B.4.3.1.1 **FxCop Rules for Member Overloading**

Default parameters should not be used

This design rule reports an error when a publicly visible method defines one or more parameters with default values.

B.4.3.1.2 **FxCop Rules for Implementing Interface Members Explicitly**

Interface methods should be callable by child types

This design rule checks that publicly visible unsealed types that have explicitly implemented interface members provide an alternate method for calling the interface member. The alternate method must have the same name as the explicit interface member. For example, a type that explicitly implements `IList.Add(Object)` should also implement a public or protected `Add(Object)` method. If the explicit interface member is `IDisposable.Dispose`, the alternate method name can be `Close()`.

B.4.3.1.3 **FxCop Rules for Choosing Between Properties and Methods**

Use properties where appropriate

This design rule reports a warning if a method has the characteristics of a property `get` or `set` accessor. For a method to have the characteristics of a property `get` accessor, the following conditions must be met:

- The method name begins with `Get`.
- The fourth letter in the name is capitalized.
- The method takes no parameters.
- The method's return type is not `System.Void` and is not an array.
- The method name is not `GetEnumerator` and is not `GetHashCode`.

For a method to have the characteristics of a property `set` accessor, the following conditions must be met:

- The method name begins with `Set`.
- The method takes one parameter.
- The method's return type is `System.Void`.
- The method does not override a base class method.
- The method is not overloaded.
- The type contains a field that matches the method name without the `Set` prefix. For example, for a method named `SetTime`, the type defines a field named `time`. The casing of the field name does not matter.

Properties should not return arrays

This performance rule reports a warning if a property returns an array. Properties that override a base class property are exempt from this rule.

B.4.3.2 **FxCop Rules for Property Design**

Properties should not be write-only

This design rule reports an error if a publicly visible property does not define a `get` accessor.

B.4.3.2.1 **FxCop Rules for Indexed Property Design**

Indexers should not be multidimensional

This design rule reports a warning when a publicly visible property is an indexer that takes more than one parameter.

Use integral or string argument for indexers

This design rule reports an error when a publicly visible property is an indexer that takes a type other than `Int32`, `Int64`, `String`, or `Object`. If the indexer's parameter is an enumeration, this rule checks the underlying type of the enumeration. This rule does not report an error for multidimensional indexers.

B.4.3.3 **FxCop Rules for Constructor Design**

Do not call overridable methods in constructors

This usage rule reports a critical warning when code in a constructor invokes a virtual member defined in its type.

B.4.3.3.1 **FxCop Rules for Type Constructor Guidelines**

Initialize reference type static fields inline

This performance rule reports a critical warning if a reference type explicitly defines a static constructor.

> ■ **MIKE FANNING**   Actually, this rule generates a critical warning if a reference type with a static constructor is not marked with the `beforefield-init` metadata. This indicates that the developer has explicitly written a static class constructor body instead of using the inline syntax to initialize static members:
>
> ```
> static int value = InitializeMe();
> static string = "someValue";
> ```
>
> If the conventions above are followed, the type will be marked `before-fieldinit`, a hint to the CLR that certain checks to ensure the class constructor has been called can be avoided altogether. This can result in a performance gain for highly performance-sensitive code.

Static constructors should be private

This security rule reports an error when a publicly visible type defines a publicly visible static constructor. If your compiler inserts a publicly visible static constructor by default, you can fix the problem by explicitly defining a private static constructor.

B.4.3.4 **FxCop Rules for Event Design**

Use generic event handler instances

This design rule reports an error when it encounters a custom event handler. You cannot comply with this rule if you are targeting versions of the .NET Framework that do not support generics.

B.4.3.4.1 **FxCop Rules for Custom Event Handler Design**

Declare event handlers correctly

This design rule is described in detail in section B.4.1.6.2 of this appendix. It ensures that event handlers conform to the relevant guidelines.

B.4.3.5 **FxCop Rules for Field Design**

Do not declare read-only mutable reference types

This security rule reports an error when a publicly visible field is a mutable reference type, because a mutable type's data can be changed even if the field is marked read-only. This rule does not report errors for fields that are value types. The following .NET Framework reference types are known to be immutable and will not cause this rule to report an error:

- `Microsoft.Win32.RegistryKey`
- `System.String`
- `System.Text.RegularExpressions.Regex`
- `System.Version`
- `System.Reflection.TypeFilter`
- `System.Reflection.Missing`
- `System.Reflection.MemberFilter`
- `System.Net.IPAddress`
- `System.EventHandler`
- `System.EventArgs`
- `System.DBNull`
- `System.Collections.Comparer`
- `System.Xml.XmlQualifiedName`
- `System.Reflection.Assembly`
- `System.Type`
- `System.Object`
- `System.ComponentModel.Design.CommandID`
- `System.Reflection.MemberInfo`

- `System.Reflection.MethodInfo`
- `System.Reflection.MethodBase`
- `System.Reflection.FieldInfo`
- `System.Reflection.EventInfo`
- `System.Reflection.ParameterInfo`
- `System.Reflection.ConstructorInfo`
- `System.Resources.ResourceManager`
- `System.Diagnostics.BooleanSwitch`
- `System.Diagnostics.TraceSwitch`
- `System.Windows.DependencyProperty`

Do not declare visible instance fields

This design rule reports an error when a publicly visible type has a publicly visible field. Be aware that the naming rules pertaining to fields do not report errors when this rule reports an error because it is more important to make sure the field is not publicly visible than to case its name correctly.

Secured types should not expose fields

This security rule reports a critical error when it detects a type that is secured with a security demand or link demand, and the type has public fields. This rule reports an error because fields are not protected by Code Access Security demands.

Non-constant fields should not be visible

This usage rule reports a warning when a publicly visible static (`Shared` in Visual Basic) field is not marked as read-only or a constant.

B.4.3.6 FxCop Rules for Operator Overloads

Do not raise exceptions in unexpected locations

This design rule reports an error when equality (==), inequality (!=), and implicit cast operators explicitly throw an exception.

Operator overloads have named alternates

This usage rule reports an error when an operator is defined and the expected named alternative method (used by languages that do not support operators) is not defined. Additionally, if this rule finds explicit or implicit cast operations in a type, the rule reports an error if it does not find a method named To<TypeName> or From<TypeName>, where <TypeName> is the name of the type.

Operators should have symmetrical overloads

This usage rule reports a critical error when a type defines an operator and does not define its symmetric counterpart. The table shows the pairs of operators that must be implemented together.

TABLE B.2: Symmetric Operators

Operator	Paired Operator
Equality ("=" or "==")	Inequality ("<>" or "!=")
Greater than (">")	Less than ("<")
Greater than or Equal (">=")	Less than or Equal ("<=")

▪ **MIKE FANNING** Symmetric operator definition is enforced by Microsoft languages that target the .NET Framework.

B.4.3.7 FxCop Rules for Parameter Design

Consider passing base types as parameters

This design rule reports a warning when a parameter appears to be more strongly typed than necessary. If a method uses only members inherited by the parameter's type (as opposed to members declared in the parameter's type), you can change the parameter to be the base type. Doing so makes the method more flexible with regard to the types of objects that it can accept for that parameter. This rule does not detect cases where the parameter type could be changed to an interface that is implemented by the parameter's type.

Parameter names should match base declaration

This naming rule reports an error if the name used for a parameter of an overriding method differs from the parameter name used in the base class declaration of the method.

B.4.3.7.1 FxCop Rules for Parameter Passing

Avoid out *parameters*

This design rule reports a warning when a publicly visible method has an out parameter. Methods that override a base class method and methods that follow the `TryParse` design pattern for exception handling described in Chapter 7 are exempt from this rule.

Do not pass types by reference

This design rule reports a warning when a publicly visible method has a parameter that takes a reference type, and the parameter value is passed by reference. Methods that override a base class method and methods in namespaces that end in "Interop" are exempt from this rule.

B.4.3.7.2 FxCop Rules for Members with Variable Number of Parameters

Replace repetitive arguments with params array

This design rule reports a warning when a publicly visible method meets the following conditions:

- The method declares more than three parameters.
- All of the parameters are the same type.
- The parameter names differ only by a numerical suffix.
- The method does not have an overload that takes an array.

For example, the following method signature would cause this rule to report a warning:

```
public void DoSomeWork(object worker1, object worker2,
                    object worker3, object worker4)
```

Use params for variable arguments

This usage rule reports an error if a publicly exposed method uses the varargs calling convention. Methods that override a base class method are exempt from this rule.

B.4.4 **FxCop Rules for Designing for Extensibility**

B.4.4.1 **FxCop Rules for Extensibility Mechanisms**

The version of FxCop provided on the companion DVD does not provide rules to enforce the guidelines for extensibility mechanisms.

B.4.4.2 **FxCop Rules for Base Classes**

The version of FxCop provided on the companion DVD does not provide rules to enforce the guidelines for base classes.

B.4.4.3 **FxCop Rules for Sealing**

Do not declare protected members in sealed types

This design rule reports an error when a sealed type declares protected members. The `Finalize()` method is exempt from this rule.

Do not declare virtual members in sealed types

This design rule reports an error when a virtual member is declared in a sealed type. The `Finalize()` method and methods on delegates are exempt from this rule. This rule does not report errors for members that override base class members.

Static holder types should be sealed

This design rule reports a critical warning if all of the type's members are static and the type is not sealed. If the compiler inserts a default public constructor in your type, this rule will not report a violation because the constructor is an instance method. To ensure that FxCop detects this issue, you must either mark the class as static if your programming language supports this, or explicitly define a private constructor.

B.4.5 **FxCop Rules for Exceptions**

B.4.5.1 **FxCop Rules for Exception Throwing**

Do not raise exceptions in exception clauses

This usage rule reports an error when a method contains a finally, filter, or fault block that throws one or more unhandled exceptions. Not all programming languages support filter or fault blocks.

> **■ MIKE FANNING**   Visual Basic and C++ are the only Microsoft languages, currently, that allow developers to define exception filters.

B.4.5.2 **FxCop Rules for Choosing the Right Type of Exception to Throw**

B.4.5.2.1 **FxCop Rules for Exception Handling**

Do not catch general exception types

This design rule reports a critical error when a method catches and does not rethrow `System.Exception` or `System.SystemException` exceptions. This rule also reports an error if a method catches and does not throw an object of type `System.Object`.

Rethrow to preserve stack details

This usage rule reports an error when an exception is caught and rethrown explicitly instead of being rethrown using an empty throw statement.

B.4.5.2.2 **FxCop Rules for Using Standard Exception Types**

Do not raise reserved exception types

This usage rule reports an error when a method throws an exception that is too general to provide useful information to the caller. This rule also reports errors when a method throws an exception that should only be thrown by the CLR. The following table identifies the exceptions that should not be thrown.

TABLE B.3: Exceptions to avoid throwing

Exception Type	Issue
`System.Exception`	Too general
`System.SystemException`	Too general
`System.ApplicationException`	Too general
`System.OutOfMemoryException`	Reserved for CLR use
`System.IndexOutOfRangeException`	Reserved for CLR use
`System.ExecutionEngineException`	Reserved for CLR use
`System.NullReferenceException`	Reserved for CLR use

Instantiate argument exceptions correctly

This usage rule reports a critical error when a method creates an instance of `System.ArgumentException` or one of its derived types provided by the .NET Framework and does not provide accurate and/or sufficient parameter data. The derived exceptions include `System.ArgumentNull-Exception`, `System.ArgumentOutOfRangeException`, `System.Component-Model.InvalidEnumArgumentException`, and `SystemDuplicateWaitObject-Exception`. This rule catches the following errors:

- The method calls a parameterless constructor.
- The method calls the `ArgumentException` constructor, which takes two parameters and supplies the name of the argument as the first parameter. The exception message should be the first parameter.
- The method calls the two-parameter constructor of one of `ArgumentException`'s derived types and supplies the exception message as the first parameter. The argument name should be the first parameter.

> ■ **MIKE FANNING** This rule performs a case-sensitive match on the parameter name as it has been declared in the method.

B.4.5.4 **FxCop Rules for Designing Custom Exceptions**

Identifiers should have correct suffix

This rule is described in detail in section B.4.1.5.1 of this appendix. This naming rule reports an error when a type inherits from `System.Exception` and does not have a name that ends in `Exception`.

Implement standard exception constructors

This design rule reports an error when a nonabstract type inherits from `System.Exception` and does not provide the following constructors:

- A public parameterless (default) constructor.
- A public constructor that takes one string argument.
- A public constructor that takes a string and an exception.
- A serialization constructor that is protected if the type is not sealed, and is private if the type is sealed.

Exceptions should be public

This design rule reports a warning when a nonpublic exception derives directly from `System.Exception`, `System.SystemException`, or `System.ApplicationException`.

> **■ DAVID KEAN**   Similar to throwing `System.Exception`, throwing an exception that violates the above rule forces consumers to catch one of the top-level exception types to handle it.

B.4.6 **FxCop Rules for Usage Guidelines**

B.4.6.1 **FxCop Rules for Arrays**

Array fields should not be read-only

This security rule reports a critical warning when a public or protected field containing an array is marked read-only (`ReadOnly` in Visual Basic).

Prefer jagged arrays over multidimensional

This performance rule reports a warning when you declare a multidimensional array instead of an array of arrays.

B.4.6.2 **FxCop Rules for Attributes**

Avoid unsealed attributes

This performance rule reports a warning when a custom attribute is not marked sealed (`NotInheritable` in Visual Basic).

Identifiers should have correct suffix

This rule is described in detail in section B.4.1.5.1 of this appendix. This naming rule reports an error when a custom attribute has a name that does not end in "Attribute."

Define accessors for attribute arguments

This design rule reports an error when the constructor for a custom attribute takes parameters, and the custom attribute does not define properties corresponding to the constructor's parameters. In the version of FxCop located on the companion DVD, this rule does not check that the names of the parameters are the same as the property names (except for casing).

Mark attributes with AttributeUsageAttribute

This design rule reports an error when a custom attribute is not decorated with the `AttributeUsageAttribute` attribute. This attribute defines where the custom attribute can be used in code.

B.4.6.3 **FxCop Rules for Collections**

`ICollection` *implementations have strongly typed members*

This design rule reports an error when a publicly visible type implements the `ICollection` interface but does not provide a strongly typed overload for the `CopyTo(System.Array, System.Int32)` method. This rule does not apply to abstract (`MustInherit` in Visual Basic) classes or generic collections implementations.

Lists are strongly typed

This design rule reports an error when a publicly visible type implements the IList interface but does not provide strongly typed overloads for the methods that take a System.Object parameter. This rule does not apply to abstract (MustInherit in Visual Basic) classes or generic implementations.

Do not expose generic lists

This design rule reports an error when a type defines a public or protected member that returns System.Collections.Generic.List<T> or uses it as a parameter type.

B.4.6.3.1 FxCop Rules for Collection Properties and Return Values

Collection properties should be read-only

This usage rule reports a warning when a type defines a set accessor for a property that exposes an ICollection. Indexer properties and permission sets are exempt from this rule.

B.4.6.3.2 FxCop Rules for Implementing Custom Collections

Collections should implement generic interface

This design rule reports an error when a type implements IEnumerable and does not implement IEnumerable<T>. The exact error, level, and certainty vary depending on whether the type extends CollectionBase, ReadOnlyCollectionBase, or provides strongly typed implementations of IList or ICollection. Implementations of IDictionary are exempt from this rule.

Identifiers should have correct suffix

This rule is described in detail in section B.4.1.5.1 of this appendix. This naming rule ensures that collections implementing IEnumerable end in "Collection." Implementations of IDictionary are exempt from this rule.

B.4.6.4 **FxCop Rules for Object**

B.4.6.4.1 **FxCop Rules for Object.Equals**

Override equals and operator equals on value types

This performance rule reports a warning when a value type does not override `System.Object.Equals` or does not implement both of the equality operators (== and !=). Enumerations are exempt from this rule.

Override `GetHashCode` *on overriding* `Equals`

This usage rule reports an error when a type overrides `System.Object.Equals` and does not override `System.Object.GetHashCode`.

Do not raise exceptions in unexpected locations

This design rule reports an error when a method overriding `System.Object.Equals` explicitly throws an exception.

B.4.6.5 **FxCop Rules for** `Object.GetHashCode`

Override `GetHashCode` *on overriding* `Equals`

This usage rule reports an error when a type overrides `System.Object.Equals` and does not override `System.Object.GetHashCode`.

Do not raise exceptions in unexpected locations

This design rule reports an error when a method overriding `System.Object.GetHashCode` explicitly throws an exception.

B.4.6.6 **FxCop Rules for URI**

B.4.6.6.1 **FxCop Rules for** `System.Uri` **Implementation Guidelines**

The next four rules examine the names of parameters and members to determine whether they represent URI data. This rule assumes that the expected data is a URI if the parameter or member is of type `string` or returns `string` and its name contains URL, URN, or URL in the appropriate casing.

Pass `System.Uri` *objects instead of strings*

This usage rule reports a warning if your code calls a member that has a string parameter with a name that suggests that the expected data is a URI, and there is an overload of the member that takes a `System.Uri`.

URI parameters should not be strings

This design rule reports an error if a member has a string parameter with a name that suggests that the expected data is a URI, and there is no overload for the member that takes a `System.Uri`.

URI properties should not be strings

This design rule reports an error if a string property has a name that suggests that it represents a URI.

URI return values should not be strings

This design rule reports an error if a method returns a string and has a name that suggests that it returns a URI.

B.4.6.7 **FxCop Rules for** `System.Xml` **Usage**

Members should not expose certain concrete types

This design rule reports an error when a public or protected member returns or defines a parameter of type `System.Xml.XmlNode`. Returning or defining a parameter using a class derived from `System.Xml.XmlNode` also causes the rule to report an error.

Types should not extend certain base types

This design rule reports an error when you define a type that inherits from `System.XmlDocument`.

B.4.6.8 **FxCop Rules for Common Operators**

Operators should have symmetrical overloads

This usage rule reports a critical error if a type implements the equality operator or the inequality operator but not both.

Override equals on overriding operator equals

This usage rule reports an error when a type implements the equality operator and does not override the `System.Object.Equals` method.

Overload operator equals on overriding value type equals

This usage rule reports a warning when a value type overrides the `System.Object.Equals` method and does not implement the equality operator.

Override equals and operator equals on value types

This performance rule reports a warning when a value type does not implement the equality operator and override `System.Object.Equals`. Enumerations are exempt from this rule.

Do not override operator equals on reference types

This design rule reports a warning when a reference type provides an implementation of the equality operator.

B.4.7 FxCop Rules for Design Patterns

B.4.7.1 Dispose Pattern

Implement `IDisposable` correctly

This design rule reports an error when a type does not implement the Dispose Pattern correctly.

This rule looks for the following scenarios:

- `Dispose()` is not public and sealed.
- `Dispose(Boolean)` is not protected, virtual, and unsealed.
- `Dispose()` does not call `Dispose(Boolean)`.
- `IDisposable` is reimplemented.
- The finalizer is re-overridden.
- The finalizer does not call `Dispose(Boolean)`.

Do not raise exceptions in unexpected locations

This design rule reports an error when a `Dispose` method explicitly throws an exception.

Types that own disposable fields should be disposable

This design rule reports an error when a type creates and owns disposable instances but does not implement `IDisposable`. Types are considered as owning a disposable instance when they assign an instance they have explicitly created to one of their instance fields.

Types that own native resources should be disposable

This design rule reports an error when a type owns unmanaged resources but does not implement `IDisposable`. Types are considered as owning unmanaged resources when they assign the result of a call to an unmanaged method to one of their instance fields of type `IntPtr`, `UIntPtr`, or `HandleRef`.

Disposable fields should be disposed

This usage rule reports a warning when a type creates and owns disposable instances but does not call `Dispose` on these instances in its `Dispose` method. Types are considered as owning a disposable instance when they assign an instance they have explicitly created to one of their instance fields.

Call `GC.SuppressFinalize` *correctly*

This usage rule reports an error when `GC.SuppressFinalize` is not called correctly.

This rule looks for the following scenarios:

- An implementation of `IDisposable.Dispose` does not call `GC.SuppressFinalize`.
- A method that is not an implementation of `IDisposable.Dispose` calls `GC.SuppressFinalize`.
- A method calls `GC.SuppressFinalize` and passes something other than "this" (`Me` in Visual Basic) as the object parameter.

> **DAVID KEAN**   I've received a lot of feedback from users confused by why this rule fires on disposable types that do not implement a finalizer. This is by design; calling `GC.SuppressFinalize` in the first type that implements the `IDisposable` interface prevents derived types that introduce a finalizer from having to reimplement `IDisposable` just to call it.

B.4.7.2 **Finalizable Types**

Disposable types should declare finalizer

This usage rule reports an error when a type implements `IDisposable` and owns unmanaged resources but does not implement a finalizer. Types are considered as owning unmanaged resources when they assign the result of a call to an unmanaged method to an instance field of type `IntPtr`, `UIntPtr`, or `HandleRef`.

Do not raise exceptions in unexpected locations

This design rule reports an error when a finalizer explicitly throws an exception.

Remove empty finalizers

This performance rule reports a warning when a finalizer is empty, calls only its base class's finalizer, or calls conditionally emitted methods.

Finalizers should be protected

This usage rule reports a critical error when a publicly visible type defines a finalizer that does not have protected accessibility.

Finalizers should call base class finalizer

This usage rule reports a critical error when a finalizer does not call the finalizer defined on its base class. Types that inherit directly from `System.Object` are exempt from this rule.

> **■ DAVID KEAN**   C# developers do not need to worry about this rule—the compiler will automatically add a call to the base class finalizer for them.

B.4.7.3 **Template Method**

Identifiers should not have incorrect suffix

This naming rule reports an error when the name of the member ends in "Impl."

> **■ DAVID KEAN**   You'll notice some older types in the Framework, such as `System.Type`, violate this particular rule by using the "Impl" suffix. Going forward, methods should use the "Core" suffix instead.

C

Sample API Specification

MANY OF THE guidelines described in this book are best considered up front during the initial design. This appendix contains an example of an API specification[1] that should be written early in the process of designing a framework feature. Although such an API specification does not describe full details of the feature, it does highlight the most important elements of the design to nail down up front. This example is heavily based on an actual specification we wrote for a feature of the .NET Framework. Its content is as simple as we could find, but it's a good illustration of the parts, flow, and priorities of a specification intended to describe framework APIs that adhere to the guidelines described in this book. Please note that the specification puts lots of emphasis on code samples showing how the APIs will be used. In fact, the code samples were written before the actual feature was implemented or even prototyped.

---

1. A full design specification document would describe many other issues, such as security, performance, globalization, and so on. The API specification is usually just the start of a much larger document.

SPECIFICATION: .NET FRAMEWORK, STOPWATCH

Executive Overview

Stopwatch class is a managed wrapper for Win32 `QueryPerformance-Counter` and `QueryPerformanceFrequency` APIs. It provides a simple API for high-precision and high-resolution measurements of elapsed time. The APIs are commonly used for performance testing, tuning, and instrumentation.

> ■ **BRAD ABRAMS**   Although I think it is perfectly fine to describe a managed API in terms of the unmanaged version to help readers quickly understand what this feature is, do not let the shape and features of the unmanaged API influence your design of the managed API. Build the right API for your customers, not a clone of the unmanaged API.

Contents

1 REQUIREMENTS

- Provide APIs to measure elapsed time with very high resolution and accuracy of `QueryPerformanceCounter`.
- Most operations should require one line of code. Time measurement functionality should not obscure the main flow of an application.

2 API SPECIFICATION

2.1 Scenarios

> **⬛ KRZYSZTOF CWALINA**   The scenario section is the most important part of an API specification and should be written right after the executive overview and the requirements sections. APIs that were designed by writing code samples before actually designing the API are generally successful. APIs that were designed before code samples were written to show how the resulting APIs should be used are often too complex, not self-explanatory, and ultimately need to be fixed in subsequent releases.

2.1.1 Measure Time Elapsed

```
Stopwatch watch = new Stopwatch();
watch.Start();
Thread.Sleep(1000);
Console.WriteLine(watch.Elapsed);
```

2.1.2 Measure Time Elapsed (Simplified)

```
Stopwatch watch = Stopwatch.StartNew();
Thread.Sleep(1000);
Console.WriteLine(watch.Elapsed);
```

2.1.3 Reuse Stopwatch (VB)

```
Dim watch As Stopwatch = Stopwatch.StartNew()
Thread.Sleep(1000)
Console.WriteLine(watch.ElapsedMilliseconds)

watch.Reset()
watch.Start()
System.Threading.Thread.Sleep(2000)
Console.WriteLine(watch.Elapsed)
```

> ■ **KRZYSZTOF CWALINA**　Note that this sample uses VB despite the author's language of choice being C#. It's very important to be familiar and write code samples in the main languages targeted by your framework. You would be surprised how many more API design issues become apparent when looked at from the perspective of different languages.

> ## Issue
>
> It would be nice to add `Restart()` that would just call `Reset()` followed by `Start()`.
> Resolution: Postponed to a future release for schedule reasons.

2.1.4 Measure Cumulative Intervals

The following sample measures how long it takes to process a list of orders. It excludes time needed to enumerate the order collection.

```
Stopwatch watch = new Stopwatch();
foreach(Order order in orders){
        watch.Start();
        order.Process();
        watch.Stop();
}
Console.WriteLine(watch.Elapsed);
```

2.2 API Design

> ■ **KRZYSZTOF CWALINA**　The API Design section is very often used during specification reviews to find issues with naming, consistency, and complexity. It gives the reviewers a similar view of the object model that the users encounter when browsing the reference documentation to familiarize themselves with new APIs.

```
namespace System.Diagnostics {

    public class Stopwatch {
```

```
    public Stopwatch();
    public static Stopwatch StartNew();

    public void Start();
    public void Stop();
    public void Reset();

    public bool IsRunning { get; }

    public TimeSpan Elapsed            { get; }
    public long     ElapsedMilliseconds { get; }
    public long     ElapsedTicks       { get; }

    public static long GetTimestamp();
    public static readonly long Frequency;
    public static readonly bool IsHighResolution;
    }

}
```

3 Functional Specification

> **■ KRZYSZTOF CWALINA** This part of the specification is usually drafted before the implementation begins but actually completed after it is finished.

public Stopwatch()	
Behavior	Creates a new Stopwatch instance.
Exceptions	

public static Stopwatch StartNew()	
Behavior	Creates a new Stopwatch, calls Start on the instance, and returns the instance.
Exceptions	
Additional Samples	Stopwatch stopwatch = Stopwatch.StartNew(); System.Threading.Thread. Sleep(milliseconds); Console.WriteLine(stopWatch.ElapsedTicks);

public void Start()	
Behavior	Starts accumulating time. If the Stopwatch is already started, the operation does nothing.
Exceptions	

public void Stop()	
Behavior	Stops accumulating time. If the Stopwatch is stopped, the operation does nothing.
Exceptions	

public void Reset()	
Behavior	Stops the stopwatch and resets the time accumulated.
Exceptions	

public bool IsRunning { get; }	
Behavior	Returns true if Stop() was not called after the last call to Start().
Exceptions	
Additional Samples	```StopWatch watch = new StopWatch();

Console.WriteLine(watch.IsRunning);
// prints false

Watch.Start();

Console.WriteLine(watch.IsRunning);
// prints true

Watch.Stop();

Console.WriteLine(watch.IsRunning);
// prints false``` |

public long ElapsedTicks { get; }	
Behavior	Return time accumulated in ticks. Start starts accumulating the time. Stop halts accumulating the time. Note: The value may overflow.
Exceptions	

Additional Samples	`StopWatch watch= StopWatch.StartNew();`
	
	`System.Threading.Thread.Sleep(50);`
	
	`Console.WriteLine(watch.ElapsedTicks);`
	`//prints 50*Frequency/1000`

public long ElapsedMilliseconds { get; }	
Behavior	Return time accumulated in milliseconds. Start starts accumulating the time. Stop halts accumulating the time. The value is computed from ElapsedTicks and the Frequency and is rounded down to the nearest millisecond. Note: The value may overflow.
Exceptions	

Additional Samples	`StopWatch watch= StopWatch.StartNew();`
	
	`System.Threading.Thread.Sleep(50);`
	
	`Console.WriteLine(watch.ElapsedMilliseconds);`
	`//prints 50`

public TimeSpan Elapsed { get; }	
Behavior	Returns time accumulated. Start starts accumulating the time. Stop halts accumulating the time. The value is computed from ElapsedTicks and the Frequency and is rounded down to the nearest millisecond. Note: The value may overflow.
Exceptions	

public static long GetTimestamp()	
Behavior	Returns the current tick count.
Exceptions	

public static readonly long Frequency;	
Behavior	Returns counter frequency on the machine. In cases when high performance counters are not supported, it returns TicksPerSecond (used by DateTime).
Exceptions	

public static readonly bool IsHighResolution;	
Behavior	Returns true if high performance counter is available on the system.
Exceptions	

Glossary

ABSTRACT TYPE: An abstract type can define members for which it does not provide implementations.

APPLICATION MODEL: A type of application. For example, the application models supported by the .NET Framework include console application, Windows Forms application, service application, and ASP.NET application.

ASSEMBLY: A set of code modules and other resources that together are a functional software unit. Usually seen in the form of a single .dll or .exe.

ATTACHED DEPENDENCY PROPERTY : A kind of Dependency Property modeled as static `Get` and `Set` methods representing "properties" describing relationships between objects and their containers (e.g., the position of a `Button` object on a `Panel` container).

ATTRIBUTES: The means in managed code of attaching descriptive information to assemblies, types, their members, and parameters.

BOXING: An operation that converts an instance of a `value` type to an instance of a `reference` type (object) by copying the instance and embedding it in a new `object` instance.

CALLBACK: User code that is called by a framework, usually through a delegate.

CLI: The Common Language Infrastructure, an ECMA standard that defines the requirements for implementing a Virtual Execution System (VES).

CLS: The Common Language Specification, which defines a set of rules for writing public APIs that allow language interoperation.

CONSTRUCTED TYPE: A generic type that has type arguments specified. For example, List<int>.

DEFAULT CONSTRUCTOR: A constructor that does not have any parameters.

DELEGATES: A callback mechanism in managed code that is functionally equivalent to function pointers.

DEPENDENCY PROPERTY OR "DP": A property that stores its value in a property store instead of storing it in a type variable (field), for example.

EVENT: The most commonly used form of callbacks (constructs that allow frameworks to call into user code). Under the covers, an event is not much more than a field whose type is a delegate plus two methods to manipulate the field. Delegates used by events have special signatures (by convention) and are referred to as event handlers.

EVENT HANDLER: Special delegate used as the type of events.

EVENT HANDLING METHOD: User code (method) that is called when an event is raised.

EXTENSION METHODS: Extension methods are a language feature that allows static methods to be called using instance method call syntax.

FINALIZERS: Finalizers provide help in releasing unmanaged resources. System.Object declares a virtual method Finalize (also called the finalizer) that if overridden is called by the GC before the object's memory is reclaimed and can be overridden to release unmanaged resources.

GENERIC METHOD: A method parameterized with the type of data it stores or manipulates. For example:

```
public class Utils {
    public static void Swap<T>(ref T ref1, ref T ref2){ ... }
}
```

GENERICS: A feature of the CLR, similar to C++ templates, that allows classes, structures, interfaces, and methods to be parameterized by the types of data they store and manipulate.

GETTER METHOD: A method of a property designed to access the property's current value.

HIGH-LEVEL COMPONENT: A component representing a high level of abstraction, for example, a component used to manipulate windows on the screen (as opposed to manipulating individual pixels).

IMMUTABLE TYPES: Instances of immutable types cannot be modified using their public members after they are instantiated. For example, `System.String` instances cannot be modified. All methods of `System.String` used to manipulate strings leave the original instance unchanged and return a new instance.

INLINING: A performance optimization in which the compiler substitutes a method call for the body of the method.

INSTANCE METHOD: A method associated with a particular instance of a type.

JIT: Just-In-Time compiler. Intermediate language (IL) instructions are compiled to machine code by the JIT before they can be executed.

LAMBDA EXPRESSION: A programming language feature for defining anonymous delegates

LINQ: Language-Integrated Query. LINQ allows for a uniform, language-integrated programming model for querying datasets independent of the technology used to store that data.

LOSSY AND LOSSLESS CONVERSION: Lossy conversion is a conversion in which some data might be lost. For example, converting from a signed integer to an unsigned integer is lossy. Lossless conversion is a conversion in which data cannot be lost. For example, a conversion from an unsigned 16-bit integer to a signed 32-bit integer is lossless.

LOW-LEVEL COMPONENT: A component representing a low level of abstraction, for example, a component used to manipulate individual pixels on the screen (as opposed to manipulating windows).

MANAGED CODE: Code for which an underlying virtual execution system, such as the CLR, provides a set of services, including walking the stack, handling exceptions, and storage and retrieval of security information.

MEMBER: Methods, properties, nested types, events, constructors, and fields of types.

METADATA: Language-independent information describing the contents of an assembly.

NESTED TYPES: A type defined within the scope of another type, which is called the enclosing type. A nested type has access to all members of its enclosing type.

OBJECTS: Instances of classes.

OVERLOADING: Defining two or more members in the same scope with the same name but different signatures.

PRE-EVENTS AND POST-EVENTS: Pre-events are raised before a side effect takes place. Post-events are raised after a side effect takes place. For example, the `Form.Closing` pre-event is raised before a window closes. The `Form.Closed` event is raised after a window is closed.

PROGRESSIVE FRAMEWORK: Framework that is easy to use in basic scenarios yet powerful enough to be used in advanced scenarios.

PROPERTIES: Essentially, smart fields with the calling syntax of fields and the flexibility of methods.

REFERENCE TYPE: A type whose instances are allocated on the heap and whose variables store locations (references) of the instances rather than storing the actual instance. Object classes and interfaces are examples of reference types.

SEALING: A powerful mechanism that prevents extensibility. You can seal either the class or individual members. Sealing a class prevents users from inheriting from the class. Sealing a member prevents users from overriding a particular member.

SETTER METHOD: A property method designed to set the value of the property.

STATIC FIELD: Fields associated with a type, not any particular instance of the type.

STATIC METHODS: Methods associated with a type, not any particular instance of the type.

THIS: A special pointer to the object on which invocations of instance members are to operate.

TYPE ARGUMENT: An argument to a generic type. For example, in the following sample, `string` and `int` are both type arguments.

```
Dictionary<string,int> map = new Dictionary<string,int>();
```

TYPE PARAMETER: A parameter in a generic type. For example, in the following declaration, `T` is a type parameter.

```
public class List<T> {
   ...
}
```

UNBOXING: When a value type instance has been boxed (embedded in an `object` instance), unboxing converts it back to a `value` type instance.

UNMANAGED CODE: Code that does not depend on the CLR for execution.

VALUE TYPE: A type whose variables point directly to its instances rather than the address of the instances, as would be the case for a `reference` type.

XAML : An XML format used to represent `object` graphs.

Suggested Reading List

The following is a list of books and blogs referenced in this text or recommended by the authors.

Abrams, B. and Abrams, T. 2004. *.NET Framework Standard Library Annotated Reference*. Volumes 1 and 2. Boston: Addison-Wesley.

Bloch, J. 2001. *Effective Java Programming Language Guide*. Boston: Addison-Wesley.

Booch, G., Rumbaugh, J., and Jacobson, I. 1999. *The Unified Modeling Language User Guide*. Boston: Addison-Wesley.

Box, D. 2002. *Essential .NET, Volume I: The Common Language Runtime*. Boston: Addison-Wesley.

Chan, P. and Lee, R. 1997. *The Java Class Libraries: An Annotated Reference*. Boston: Addison-Wesley.

Clarke, S. 2004. Measuring API Usability. *Dr. Dobb's Journal*, Special Windows/.NET Supplement 9(5): S6–S9.

Coplien, J. 1992. *Advanced C++ Programming Styles and Idioms*. Boston: Addison-Wesley.

Fowler, M., Beck, K., Brant, J., Opdyke, W., and Roberts, D. 1999. *Refactoring: Improving the Design of Existing Code*. Boston: Addison-Wesley.

Gamma, E., Helm, R., Johnson, R., and Vlissides, J. 1995. *Design Patterns: Elements of Reusable Object-Oriented Software*. Boston: Addison-Wesley.

Green, T. R. G. and Petre, M. 1996. Usability analysis of visual programming environments: A "cognitive dimensions" framework. *Journal of Visual Languages and Computing* 7: 131–174.

Hanson, D. 1997. *C Interfaces and Implementations: Techniques for Creating Reusable Software*. Boston: Addison-Wesley.

Hejlsberg, A., Wiltamuth, S., and Golde, P. 2004. *The C# Programming Language*, 2nd ed. Boston: Addison-Wesley.

Hoc, J.-M., Green, T. R. G., Samurcay, R., and Gilmore, D. J. (eds.). 1990. *Psychology of Programming*. London: Academic.

Jacobson, I. 1992. *Object-Oriented Software Engineering, a Use Case Driven Approach*. Boston: Addison-Wesley.

Kernighan, B. and Ritchie, D. 1988. *The C Programming Language*, 2nd ed. Upper Saddle River, NJ: Prentice Hall.

McConnell, S. 2004. *Code Complete*, 2nd ed. Redmond, WA: Microsoft Press.

McLellan, S. G., Roesler, A. W., Tempest, J. T., and Spinuzzi, C. I. 1998. Building More Usable APIs. *IEEE Software* 15 (3): 78–86.

Miller, J. and Ragsdale, S. 2004. *The Common Language Infrastructure Annotated Standard*. Boston: Addison-Wesley.

Newkirk, J. W. and Vorontsov, A. A. 2004. *Test-Driven Development in Microsoft .NET*. Redmond, WA: Microsoft Press.

Norman, D. 2002. *The Design of Everyday Things*. New York: Basic Books.

Richter, J. 2006. *CLR via C#*. Redmond, WA: Microsoft Press.

Shalloway, A. and Trott, J. 2004. *Design Patterns Explained: A New Perspective on Object-Oriented Design*, 2nd ed. Boston: Addison-Wesley.

Stroustrup, B. 1994. *The Design and Evolution of C++*. Boston: Addison-Wesley.

Syme, D., Granicz, A., and Cisternino, A. 2007. *Expert F#*. Berkeley, CA: Apress.

Vick, P. 2004. *The Visual Basic .NET Programming Language*. Boston: Addison-Wesley.

Watkins, D., Hammond, M., and Abrams, B. 2003. *Programming in the .NET Environment*. Boston: Addison-Wesley.

Weinberg, G. M. 1971. *The Psychology of Computer Programming*. New York: Van Nostrand Reinhold.

Blogs

http://blogs.msdn.com/kcwalina

http://blogs.msdn.com/brada

http://blogs.msdn.com/stevencl

Index

System.Uri. *See* Uri, usage guidelines
System.ValueType, 103
System.Xml, usage guidelines, 284–286, 401

T

TDD (test-driven development)
 defined, 15
 framework design and, 6–7
 scenario-driven design, 19
 unsealed classes, 195
Technology namespace groups, 59–60
Template method, 404
Template Method Pattern, 203, 354–356
Tense, for event names, 70–71
Test-driven development. *See* TDD (test-driven development)
Tester-Doer Pattern, 219, 241–242
ThenBy method, Query Pattern, 343
This, defined, 421
Throwing exceptions, 216–221. *See also* Exceptions, choosing type to throw
TimeoutException, 357
Timeouts, in API design, 356–358
TimeSpan, 356
ToString method, 240, 271–273
Trade-offs, design, 5–6
Transparency, Aggregate Components, 290
Try-Parse Pattern, 219, 242–243
Type arguments
 calling generic methods with, 350
 in constructed types, 418
 defined, 421
Type constructors
 defined, 144
 designing, 151–152, 389
Type converters, and XAML readers, 359–360
Type design guidelines
 abstract classes, 95–97
 adding values to enums, 114–115
 assembly metadata and, 118–119
 choosing class vs. struct, 84–88
 choosing classes vs. interfaces, 88–95
 flag enums, 109–114
 FxCop rules for, 384–386
 interfaces, 98–101
 namespaces and, 79–84

nested types, 115–117
overview of, 77–79
simple enums, 103–109
static classes, 97–98
structs, 101–103
Type members, naming, 68–73
 conflicts with namespace names, 58–60
 designing self-documenting APIs, 28–30
 events, 70–72, 382
 fields, 72–73, 383
 methods, 68
 PascalCasing for, 39–40
 properties, 68–70, 381
Type parameters, 64, 421

U

UEFs (unhandled exception filters), 215
Unary operators, 366
Unboxing, 421
Underscores (_), 73, 75
Unhandled exception handlers, 214–215
Unmanaged code, 421
Unmanaged resources, 319
Unsealed classes, 194–195
Uri, usage guidelines, 283–284, 400–401
UrtCop (Universal Runtime Cop), 373
Usability, consistency for, 31–32
Usability studies, API, 19–21, 25
Usage errors, 222–223
Usage guidelines, 245–287
 arrays, 245–247
 attributes, 247–250
 collections. *See* Collections, usage guidelines
 DateTime and DateTimeOffset, 261–263
 equality operators, 286–287
 ICloneable, 263–264
 IComparable<T> and IEquatable<T>, 264–266
 IDisposable, 266
 Nullable<T>, 266–268
 Object, 268–273
 serialization. *See* Serialization, usage guidelines
 System.Xml usage, 284–286
 Uri, 283–284

DVD-ROM Warranty

Addison-Wesley warrants the enclosed DVD-ROM to be free of defects in materials and faulty workmanship under normal use for a period of ninety days after purchase (when purchased new). If a defect is discovered in the DVD-ROM during this warranty period, a replacement DVD-ROM can be obtained at no charge by sending the defective DVD-ROM, postage prepaid, with proof of purchase to:

Disc Exchange
Addison-Wesley
Pearson Technology Group
75 Arlington Street, Suite 300
Boston, MA 02116
Email: AWPro@aw.com

Addison-Wesley makes no warranty or representation, either expressed or implied, with respect to this software, its quality, performance, merchantability, or fitness for a particular purpose. In no event will Addison-Wesley, its distributors, or dealers be liable for direct, indirect, special, incidental, or consequential damages arising out of the use or inability to use the software. The exclusion of implied warranties is not permitted in some states. Therefore, the above exclusion may not apply to you. This warranty provides you with specific legal rights. There may be other rights that you may have that vary from state to state. The contents of this DVD-ROM are intended for personal use only.

More information and updates are available at:

informit.com/aw